SPIRITUALIZING POLITICS WITHOUT POLITICIZING RELIGION

The Example of Sargent Shriver

Spiritualizing Politics without Politicizing Religion

The Example of Sargent Shriver

JAMES R. PRICE AND KENNETH R. MELCHIN

UNIVERSITY OF TORONTO PRESS
Toronto   Buffalo   London

ISBN 978-1-4426-4252-2 (cloth)
ISBN 978-1-4426-9421-7 (EPUB)
ISBN 978-1-4426-9420-0 (PDF)

Library and Archives Canada Cataloguing in Publication

Title: Spiritualizing politics without politicizing religion : the example
of Sargent Shriver / James R. Price and Kenneth R. Melchin.
Names: Price, James R., author. | Melchin, Kenneth R., 1949– author.
Description: Includes bibliographical references and index.
Identifiers: Canadiana (print) 20210325615 | Canadiana (ebook)
2021032578X | ISBN 9781442642522 (cloth) | ISBN 9781442694217 (EPUB) |
ISBN 9781442694200 (PDF)
Subjects: LCSH: Shriver, Sargent, 1915–2011 – Religion. | LCSH: Politicians –
United States – Biography. | LCSH: Ambassadors – United States – Biography. |
LCSH: Religion and politics – United States. | LCGFT: Biographies.
Classification: LCC E840.8.S525 P75 2022 | DDC 973.924092 – dc23

We wish to acknowledge the land on which the University of Toronto Press
operates. This land is the traditional territory of the Wendat, the Anishnaabeg,
the Haudenosaunee, the Métis, and the Mississaugas of the Credit First Nation.

University of Toronto Press acknowledges the financial support of the
Government of Canada, the Canada Council for the Arts, and the Ontario Arts
Council, an agency of the Government of Ontario, for its publishing activities.

For Tim Shriver, with thanks for his patience and steadfast belief in this project

Contents

Preface   ix

1 Religion and Politics: Doing Things Differently   3
Sargent Shriver   4
The Mess We're In   7
Doing Things Differently   9
Interiority and Method   13
Shriver the Peacemaker   15
Outline of the Argument   19

2 The Public Faith of Sargent Shriver, 1955–1959   23
Shriver's Religious Vocation to Public Life   24
Catholics and American Politics   27
Religion, Schools, and the "Wall of Separation"   31
Shriver's Vision: Religious Resources for Guarding Diversity   35
The Campaign Against Racism   40
The Turn to Interiority   44
Concluding Remarks   47

3 Shriver on Spirituality and Politics, 1961–1964   48
Shriver's Vocation and the Peace Corps Years   49
The "Wall of Separation"   52
Political Backlash   55
Differentiating and Relating Spirituality and Politics: What Shriver Said   57
From Charity to Spirituality and Compassion   62
Spirituality, Politics, and the Peace Corps: What Shriver Did   67
Concluding Remarks   71

Contents

4 Explaining What Shriver Did   75
Religion and Politics: Shriver's Catholic Tradition   76
Coming to Terms with Diversity   82
Transposing the Tradition: Diversity and Interiority   90
Interiority and Conflict: The Insight Approach   95
Religion and Politics Revisited   100
Concluding Remarks   104

5 Religion, Politics, and the Peace Corps   106
The Peace Corps   107
How the Peace Corps Works   110
Interiority and Spirituality   115
Spiritual Values and the Peace Corps   118
*Resolving Conflicts and Building Peace: The Peace Corps
and the Insight Approach*   123
Concluding Remarks   131

6 The Way Forward   133
Comprehensive Doctrines   134
Philosophical Method   136
Exemplary Figures   139

Notes   141
Bibliography   161
Index   179

Preface

Working together on this book has been a pleasure and a privilege on many levels. It would not have been possible without the aid, support, and input of many friends and colleagues along the way, or without the inspiration provided throughout by the spirit, integrity, and achievements of Sargent Shriver. To explain the context of our work together and our aims in this book, we begin first with a few words in our own voices before returning to a common account.

J.R.P.: In 2002, I received a phone call from Tim Shriver, a friend and former student from my time at the Catholic University of America, inviting me to engage with him in the work that has led to the writing of this book. Tim had just secured funding for the launch of a peace institute to be named for his father, Sargent Shriver, the founding director of the Peace Corps and a man who through Tim had become a friend of mine over the previous fifteen years. Tim was seeking my help in thinking through what it would mean to educate and train future peace builders in the manner and methods of Sargent Shriver – a prospect that was immediately intriguing to me. Looking back, it is clear that neither of us had any idea what a complicated, multifaceted challenge this would prove to be, or that puzzling out the answer to this question would become the capstone of my life's work.

At the time, all we knew about Sarge's approach to peacebuilding was that it provided a stark contrast to the contemporary political realism associated with Thomas Hobbes and his notorious dictum that, absent the constraints of civil society, human living is at root "a war of all against all." For his part, Sarge was happy enough to concede that, left to our own devices, the decisions and actions of human beings would not and could not usher in a world of peace. But he also insisted that, in cooperation with the Spirit, we not only could but also must work in a spirit of compassion and service to overcome the obstacles to peace and friendship created by our experiences of difference in race, creed, culture, and politics. Sarge's forthright spiritual realism guided every program he ever conceived or built, including, notably, the Peace Corps. Therefore, Tim and I decided that any peace institute named for Sargent Shriver would need to be grounded in and oriented by Sarge's spiritual realism. But this opened up two problems that needed to be solved.

Problem number one was the question of explanation. In his public addresses, Sarge regularly made declarative statements about religion and politics, such as his remark to graduates at Fordham University in 1963 that the "Peace Corps is an example of the need for spiritual values in the work of government. And its work is, in the deepest sense, the work of reconciliation." By his own admission, Sarge was a public servant, an attorney, and a social entrepreneur, not a methodologist, so he never took the opportunity to formally explain the connections he routinely discerned between spiritual values, public policy, and peacemaking. He just made them and ran with them. So it fell to the Sargent Shriver Peace Institute to work out those explanations. As Tim and I saw it at the time, the fundamental task of the Sargent Shriver Peace Institute would be to discover answers to three main questions: What did Sargent Shriver do when he was building peace? How did he do it? How can other people do likewise?

This in turn gave rise to problem number two: it was much easier to formulate these methodological questions than to answer them. This is because there was precious little methodological or practical wisdom available in North American religious and political culture for attacking these questions – riven as it is by the fog of the contemporary culture wars, the imperious proliferation of doctrinaire religious conviction, and the growing secularism of the academy and the public square. In effect, the challenge was to recover a way of thinking about the spiritual component of political action and institution building that was spontaneously apparent to Sarge, but obscure, incoherent, or downright wrongheaded to many people oriented by contemporary political culture. One of my first steps was to turn to my friend Ken Melchin to tell him about the amazing opportunity that Tim Shriver had brought to me.

K.R.M.: I learned of Jamie's work on Shriver in June 2005. We had known each other as Lonergan scholars since 1984. But the occasion for closer collaboration was provided by an invitation to present a paper at the Boston College Lonergan Workshop on research I was doing with my colleague, Cheryl Picard, on insight and conflict. The paper was a progress report on a book Cheryl and I were writing, *Transforming Conflict through Insight*, that drew on Lonergan's insight theory to help explain what she was doing when she was resolving conflicts in her mediation practice. Jamie caught up with me at lunch one day and began sharing ideas about the convergence of our two lines of work. Very quickly I found his ideas compelling. Jamie's project opened new vistas for exploring and expanding the range of applications of insight theory in the fields of peace and conflict. And in the months that followed, we kept up conversations about some of the strands of analysis that appear in this book: Supreme Court decisions, the insight approach, religion and conflict, religion and politics, and the culture wars.

What impressed me about Jamie was that he took the task of understanding seriously. He had been researching and writing draft chapters on Shriver, religion, politics, and peace, and in 2005 was invited to present a paper on his work at Trinity College, Dublin. After our meeting, he took it upon himself to travel to meet Cheryl Picard in person and signed up for two insight mediation training workshops with her in Ottawa. He did not rest content with "talking the talk"; he insisted on the more complex learning path of "walking the talk." This is not easy. I had taken mediation training and had come to realize that scholars often do not commit the time required for the difficult work of practice-based skill development. Learning mediation skills had changed my own horizons dramatically, and I developed a special interest in scholars who were willing to engage seriously in hands-on learning.

My earliest research notes for the book are from 2008, but our work together on Shriver began in 2006 in the context of a series of sessions at Columbia University with Andrea Bartoli. Jamie and I had begun meeting with a wonderful group of colleagues called the Insight Peace and Conflict Group, and Andrea invited us to New York City in May and December of 2006 to explore opportunities for promoting and developing the insight approach. It was during these sessions that Jamie told me about Sarge. By the time he asked me to work with him on the book, I had learned enough about Shriver to appreciate what an honor this would be. I have since come to consider Sarge an important part of my life, and I have since come to consider Jamie one of my dearest friends.

J.R.P. and K.R.M.: Our work together on the book developed in the context of sessions we were able to coordinate with regular meetings of the Insight Peace and Conflict Group. Between 2006 and 2011, we held meetings every February at the time of the Annual Conflict Symposium in Ottawa. In addition, the School for Conflict Analysis and Resolution at George Mason University in Arlington, Virginia – now named for Jimmy and Rosalynn Carter, and which invited Jamie to join at the faculty as a Reseach Professor – provided both formal and collegial opportunities related to our work. Our concern at each step along the way was both theoretical and practical. Insight theory provided us with tools for understanding Sarge's words and deeds in totally new ways. But we also wanted practical applications to help present and future peacebuilders do likewise.

In June 2009, Jamie developed an application of our research to the field of economics in a paper titled "Circulating Grace: Resources for a Just Economy," presented at the Seton Hall University Conference on Lonergan and Economics. Then, in August 2009, we submitted a paper on an application of our work to the field of poverty law, "Recovering Sargent Shriver's Vision for Poverty Law: The Illinois Familycare Campaign and the Insight Approach to Conflict Resolution and Collaboration." Both papers were practical applications and were published in 2010, the first in *The Lonergan Review* and the second in *Clearinghouse Review*. When Sarge passed away in 2011, Jamie was invited by *Commonweal* magazine to contribute an article, and he drew on our research to paint a portrait of another practical application of Sarge the peacemaker in "Practical Idealism: How Sargent Shriver Built the Peace Corps."

By June 2012, we had enough material on the book assembled to present an overview of the argument at the Lonergan Workshop at Boston College. The interest this generated resulted in our being invited back in 2015 and 2018. Along the way, numerous other paper presentations accompanied the development of our research, and readers can find details on ten published articles that arose from this work in the bibliography of the book. We submitted the final manuscript to the University of Toronto Press in 2019, and since then have been pleased to observe considerable interest in the fruits of our research.

Our work together on the book has been guided by the three questions at the heart of the mission of the Sargent Shriver Peace Institute: What did Sargent Shriver do when he was building peace? How did he do it? How can other people do likewise? We draw on Lonergan's insight theory to help answer these questions, and our focus is on the early years of Sarge's public life. Much of our research arises from a careful study of Sarge's speeches. But we also situate his words and actions within analyses of wider theological and political currents of the times as well as biographical material on Sarge. Our questions are historical, but they are also theoretical and practical, and they are so because Sarge's words and deeds, understood through the lens of insight theory, provide novel explanatory insights that can ground present and future practice. If there is a center point that might be called the "micro-focus" of the book, it is the question of religion and politics – thus the title.

We could not have arrived here without the aid, support, and input of many friends and colleagues. Our special thanks go out to Tim Shriver and the board of the Sargent Shriver Peace Institute (SSPI) for support through thick and thin. SSPI's services and resources related to Shriver and Peace Corps have been invaluable.

The Insight Peace and Conflict Group provided friendship and scholarly competence on the theory and practice of Lonergan's work as applied to the field of conflict. Our thanks go out to Cheryl Picard, Andrea Bartoli, Morag McAleese, Derek Melchin, Vieve Price, and Neil Sargent. We thank Fred Lawrence, Director of the Lonergan Workshop, for the opportunity to present and receive feedback on early research materials in 2012. Double thanks go out to Fred for inviting us back again to present our work on Sarge in 2015 and 2018.

We thank Research Services at Saint Paul University for their support along the way. The Lonergan Centre at Saint Paul University has been helpful, and we thank Amy Pauley, Morag McAleese, Susan Gray, and Elisabeth Nicholson for their contributions. We thank Marnie Jull and Megan Price for opportunities for presentations at the annual Insight Summit at the University of Prince Edward Island, Charlottetown, in August 2019, and Royal Roads University, Victoria, BC, in July 2020. With the launch of Insight Collaborations International, these opportunities continue and are assured in future years.

We are grateful for the patience and support offered by Daniel Quinlan of the University of Toronto Press. The project took longer than expected, and when we finally completed the book we wondered whether UTP would still be interested. Thankfully, Daniel liked the manuscript and the Press agreed. We are grateful for the comments provided by the readers. It was a delight to have the team at Apex CoVantage guide us through the copyediting and page proof stages. Our thanks go out to Lucy Di Rosa at SSPI for her contribution to communications and marketing.

We thank the editors of *Theoforum* for permission to reprint selected passages from "Religion and Politics in the Early Public Life of Sargent Shriver," *Theoforum* 50 (no. 2, 2020): 315–44, by Kenneth R. Melchin and James R. Price, © Peeters Publishers. Research for this book was carried out with the aid of financial support from the Sargent Shriver Peace Institute, and the volume was published with the aid of a grant from SSPI.

Two more notes. Readers who follow Shriver's speeches chronologically on the website of the Sargent Shriver Peace Institute from the 1950s to 2005 will observe his language changing to reflect the shift to gender sensitivity and inclusivity. Our focus in this book is on his early public life, and so the speeches quoted reflect the language of the times. In the interest of historical accuracy, we cite the speeches as they were delivered. Instead of interjecting comments reminding readers of the need for inclusive language, we have chosen to let Shriver's record speak for itself. We also wish to say a few words about our positive treatment of Sarge. It has become commonplace to expect authors to criticize historical figures. Instead of following the standard path, our portrait offers Sarge as an exemplary figure worth following as we work through one of the difficult challenges of our age, thinking responsibly about politics and religion. We trust other authors will offer whatever criticisms might be needed to remind us of Sarge's humanity.

Finally, our thanks go out to our partners, Vieve and Sandie. You have been friends and companions at every step along the journey. We could not have done it without you.

SPIRITUALIZING POLITICS WITHOUT POLITICIZING RELIGION

The Example of Sargent Shriver

Chapter One

Religion and Politics: Doing Things Differently

Not since the days of established churches in colonial times has the clash of religion and politics so polarized North America as it does today. Conflicts rage on diverse fronts, and citizens find themselves gathered in liberal and conservative camps, taking sides against each other over the role religion should or should not play in politics. In the US, both camps invoke the power and authority of the First Amendment, and both marshal arguments in light of visions of the common good: guarding diversity and protecting politics against the caustic influence of religion; or infusing political life with religion's healing and sustaining power. The flashpoints are known to all: religion in schools, public prayer, creation and evolution, religion and violence, abortion, euthanasia, and gender relations.

For one camp, the critique focuses on American Supreme Court decisions, beginning in the 1940s, that apply the religion clauses of the First Amendment to build a "wall of separation" between church and state. They believe such a dramatic separation of religion and politics is a mistake and an illusion. Secular belief simply ends up imposing its own religion on politics. Americans in this camp believe this misinterprets the First Amendment, unconstitutionally circumscribing the rights of all believers in public spaces, and unconstitutionally prohibiting public officials from bringing religious beliefs into political practice. Traditional religion, they argue, nurtures the moral values required for public life, and this means religion has a role in politics.

A second camp, alarmed by the religious motives and political successes of the first, thinks that bringing religion into politics undermines America's historic commitment to diversity, civic liberty, and freedom of belief. Americans in this camp believe we need the wall of separation to keep religious belief from compromising citizens' legal and political status in America. Diversity, they argue, is the essence of democracy, and this means religion and politics must be kept separate.

The trouble with all this is many citizens resonate with arguments on both sides. The challenge they face is finding a forum for working through the issues carefully, exploring ways that values from both camps can be appreciated and related within fresh horizons. The conflicts raging in public spaces seem to prevent this work of thoughtful reflection. The issues now seem to be bigger than any individual or group, and they unfold within the charged atmospheres of the highest courts, legislatures, and media outlets. Some feel they threaten to paralyze governance of the land. The conflict sweeps Americans up, presses them to take sides, and divides them from one another.

Most problematic is the import of this clash for the pursuit of peace. Politics, if it is to prove its worth, needs to bring peace to citizens both abroad and at home. Yet the highly charged debates seem to celebrate a conflict that makes a mockery of the very peace it is supposed to achieve. Religions of the world claim a special place in the enterprise of peace-building. Without a clear consensus on their role in politics, however, religions are either shackled or left to run amok in the delicate work of achieving peace amidst diversity.

If we are to find our way through these difficulties, citizens will need some new habits of mind. In particular, we will need new horizons that enable us to explore and articulate values on all sides of the issues – horizons that enable us to work through and free ourselves from the misunderstandings, recriminations, and crossed purposes that mark the conflict today. Specifically, we need an approach that can, on the one hand, affirm the religion-politics distinctions that guard freedom of conscience and diversity of belief, and on the other, affirm the religion-politics relations that ensure religious involvements in nurturing values essential for public life.

In this book, we argue for an approach we believe enables this horizon. To portray this approach, we offer a profile of a prominent American Catholic, heralded as "one of the major figures of the second half of the twentieth century,"[1] who upheld values of both conservatives and liberals and put them to practice in the pursuit of peace: Sargent Shriver.

Sargent Shriver

Sargent Shriver was a deeply faithful Catholic, steeped in the most ancient traditions of his church, and committed to the values and beliefs articulated by church leaders of his time. His religious faith inspired a vocation to political life that never ceased to shape the substance and direction of the policies and programs he launched and supported. Yet, throughout his career, Shriver was adamant in upholding the values of religious liberty, embracing cultural and religious diversity, and promoting the most aggressive public programs for peace and social justice.

His public life began in the years generally regarded as the most turbulent and transformative in the recent history of his Catholic tradition, the years surrounding the Second Vatican Council. While conflict was brewing in the US over the role of religion in politics, a parallel conflict between conservatives and liberals was developing within Catholicism that would see the warring camps align with those of the political battle. The Council began at the end of an historic era that has been called "classicism." It was an era in which conservative church leaders held to a world view rooted in a traditional interpretation of Thomas Aquinas, proclaimed the church as essential for salvation, upheld the ideal of perennial truth, drew upon a natural law framework for developing and implementing moral rules, deeply mistrusted both liberalism and science, focused on family values and a traditional role for women in family and church, and held to an understanding of church-state relations that often was regarded as a threat to American political life. Conservative Catholics supported the involvement of church in the affairs of state to maintain the objective values required for the proper functioning of politics.

During the Council, there emerged an expression of a radically new Catholicism that would be as different from classicism as night is from day. Liberal Catholicism was rooted in a world view shaped by the natural and historical sciences, it recognized diverse cultural expressions of faith and authentic religious experiences in other traditions, opened doors to multiple moral frameworks and moral judgements, found a way of living with core affirmations of both liberalism and science, championed social justice and equality for women in family, society, and church, and found a place alongside other traditions respecting religious freedom and diversity in American political life. Liberal Catholics expressed sympathy for the "wall of separation" between church and state that ensured the liberty, diversity, and freedom of conscience that were a necessary part of the Catholic Church's transition to modernity.

Where the two Catholicisms collided was on the issue of objective moral values. Many conservative Catholics were vaguely sympathetic to ideas of democracy and cultural diversity. But in their view, liberal Catholics purchased their openness to diversity at the cost of objectivity. One of the central pillars of the Thomist intellectual tradition, undergirding the convictions of classic Catholicism, was its strong natural law framework for affirming objective values. The liberal Catholicism of Vatican II, in its effort to embrace liberty and diversity, distanced itself from the natural law tradition. But in doing so, it seemed unable to deliver a satisfactory response to the question of objectivity.[2] The result was a growing divide on all the issues championed by conservative and liberal Catholics. And in America, a flood of Catholics aligned their faith stance with one or the other of the warring camps in the battle of religion and politics: conservatives insisting on the involvement of church in politics to ensure the objective values essential for politics; and liberals insisting on the separation of church and state to ensure the liberty of conscience essential for democracy and diversity.

Throughout his public life, Sargent Shriver was able to live the tensions of these conflicts with an authenticity and grace that transcended the prevailing climate of mutual recrimination. Shriver was not a philosopher or a theologian. He was a man of action. Yet, he was well read in philosophy and theology, and his actions were deeply thoughtful; in many ways he was a man ahead of his time. His life bore witness to the oldest and most authentic intellectual currents of the Thomist Catholic tradition. His was a commitment to nature and grace, the natural law, the Aristotelian-Thomist architecture of truth, the value of fidelity, the theological virtue of charity, and the church's role in mediating grace to the world. Yet his was also a commitment to discerning the spectacular presence of the Holy Spirit in diverse cultures and traditions. He recognized an authenticity in diverse forms of spirituality, and was clear in his commitment to the liberty of religious conscience. He celebrated the role of science in revealing the wonders of God's work in the world. And his life was an authentically religious vocation devoted to justice and peace.

Most compelling was Shriver's commitment to peace. In January 1961, when John F. Kennedy was newly sworn in as the thirty-fifth president of the United States, he summoned Shriver from Chicago to take the lead in designing and developing the Peace Corps. It was a new idea; nothing like it had ever been tried by the US government, and it was Shriver's tough-minded, practical answer to a question just as pressing to Americans today, both at home and abroad, as it was when he asked it then: "If you believe men must live together in a different way in this new world of the hydrogen bomb how is this going to come about?"[3]

At the center of the Peace Corps was Shriver's commitment to the enduring power of people-to-people contact in the making of peace. Peace Corps workers would be living examples of the "most powerful idea of all":

> The idea that free and committed men and women can cross boundaries of culture and language, or alien tradition and great disparities of wealth, of old hostilities and new nationalisms, to meet with other men and women on the common ground of service to human welfare and human dignity.[4]

Shriver's Peace Corps was arguably the most significant achievement of his life's vocation of service to human dignity. There can be no doubt that Shriver lived his public life as a religious vocation inspired by the model of Christ. Yet with the Peace Corps, he was able to take his vocation into politics and transpose core elements of his faith into a public program that championed peace and justice. Shriver not only bridged the worlds of religion and politics, he lived core values from both sides of the conservative-liberal divide, and he transposed the values at the heart of his faith into a political program that reached out to touch the hearts of women and men from diverse religious and secular belief traditions in the service of peace. In the chapters that follow, we explore the life of Sargent Shriver and ask: How can we explain his achievement? How can we do this sort of thing today? In answer, we propose a method for carrying forward the practical idealism of Shriver.

The Mess We're In

When contemplating the task of navigating the challenges of the religion-politics debate, it is helpful to recall that, as Americans, we have been here before. In the colonial period, Americans created a world of religion and politics in which it seemed reasonable and necessary to use the power of the state to enforce religious loyalty and obedience. All thirteen of the original colonies required a test of religious orthodoxy for anyone holding positions in the government or the military, and nine of the colonies had legally established churches. Yet, plausible as these laws obviously were at the time, they created political conflict and strife in colonial America. For, by integrating religious belief into the laws of the land, the colonies not only divided Americans from each other along religious lines, they institutionalized an adversarial relationship between the government and groups of religiously committed Americans.

Of course, Americans transformed the legal and political foundations of this conflict when they ratified the Constitution in 1789 and adopted the Bill of Rights shortly thereafter. Article VI, section three of the Constitution bans religious tests for public officials and office holders, and the Religion Clauses of the First Amendment forbid Congress from making laws that either require adherence or prohibit religious practice.[5] The lesson here for meeting the challenge of today, however, is to recognize that behind this political achievement lay a philosophical effort, championed by Thomas Jefferson among others, that transformed the way colonial Americans understood the relationship of religion and politics.

Operating with a perspective on religion and politics that has since become the political common sense of America, Jefferson argued that genuine religious conviction is a matter of conscience, not coercion, and people are answerable to their god and to themselves, not to the government, for the integrity of their religious beliefs. In making his case, Jefferson helped his fellow Americans cultivate a perspective on religion and politics that highlighted the role of interiority in framing the question. The core of the issue for Jefferson was conscience. Recognizing the significance of conscience had the effect of placing the interior operations of human meaning at the core of the problem and its solution.

In his day, Jefferson's analysis had the effect of emphasizing the distinction between the institutions of political power and the religious institutions whose role it was to oversee the cultivation and exercise of religious conscience. Today, however, the conflict takes for granted this distinction, but asks a new question, a question about the relations between religion and politics. This question arises because of a new level of cultural diversity and a new diversity of institutional involvements. Political and religious institutions now deliver wide ranges of public goods to communities of citizens affiliated with more diverse religious and secular belief traditions. In this new context of increased diversity of belief and institutional involvements, formal affiliations and formal institutional distinctions no longer provide adequate criteria for assessing which forms of religion-politics relations are permissible and which are not. We argue that, with Jefferson, responding adequately calls for another step in the turn to interiority that proved relevant in Jefferson's day.

In Chapters 2 and 3, we offer brief overviews of significant events in the background context that shaped the contemporary religion-politics debate. The impact of the separation of church and state has been formidable. Many Americans forget, however, that historically in North America, unlike in Europe, the purpose of the distinction was not to keep religion out of politics, but to keep the institutions of church and state separate so that religion, cultivated and expressed in the liberty required by a free conscience, could relate to politics in diverse ways through diverse traditions.[6] Americans of Jefferson's era had no doubt that religion related to politics. Americans of today, however, nurtured by a series of events that stressed the distinction, and faced with a bewildering diversity of affiliations and involvements, have now come to ask new questions about the relations.

We suggest that navigating this challenge requires thinking differently about religion, and this means attending to how we think and feel about things ultimate, comprehensive, religious, or spiritual. There is a commonplace horizon that tends to identify religion exclusively with the beliefs and practices of organized institutions. Thus, "being religious" is defined by the expressed identity and claims of such institutions. This approach judges books by their covers, and identifies religious realities by the ways they are ordinarily discussed in common sense terms. It is a pragmatic orientation that takes commonplace social forms as identifying markers for religious or spiritual realities.

What this approach overlooks, however, is the interior life of our significant experiences – in particular, the spiritual experiences that transform all of us and dynamize our deepest, most comprehensive cares and questions. This is important today because these experiences and their related convictions now find expression in diverse languages – often in languages of belief traditions that do not self-identify as religious. We think of ours as a "Secular Age."[7] Political philosophers like Charles Taylor and Eric Voegelin have probed the origins and prospects of these traditions, and shown us how secular belief traditions, like traditional religions, evoke the habits and convictions of ultimate or comprehensive moral purpose that dynamize and sustain involvement in political life. Yet they also remind us of the dark side – the historical record of fanaticism and violence that some secular traditions share with the worst forms of institutional religion. We can no longer imagine that distance from religious institutions assures freedom from fanaticism.

Gaining an adequate framework for thinking wisely about religion and politics requires attending to the interior life of both secular and religious belief traditions. It requires thinking more carefully about how diverse types of traditions now influence political life, both for better and for worse. It requires understanding and assessing ways that institutions affiliated with diverse traditions cooperate with political agencies, particularly via public funding. And it invites us to identify and celebrate exemplary figures like Shriver who navigated religion-politics issues with an eye to both the religious diversity that politics must guard and the religious involvements that politics needs to do its work, most notably its work of building peace.

Doing Things Differently

Gaining insight into appropriate forms of religion-politics relations and distinctions requires taking a cue from Jefferson. His resolution to the conflict of colonial America was based on an inward turn, a turn away from an outer-directed or extroverted way of thinking, towards the interior world of conscience. Jefferson turned his attention to the realm of *interiority*. This is the realm where transformative experiences are formative, where religious convictions are nurtured and cultivated, where questions reflect on experiences, where insights are gained and judgements pronounced, and where decisions are made to live out the convictions that matter for personal and public life.

We propose that developing this turn to interiority can provide a method for raising and exploring questions about religion and politics.[8] It is a method that attends to elements frequently overlooked in the commonplace approach. Its point of departure is an attention, not to the outer formulations, institutions, and pronouncements of a religion, but to interiority – the inner religious, spiritual, or philosophical questioning itself: the questioning about transformative experiences, ultimacy, the meaning of life, what is worth living and dying for, the goodness of the universe, my role in the cosmos, and what lies beyond. Most important, this method provides tools for transposing traditional values into novel and diverse contexts.

The focus of interiority is not, first and foremost, on answers to religious questions, but on the ultimate or comprehensive character of the questioning itself and the transformative experiences that dynamize the questioning. The focus is on this questioning as it emerges within us all, and the way it shapes all aspects of our living. This questioning is a dynamism that can take us along paths of traditional religions or along alternate paths of spiritual or secular belief traditions. Attending to our ultimate or comprehensive questioning gives rise to novel ways of thinking about matters that have been the concern of traditional religions but now are the concern of a wide array of belief traditions, both religious and secular. The turn to interiority offers a method for understanding and critically assessing the political impacts of assumptions and claims arising from both religious and secular belief traditions. And it offers ways of transposing resources from past ages into contemporary conversations while retaining grounds for objectivity on matters relevant to public life.

In Chapters 2 and 3, we offer a portrait of how this turn to interiority was lived out by Sargent Shriver in the period when he developed the most enduring policies and programs of his career. Shriver's speeches offer a wealth of data on how he approached issues of religion and politics, and one of his most compelling ideas was the claim that politics actually needs religion to do its work. In his 1963 address to the National Conference on Religion and Race, Shriver holds fast to the separation of the institutions of church and state.[9] But he is strident in his argument that religion is not only permitted in politics, it is essential.

> But laws and government are, at best, coarse and inefficient instruments for remolding social institutions or illuminating the dark places of the human heart. They can deal only with the broadest and most obvious problems ...

If we recognize that laws alone are inadequate, that legislatures and presidents cannot impose moral convictions, then we must look to those institutions whose task it is to teach moral values, to restate eternal principles in terms of today's conflicts, and to conform the daily conduct of men to the guiding values of justice, of love and of compassion. Pre-eminent among those institutions is religion and the church.[10]

Shriver's focus here is on the "dark places of the human heart." His claim is that a nation's political life is only as good as the "moral convictions" of citizens. On their own, laws and government are limited in what they can achieve, and this means that most of the work of politics actually gets implemented as it is lived out by citizens. Politics involves institutions, but it requires that citizens have an adequate interior formation for their work to bear fruit, and this involves principles that are "eternal" or ultimate or comprehensive. Shriver's attention here is on religious institutions, but his concern is their role in forming the interiority of citizens.

While Shriver refers to churches and religions, he speaks of these as institutions "pre-eminent" among others, and his reference is to other institutions and traditions that also engage in this work of teaching values, restating eternal principles, and shaping the habits that inform daily conduct. The work of religions is identified, not first and foremost by traditional traits or markers, but by the very things they share with contemporary secular belief traditions. The role of all traditions, religious and secular, is to cultivate the interiority of citizens in light of "the guiding values of justice, of love and of compassion."

The focus on interiority provided Shriver with resources for reaching out to women and men from diverse belief traditions. Yet what is compelling is the core of his message and the ground of his convictions; they were among the most traditional elements of his Catholic faith: the natural-supernatural distinction, the natural law, and the theological virtue of charity. From his earliest days of public life in Chicago in the 1950s, his preoccupation with the liberal issues of racism, poverty, and peace was expressed in the conservative language of the natural law. His commitment to justice was framed within the traditional Catholic language of the supernatural destiny of humanity. Most important, his commitment to peace was rooted in his own appropriation of the theological gift of charity. His was the traditional Catholic language of nature and grace. But while Shriver used the traditional Catholic language in the speeches of the 1950s in Chicago, and while he continued to draw on these ideas throughout his later years, by the 1960s he had transposed them into a broader framework that spoke effectively to citizens from diverse traditions, and he institutionalized these ideas in political programs that reached out to all.

Influenced as he was by the work of Catholic philosopher, Jacques Maritain, a prominent contributor to the drafting of the 1948 United Nations Universal Declaration of Human Rights, it is not difficult to understand how Shriver's natural law framework led him to believe that a universal language of justice and peace was indeed possible.[11] Yet while this tradition influenced his thinking, his approach was to go beyond older, more rigid conceptions to explore the interior life of conscience as a principle he could enshrine in political programs that were effective in reaching women and men from diverse traditions. His speeches of the early 1960's reveal an ability to transpose the natural law from an extrinsic, static, and culture-bound formulation to an interior principle that engages women and men everywhere in a program of service to others.

What is most impressive is how Shriver transposed the religious virtue of charity into broadly accessible terms. As a traditional Catholic, Shriver believed that moral life could never be reduced to our own self-making. Ours is a life lived in close relationship with God, and in this relationship, God is an actor, dynamizing, healing, and elevating our own efforts through transformative experiences of love. The traditional Catholic view had been that this grace is dispensed through the prayer and sacramental life of the church, and Shriver never ceased to avail himself of these sources. But he also understood that the work of the Spirit is in no way restricted to Catholic practice. He knew that women and men encounter transformative experiences of love as charity in diverse cultures and traditions: experiences that shift them from despair to hope, from hatred to love, from resentment and rage to generosity and joy. He knew this was how the theological virtue of charity worked. In the early 1960s, the years of the Peace Corps, we observe Shriver focusing resolutely on these transformative experiences of love, but now in the transposed language of "spirituality" and "compassion." Moreover, Shriver structured the policies and procedures of the Peace Corps to help create conditions for these transformative experiences. He was able to do this by making the turn to interiority in appropriating and transposing core elements of his Catholic tradition.

Shriver shared with conservatives the concern for the relevance of religion for politics. Yet he framed this relation in a way that was open to diversity. His focus was a universally human moral capacity and the transformative experience of love that mobilizes and enables this capacity to work on behalf of peace and justice for all. He never lost his critical edge or his concern for objectivity, but he trusted that diverse belief traditions can indeed do the work of cultivating the inner resources of justice, love, and compassion that are essential for politics. Throughout the chapters of the book, we explore the speeches of Shriver and offer a portrait of an alternative approach to religion and politics that centers on human interiority. Our focus is on a method for reflecting on interiority, and we explore how this method provides a framework for meeting challenges arising in religion-politics conversations of today.

Interiority and Method

The turn to interiority is not new, it is an idea whose elements began to emerge in the eighteenth century and whose development came to expression during the religious and cultural transitions that shaped Sargent Shriver's public life. The philosopher-theologian Bernard Lonergan has been credited with explaining this tumultuous period as a transition from classicism to historical consciousness.[12] His argument is that the classical religious heritage of the West contains profound elements that remain valid to this day, but since the seventeenth and eighteenth centuries, important revolutions have occurred that require a transposition of these elements into a new framework. These revolutions are modern science and historical consciousness.

Many of the features of modern science are well known, but what is less well known is the transformation in consciousness that occurred in Western civilization as we came to understand the diverse cultures both beyond and within our borders and the diverse horizons that marked earlier periods in our own historical development. This discovery of diversity gave rise to a discovery about meaning itself. It transposed us into an awareness of meaning as constituting culture. Ultimate beliefs and convictions are acts of meaning, and understanding how they unfold in diverse traditions requires a method for attending critically, not simply to their outward forms of expression, but to the operations underlying their performance.

Our argument is that religion-politics conflicts are rooted in a transition from classicism to historical consciousness that began in the past two centuries but remains to be completed in the present century by a method that turns its attention to interiority. Many commentators have heralded the argument for historical consciousness, but most have understated the role of interiority in the transition. The discovery of historical consciousness does not, by itself, provide the tools for navigating the challenges of historical consciousness. The discovery of our historicity arose from a focus on the outward forms of institutions and the outward objects of meaning and culture. This extroverted religious imagination accentuates diversity. But while attention to outward forms yields a preoccupation with diversity, gaining an adequate understanding of diversity requires attending to the interior operations of meaning that undergird the outward forms. This is the turn to interiority. What is achieved in this turn is a discovery of commonalities that bind us together, critical tools for navigating towards objectivity in our judgements, and resources for meeting the challenges that arise as we wrestle with matters of ultimate or comprehensive concern.

In Chapters 2 and 3, our portrait of Sargent Shriver's vocation to public life illustrates this turn to interiority at work in public life, and in Chapter 4, we offer an analysis of the turn to interiority as a method for explaining Shriver and appropriating the operations of meaning at work at the intersection of religion and politics. Shriver's speeches from his early years of public life provide a wealth of insight on the way traditional religious values dynamized his remarkably open and innovative political career. Shriver lived his life in full commitment to the conservative values of objectivity, fidelity, and respect for tradition, but he managed to marry these with an openness to the liberal values of diversity, agency, and liberty. He managed to transpose traditional religious ideas into programs that engaged men and women from diverse belief traditions in service of peace and justice for all.

Running through his speeches is the conviction that public life makes a dramatic, existential claim on the "hearts" of citizens. Working in politics during some of the darkest years of the Cold War abroad and the war against racism at home, his was an odd response to these wars. Shriver argued that the politics of his nation was only as good as the "hearts" of its citizens. Democracy is a high calling for all citizens, and Shriver's campaign was for mobilizing the resources of philosophy, culture, art, and religion to shape these "hearts" towards the pursuit of charity and justice in political life.[13] His turn was to a vision of the interior life of conscience that recognizes the role of free human agency, but he discerned an accountability in this agency. We are free citizens, but our freedom is grounded in a conscience that is not arbitrary, rather, it has an inner structure that calls us out of ourselves to a life of transcendence and responsibility in the pursuit of peace, justice, and service.

His understanding of this calling was rooted in his own traditional vocation to public life. His was a true "vocation," a muscular form of self-sacrifice and service to others that he understood as a path following the model of Christ and rooted in the traditional Catholic principles of natural law and charity. He saw his life as a participation in a cosmic drama whose stakes were nothing less than world peace. His own direction through this drama was forever guided by the spiritual values of openness, friendship, justice. He was able to articulate his message to both religious and secular audiences in languages diversely appropriate to each as required. Yet regardless of context, his meaning never wavered, it was a meaning that reached out to conservatives and liberals and to women and men of all belief traditions with an invitation to the exercise of liberty in the cosmic drama of service to others. Shriver's ability to combine faith, tradition, and truth with a commitment to reason, diversity, and justice provides an example that the journey through the challenges of historical consciousness can indeed be navigated in public life.

Shriver the Peacemaker

On January 18, 2011, Sargent Shriver died at the grand old age of 95. His passing came half a century – almost to the day – after John F. Kennedy summoned him to develop the Peace Corps that Kennedy had pledged in his campaign. The nation greeted it with widespread enthusiasm – one Harris poll showed over 70 per cent of Americans favoured its creation. Today we are no longer as curious about the organization and what it does; with familiarity has come the easy assumption that we already know all we need to know about the Peace Corps. It is now easy to overlook the distinctive approach to politics and peace that Sargent Shriver and his staff built into the program.

The Peace Corps came about with astonishing speed. Immediately after Kennedy's inauguration, Shriver returned to Washington, where he set up temporary headquarters at the Mayflower Hotel. In short order he gathered a team of talented people from across the country, galvanized a freewheeling dialogue that brought their best insights to light, and pushed hard to deliver a report to the president just four weeks later. The report recommended starting the program immediately, by executive order, with congressional authorization to follow. On March 1, five days after receiving Shriver's report, Kennedy issued the order that created the Peace Corps, and he quickly appointed Shriver its first director. To be sure, not all were enthusiastic – certainly not the editors of the *Wall Street Journal*, at any rate, who greeted the announcement of the corps and its new director with a scathing rhetorical question: "Who but the very young themselves can really believe that an Africa aflame with violence will have its fires quenched because some Harvard boy or Vassar girl lives in a mud hut and speaks Swahili?"[14]

Shriver, for his part, was not young. He was 45, a graduate of Yale Law School who had seen action as a gunnery officer in the Battle of Guadalcanal, and gone on to work as a reporter for Newsweek in New York City. After moving to Chicago, he helped Joseph P. Kennedy build the

Chicago Merchandise Mart into an extraordinarily successful enterprise and then served as chairman of the Chicago School Board. Far from being naive, he was in fact savvy enough to understand that in creating the Peace Corps he had introduced into the heart of the US government a fundamentally different approach to conflict and peace.

In a commencement address delivered at Fordham University on June 12, 1963, Shriver speaks explicitly about the spiritual dimension of the formula practised by the Peace Corps: the Peace Corps is based on "the infusion of spiritual values into secular affairs."[15]

> I speak to you not as a philosopher or theologian or even as a political scientist. For I am none of these. I am only a public servant. But my work has taken me to thirty countries. It has enabled me to send young Americans of every religious persuasion to almost fifty countries of mixed beliefs. I have seen firsthand how *basic spiritual beliefs and deeds can shatter barriers of politics and creed.*[16]

He points specifically to the connection between the "basic spiritual beliefs and deeds" the volunteers put into practice in their service assignments, and the possibilities this opens up for shattering the "barriers of politics and creed" that divide people from each other. He not only distinguishes the outer, cultural referents of religious meaning (religious persuasion, belief, creed) from their grounding in interiority (basic spiritual beliefs and deeds); he also relates the spiritual values to political life: "basic spiritual beliefs and deeds can shatter barriers of politics and creed." Indeed, Shriver sees the role of spiritual values in the Peace Corps to be an example of the broader "need for spiritual values in the work of government."[17]

In building the organization, Shriver and his staff consciously built program policies and procedures that would implement these spiritual values in the day-to-day operations of the Peace Corps. They structured service assignments to maximize possibilities for cross-cultural understanding and opportunities for the personal growth needed "to meet with other men and women on the common ground of service to human welfare and human dignity."[18] In a speech to the Commonwealth Club of California, Shriver described this "formula for practical idealism":

> The rules are few and simple. First, learn the language of the people with whom you work. Second, make up your mind that the work of developing nations is worth the price of personal sacrifice. Third, anchor yourself in the customs and traditions of the country where you are serving. Fourth, take your standard of living down near enough to the local level to make

it possible to mix freely and easily with the people – get down to eye level with them. Fifth, believe in the power of personal integrity, humility and determination.[19]

These "simple rules" channel the skills and energy of the volunteers, they put the core values of the program into action, and concretely structure the way volunteers treat the people they meet in their host countries. This set of practical program guidelines – learn the language, commit personally to development work, embrace local customs, live at or near local standards of living, cultivate personal integrity, humility, and determination – patterns the personal relations of the Peace Corps volunteers towards openness and engagement with the humanity at the core of the diverse customs and traditions of host country nationals. By putting themselves in service to human welfare and human dignity, volunteers open themselves to the transformative experiences that both attune them to difference and level the barriers of difference, creating possibilities for personal meeting on "common ground." The spiritual values of dedication, sacrifice, charity, and service are among the most traditional values of Shriver's Catholic faith. Yet their effect is to cultivate an openness to diversity and a dedication to service that are at the center of the Peace Corps vision of peace.

In Chapter 5, we explore the distinctive understanding of peace at the heart of the Peace Corps. We show how the turn to interiority can explain how it works, how it offers insights into a positive role for spiritual values in politics, and how Shriver's faith shaped a program whose openness and commitment to service could reach out to touch the hearts of all.

We also explore how the Peace Corps embodies a distinctive approach to resolving conflicts and building peace. We argue that Shriver's "simple rules" reflect novel insights into how volunteers engage in the resolution of personal and political conflicts in their work. It is not difficult to imagine – based on what we know and believe about America's exercise of international power – how women and men of a host community might feel suspicious, even hostile at the prospect of an American coming to live and work among them. We would feel the same in their situation. We would feel the defensiveness and anger that always accompanies the sense of threat. Why has she come? What reason could she have other than to exploit us or to use us? She should not be here. She should go back to where she belongs, and she should take the United States government with her.

From this vantage, the question for peacemaking becomes: What would it take for us to allay our sense of threat and begin to question our sense of certainty about her intentions? Indeed, what would it take to become genuinely curious about who she is, why she is here? What would it take to begin to trust her, to work collaboratively with her? Shriver knew that making peace is a difficult business. He knew that once a foreign national adopts a wary and defended stance regarding the United States, it is difficult to allay their suspicions and defuse their sense of threat. Claims of innocence won't bridge the distance in the relationship or mend the rupture. Neither will assertions of good intention. As we all know from personal experience, there is little hearing for such protests once something we say or do triggers another person's sense of suspicion or threat.

When we feel threatened, it is very difficult to make peace. This is because an experience of threat sharply narrows the framework we use for interpreting our experience and choosing our response. We are on alert, we are wary. We are not at all curious about the other person's intentions, or if we are, it is only to discern a better way of mounting an attack or defence. We already know they jeopardize something we care about. We are focused on how to defend against the threat. What would it take to allay our suspicions about the Peace Corps volunteer, to shift from a posture of threat and suspicion to a horizon of curiosity and trust? Shriver's answer is inscribed in the principles and "simple rules" of the Peace Corps: service to human welfare and human dignity. He called it "the most powerful ideal of all."[20]

By sending volunteers overseas to engage in service to welfare and dignity, Shriver established the path for resolving conflicts and building peace both locally and in the broader international arena. Shriver knew that the core of politics was interiority, that politics involved changing "hearts." And he knew this is what the Peace Corps does. Shriver acknowledged that this approach was unusual. He referred to the volunteer as a "rare bird."

> A Peace Corps Volunteer, therefore, is really a "rare bird." He is unique. He goes to a foreign country to work within that country's system; he helps fill their needs as they see them; he speaks their language; he lives in the way they live and under their laws; he does not try to change their religion; he does not seek to make a profit from conducting business in their country; he does not interfere in their political or military affairs.
>
> And because of this he has been welcomed where others were turned away.[21]

To learn that a volunteer is serving welfare and dignity – to learn she is serving our community as a teacher, a youth development specialist, or a nurse; to learn she is working with and supervised by a counterpart from our community; to learn that she would not be here had our country not requested her – all this is to learn that there is reason to question our original suspicion and hostility. This learning involves experiences that are transformative. It raises doubts about our original interpretation of her intentions, and this releases our curiosity. "If she is not here to push her own agenda, then why is she here?" It releases our spontaneous desire for contact, for fellowship, for the breaking down of barriers. "Who is she? Why would she come all this way to serve us? A representative of the American government would do that?" The result is the feelings of threat that fuel the conflict begin to give way.

The analysis of Chapter 5 draws on the turn to interiority of the Insight approach to conflict to explain how we understand Shriver's work in the Peace Corps.[22] The focus on interiority is an interesting approach currently pursued within the field of peace and conflict studies, and authors advancing this approach investigate how spiritual values work to shift the direction of conflicts and establish conditions for peace. Central to this is the analysis of conflict as a process where *learning* functions both to construct conflicts and to open avenues for resolution and peace. The significant learning that transforms conflicts is the person-to-person learning that de-links hardened feelings of hostility and threat and opens new avenues for curiosity. Our analysis engages this approach and focuses on Shriver's "simple rules": how they go to the heart of this learning process; how they reveal insights into the role of spiritual values in facilitating the resolution of conflict and the building of peace; and how they arise from a turn to interiority that enables the transposition of core elements from faith tradition into a public institution that engages women and men from diverse traditions in the service of peace.

Outline of the Argument

In this book, we offer Sargent Shriver as a compelling example of an approach to religion and politics that, we believe, can help contemporary North Americans navigate the perils of liberal-conservative divisions. Our focus is on Shriver's early years, the first decade of his public life and the early years of the Peace Corps. In many ways, these are most interesting because Shriver's Catholic faith tradition was only beginning to experience the dramatic transformations wrought by the Second Vatican Council, and American society was just beginning to become a community divided by the conflicting convictions of conservative and liberal belief traditions. Our focus is on the Peace Corps as a mature expression of a set of ideas on religion and politics that we believe merit consideration in the present-day context.

The focus is on Shriver, but the book is not a biography. Rather, we present Shriver as an example of a set of ideas we believe explain his life and work in ways that are relevant today. These ideas have roots in Shriver's Catholic faith tradition. Yet ours is not the standard way this tradition is presented. In fact, Catholics from both the left and the right will likely find aspects of the presentation rather odd. We present the core ideas as a method we call the turn to interiority. We draw on the philosophy of Bernard Lonergan to develop this method, and throughout the book we provide background material to help understand the core ideas. Yet this is not a text on philosophical or theological theory. It is a book that argues for the value of attending to interiority and explaining Shriver's continued relevance to religion-politics conversations today.

Shriver is addressed in Chapters 2, 3, and 5, and our method is to begin with an analysis of his speeches. Shriver reveals a great deal about himself in his speeches. His public addresses are to diverse audiences, yet it is not difficult to observe central themes that come back time and again. These themes tell us a lot about how he understood his work and why he did what he did. Shriver is now regarded as one of the most influential figures in the last half-century of American politics. His biographer, Scott Stossel, makes clear the extraordinary influence of his religious faith on all aspects of his work in politics.[23] Our effort is not to critically assess Shriver but to gain some insight into what, precisely, this influence was, how it worked, how he was able to navigate the challenges of his day, and how he provides a way forward for Americans today. The projects Shriver built have been shaped by his faith, but they have reached out to find resonance in the hearts of women and men from diverse secular and religious belief traditions. This is remarkable. Our effort in this book is to help explain this achievement so we might do likewise today.

Our argument is that religion-politics issues can no longer be handled by simplistic appeals to either separation or fusion. The political context for current debates involves a series of historical events, notably Supreme Court Decisions and reactions to these decisions, that progressively polarized liberals and conservatives into emphasizing either separating or fusing the two. Neither, on its own, is adequate. The basic elements of the institutional distinction and the primacy of conscience were established in colonial days, but they must now be developed further to deal with new challenges. New forms of formal and informal involvements by both religious and political groups have arisen to deliver diverse public goods to communities with diverse allegiances. Secular belief traditions have now joined the ranks of traditional religions in offering "comprehensive doctrines" that pronounce on matters of ultimate concern, and these influence politics both explicitly and implicitly in ways that require subtle and precise tools for analysis and assessment.[24] Thinking adequately through the issues now requires criteria for case-specific insights into permissible and non-permissible forms of religion-politics relations. Most important, however, is the spirit that needs to guide the project, the spirit of peace.

Navigating appropriate distinctions and relations between religion and politics now calls for care and precision. Most important, it calls for a philosophical method that incarnates the very spirit of peace that must shape the project of politics. It needs to be a philosophical method that can mediate between diversity and objectivity; a philosophy with a method and criteria for precise distinctions and relations that permit the assessment and cultivation of objective values while remaining open to diversity. We suggest that such a philosophy can be found in the turn to interiority and that Shriver provides an example of interiority in practice. Shriver's speeches reveal the liberal commitment to diversity and the religion-politics distinction that is required to guard this diversity. But they also reveal the conservative commitment to objective moral values and the religion-politics relations that are required to nurture these values. Most important, they reflect an innovative adaptation of traditional analytic tools, via interiority, that enabled him to achieve in practice what we seek to explain in the theory.

Chapter 2 explores the early years of Shriver's public life in Chicago from 1955 until 1959. Our interest, here, is in his public life as a "vocation." The speeches of these years reveal a great deal about the elements from his Catholic faith that shaped Shriver's self-understanding, most notably the natural law and the theological virtue of charity. We explore the role these elements from his conservative faith tradition played in opening his life to the service of others from diverse traditions. We can discern in these years the beginnings of core ideas that would find fuller expression in the Peace Corps. In this chapter we also offer a brief overview of key elements of the background context. The notable events were the Supreme Court Challenges related to religion and schools. We examine how these events galvanized American public opinion into opposing camps, and we offer an analysis that provides insights into possible ways forward.

In Chapter 3 we focus on Shriver's speeches from the Peace Corps years, 1961 to 1963, in particular his January 1963 address to the National Conference on Religion and Race and his June 1963 commencement address delivered at Fordham University. These speeches offer his clearest insights into how we can differentiate religion and politics while exploring forms of religion-politics relations that could remain open to both conservative and liberal values: objectivity and diversity; family and social justice; liberty and peace. The analysis explores how Shriver transposed the traditional principles of natural law and charity from his Catholic tradition into a public language fit for the arena of public life in politics. We begin exploring core questions arising currently in debates over religion and politics. And the analysis sets out the turn to interiority as a framework for effecting this transposition both in Shriver's day and today.

In Chapter 4 we offer an overview of central features of the philosophy that informs the method of interiority that is central to our analysis of Shriver. We develop the framework for explaining Shriver's achievements, and to do so we draw on the work of Bernard Lonergan and situate Lonergan's work within the Catholic tradition that shaped Shriver's life and work.

Chapter 5 focuses on the Peace Corps as the fullest expression of Shriver's vision of religion and politics.[25] The speeches are those from his years as director of the Peace Corps, but they also include later addresses that reflect on the Peace Corps experience and its achievements. The analysis highlights the relevance of the turn to interiority and draws on insights from the field of conflict studies that are rooted in the Insight approach to conflict.[26] We propose a method that champions the turn to interiority. And we offer the Peace Corps analysis as an example of how we might follow Shriver and build on his legacy in relating religion and politics in present and future years. The guiding questions are those of the religion-politics debate, and the analysis reveals the significance of Shriver, not only as a great figure in American politics, but also as a true holy man of our age.

Finally, in Chapter 6, we offer concluding reflections on ways forward in addressing core challenges in the religion-politics conversation. Shriver lived his public life as a religious vocation inspired by Christ, yet he took his faith into public life as a champion of justice and peace. He bridged the worlds of religion and politics, he lived core values from both sides of the liberal-conservative divide, and he built successful public institutions on the principles of peace at the heart of his faith tradition. We offer an analysis of this achievement that, we believe, offers direction for present and future years.

Chapter Two

The Public Faith of Sargent Shriver, 1955–1959

Sargent Shriver offers a compelling example of a public figure whose Catholic faith influenced the development of political programs that, to this day, are lauded as exemplary in American history: the Peace Corps, Head Start, the Job Corps, VISTA, Poverty Law, the Special Olympics, to name a few.[1] The most significant, we argue, is the Peace Corps. He has been heralded as "one of the major figures of the second half of the twentieth century,"[2] and his spirituality played a decisive role in influencing his politics in directions towards openness, generosity, and humanity. Shriver held traditional Catholic convictions about objective moral values and the important role of religion in politics.[3] Contrary to popular expectations, however, the influence of religion on his politics was not towards closure or exclusion. He upheld the distinction between religious and political institutions that guarded respect for diversity and the primacy of conscience. His was a commitment to global humanity and a vision of peace and justice that found resonance in the hearts of women and men from diverse secular and religious belief traditions.

His faith and work bear witness to what Bernard Lonergan has called a shift to interiority – a recognition of openness and diversity that discovers a common humanity and spiritual dynamism in the interior life of all citizens. We suggest that the methodical discernment of this spiritual dynamism provides resources for a new path for thinking about religion and politics; one that opens doors for a commitment to objective values in the midst of diversity and the pursuit of justice and peace. For Shriver, central to this was the theological virtue of charity that dynamized a public life of service to peace.[4] We argue that interiority and charity played key roles in shaping Shriver's life and his programs. And in the essays that follow, we offer an explanation, rooted in insights from Lonergan, for understanding and appropriating Shriver as one of the great peacemakers of our age.

Shriver's Religious Vocation to Public Life

Shriver's speeches from his early years of public life in Chicago (1955–9) provide a wealth of insights on the way religious values shaped his open and innovative political career. Working in politics during some of the darkest years of the Cold War abroad and the war against racism at home, his response to these wars was to argue that politics is only as good as the hearts of citizens. Politics is a mission of service to humanity, and religious values play an essential role in dynamizing these "hearts" in the direction of justice and human flourishing.[5]

For Shriver, no religious virtue is more important than charity in this work of service to public life. In April 1956, just months after being elected to his first major role in public life as President of the Chicago Board of Education, Shriver delivered a speech on racism to DePaul University. He opens one of the earliest addresses of his public career with the following words:

> No subject is more controversial than the topic of race relations, interracial justice, segregation. Call it what you will, this subject of racial discrimination arouses hotter passions than any other in America today. My first thought, therefore, is this: I am NOT here to arouse passion, excite enmities, or plead for doctrinaire solutions to complex human problems. I'm here to plead for CHARITY, and patience, for hope and GOOD WILL.[6]

The religious virtue of charity is everywhere in Shriver's speeches.[7] In March 1957, in his address to educators at the Livingston County Institute, Shriver concludes by situating education at the center of the drama of human civilization, and he invites his audience to a cosmic vision of their work:

> Today hydrogen or atom bomb explosions could literally devastate the world, destroy knowledge, cause tongues to cease, make prophecies void. But, as St. Paul said – even then, charity would not fall away.
> You teachers are daily practitioners of charity, and your work will not fall away. For you give of yourselves to children, every day, all day.
> There is no more noble charity, no more exalted work than yours.
> Impervious to threats, dedicated to children and the welfare of others, may you carry on your charity and gain the eternal rewards you so richly deserve.[8]

Again, in his Chicago address to the Sixteenth Annual Vocational Conference, March 14, 1957, his topic is "Citizenship," and he uses the language of "love" to speak about the religious gift of charity:

We can change Chicago. That's easy. The hard part is to change ourselves – to change ourselves from men and women looking for the easy job with "the most in it for me" as the popular expression puts it.

Such a job may pay well – in dollars. And the absence of work may be pleasant – for a while.

But if like a scientist you will take the raw materials of your mind and your body and process them through the laboratory of humility, prayer and neighborly love, the result will be a second explosion heard 'round the world.

You will be raised into a life of overwhelming love, great peace, and heroic achievement. And these things no man will ever be able to take from you.[9]

We suggest that Shriver's understanding of religion and politics was rooted in his own religious vocation to public life. His work mirrored his own interiority. His was a true "vocation," a muscular form of self-sacrifice and service to others that he understood as a path following the model of Christ.[10] He speaks of his role in public life as a form of "stewardship," a public trust that has been handed down to him and which he is charged to hand on again to others.[11] He evokes a vision of American citizenship as one of service to those in need around the world, whose exercise is to be dynamized by "true religion," "hard work," "fervent prayer," and "humility."[12]

Shriver's Catholic faith was deeply traditional – today we would certainly call it conservative. References to "the home, the church, and the school" arise frequently in his speeches, and Shriver speaks of these as "three great bulwarks of American democracy."[13] His vision is of a strong role for religious institutions involved in public life, nurturing objective moral values. He argues for "Stable, happy homes" as "the most important foundations for a just, democratic society," and he praises the Christian Family Movement for its role in preparing and supporting good Catholic family life.[14] Shriver's biographer, Scott Stossel, speaks of his practice of attending mass daily, even in the midst of hectic political campaigns. He notes Shriver's early affiliation with the conservative Catholic organization Opus Dei and its influence on Shriver's vision of work as a "spiritual calling."[15] When Shriver passed away in January 2011, Ross Douthat praised him as "the last abortion critic to find a place on the national Democratic ticket."[16]

His traditional faith had roots in early years of family life.[17] In 1910 his Catholic mother, Hilda, sought and received a special dispensation from the Archdiocese of Baltimore to marry a non-Catholic, Robert Sargent Shriver, and soon after, Robert converted to Catholicism. Sarge's parents became active Catholics, involved in numerous Catholic organizations, and were personal friends of Cardinal Gibbons, Archbishop of Baltimore. Sarge and his siblings became altar boys, serving at masses of the cardinal during their summers at the Shriver family home in Union Mills, and they socialized frequently with the nuns, priests, bishops, and seminary students who were welcomed into the home as visitors.

He began his education at St. John's Catholic Parochial School in West-minster, he continued at the Cathedral School when the family moved to Baltimore in 1923, and he spent his high-school years at Canterbury School in New Milford, Connecticut, a Catholic prep school dedicated to preparing Catholic students to enter non-Catholic Ivy League Colleges.[18] He maintained and deepened his Catholic religious practice and his theo-logical education during his years at Yale where he joined the St. Thomas More Society and took it upon himself to read systematically through the works of Thomas Aquinas.[19] He was deeply traditional in his commitment to sexual abstinence before marriage, he turned frequently to the Catholic Chaplain at Yale for spiritual consolation and support, and maintained his faith practice through his years in the navy during World War II.[20]

Shriver's faith was traditional, yet his was never a purely "other-worldly" faith. His religious dedication was to the service of others. For Shriver, politics in a democracy makes demands on citizens and leaders, and a life dedicated to public service could be a true "vocation" – a calling rooted in a spirituality that focuses on the religious virtue of charity. His campaign was for mobilizing the resources of philosophy, culture, art, and religion to shape the interiority of citizens to live out their diverse roles in democratic service to others.[21] We are free citizens in a democ-racy, but our freedom is grounded in a deeper human life that calls us out of ourselves to transcendence and responsibility. The highest form of this transcendence is a dedication to peace and justice that is grounded in the Divine gift of charity.

On January 21, 1958, in his address to The Jewish Big Sisters Standard Club, Shriver puts forward a model of leadership in American public life that can only be understood as one he sought to realize in his own role of service to the Chicago Board of Education:

> We have honored businessmen, lawyers, doctors, bankers and management experts, but America needs sages, saints, scholars and statesmen master-minds and master-spirits. We shall never get an adequate supply of them, however, until superhighways and supermarkets take second place to super-schools and super-churches.[22]

One month later, Shriver adds further substance to this vision:

> If in the United States by the time of the 21st century we could perfect an education of the type I describe, we could begin to prove ... that the U.S. is

the proper leader of a united world based on knowledge and love as compared to a Soviet world based on fear and hate.[23]

And on June 4, 1959, he concludes his address to St. Procopius College:

Great and good as our former achievements have been, let us dedicate ourselves to future accomplishments based on the mind and soul of man, not on his stomach or back. Then we shall be fulfilling our main purpose and true vocation. Then you will be achieving your greatest happiness and success.[24]

Shriver saw his life as a participation in a cosmic drama whose stakes were nothing less than world peace and the future of civilization.[25] His own role in this drama was forever guided by his faith, particularly the gift of charity, understood as a transformation to a new habit of loving dedication to others that is grounded in the gift of Divine love and ordered towards a cosmic, supernatural destiny. He expressed his message to both religious and secular audiences, yet regardless of context, his meaning never wavered. It was a meaning that reached out to women and men of diverse religious and secular belief traditions with an invitation to mobilize the resources of their religious traditions in the cosmic drama of self-giving service to others.

Catholics and American Politics

The account so far is of a public figure whose Catholic faith seemed ready and fit for application to American politics. In the early years of Shriver's public life, however, the reality was disturbingly different. In fact, when John F. Kennedy campaigned for President in 1960, it was not clear to Americans that a Catholic could fit in with the American vision of democracy. This was because of a long history of Catholic suspicion of liberalism. In his contribution to the Cambridge volume, *Catholicism and Liberalism*, Joseph Komonchak paints a dramatic portrait of two centuries of popes, bishops, and apologists issuing vitriolic condemnations of a liberalism that was judged nothing short of Satanic.[26] The focus of the critique was an extreme individualist version of liberalism that claimed that religion must be private, that social and political life must be freed from all forms of influence from religion, that economic life must be left to operate automatically, free from moral guidance, and that philosophy must function autonomously, accountable to no higher authority. The Church's response was to urge the construction of a separate Catholic society, insulated from liberalism's diabolical influences, equipping

Catholics to "undertake the battle to restore Christ's rights."[27] It is not difficult to observe parallels in contemporary political life.

The Second Vatican Council (1962–5), however, marked a dramatic shift in this vision. At the Council, Catholic philosophers and theologians began articulating an alternate version of liberalism that opened doors for diverse forms of Catholic participation in democratic life. Shriver's formative years were before the Council, and the Peace Corps was launched as the Council was in session. But the transformative effects of the Council arose as a result of forces that were at work during the first half of the twentieth century, and Shriver was shaped by these forces. These decades witnessed the development of a community of American Catholics who would anticipate the Council by living out their faith as participants and leaders in American political life.[28] Shriver grew up part of this community.

In 1929, when Shriver was 13, he moved from their Baltimore home into a New York City apartment where his parents, Hilda and Robert, teamed up with Richard Dana Skinner to support and promote the newly founded *Commonweal* magazine.[29] The magazine exerted considerable influence on American Catholic life in the decades leading up the Council and beyond, and it came to be associated with a view of liberalism that advocated the separation of church and state but respected the role of religion in politics.[30] *Commonweal* liberals had a focus that was different from the extreme individualist liberalism that was the object of the traditional Catholic critique. They were critics of despotism, advocates of representative government, and champions of freedom of conscience.

At the core of their vision was the conviction that church and state must remain institutionally separate in order to safeguard their proper spheres of responsibility; the church for the spiritual, and the state for the political. In the American tradition, however, this form of liberalism developed, not to keep religion out of politics, but precisely because religion has a specific role in politics that is to be exercised through the conscience of citizens. Their goal was to define this role in a democracy in order to safeguard diversity and freedom of conscience and safeguard the role of individual conscience in drawing on religion for guidance and leadership in politics. *Commonweal* liberals were committed to guarding the sphere of religion from meddlesome interference by the state, maintaining a political context for diversity and freedom of conscience, and ensuring that religion's influences on politics would be channeled through the proper democratic processes.[31]

Commonweal developed into a voice against Catholic separatism.[32] The magazine's editors affirmed the American form of democratic life and promoted the involvement of Catholics in this project. Their vision recognized the pluralism of American society, the responsibilities of Catholics in this society, the importance of government involvement in broader ranges of social and economic life, and a sort of third way between a strong critique of Communism and a McCarthyism whose anti-Communism proved corrosive for democratic life.[33] Part of the philosophy was an accepted version of "Americanism" that tended to indulge readers in a rather self-congratulatory assessment of America's role in the wartime conquest of totalitarianism.[34] Yet the magazine remained self-conscious and self-critical, and the editors sought to combine the positive affirmation of Catholic participation in American politics with a critical assessment of problems that arise when this participation succumbs to ideology.[35]

One of the defining influences on Shriver was Catholic philosopher, Jacques Maritain.[36] Maritain's ideas were welcomed in *Commonweal* and he was influential in developing a natural law framework for a "Christian humanism" that could reach out to diverse beliefs and traditions.[37] He played an important role in defending the compatibility of Catholic faith and American democracy. His analysis included an appeal to three core ideas: the tradition's classic distinction-relation between the natural and the supernatural; the natural law framework; and the theological virtue of charity.[38] The natural-supernatural distinction, worked out by Catholic theologians in the middle ages, carved out a sphere where human intelligence can do its proper work of understanding and guiding personal and social life.[39] Politics falls within the capacities of natural reason. The Thomist natural law framework emphasized reason's ability both to understand the natural world and to organize human life by applying its talents to the affairs of family, commerce, society, and politics. Contrary to much contemporary thought, the term "natural" did not refer to the world of plants and animals. The focus of Maritain's analysis, rather, was a distinctive feature of our *nature* as humans, an inner normativity that is operative as an inclination in human intelligence that we can discern, formulate, and implement in the decisions we make to organize ourselves in personal, social, and political life.[40] Finally, the theological virtue of charity enables us to fulfill our nature and live out our highest capacities as persons.[41]

Maritain's framework for relating these three sets of ideas was provided by his understanding of the Catholic tradition of natural law. This was an impressive Aristotelian philosophy for understanding both the nature of human persons and the moral basis for social and political life. It was a framework that understood persons as having both lower faculties that are shared by animals, and higher intellectual, volitional, and spiritual faculties that are distinctively human. Acting responsibly involved cultivating virtues or habits that promoted the higher faculties, and this required bringing the excesses of the lower faculties under the control of the higher by discerning and acting in accordance with an inner inclination operative in our nature as intelligent. All of this required the development of character through a life of devotion to practice, analysis, and discipline in diverse spheres of social and political life. Most important, the work of politics falls within the proper range of reason, and because reason has a universal structure, we can expect to find a basis for some measure of agreement among women and men from diverse cultures and religions in a pluralist democracy.[42]

But the Thomist approach to natural law also required a life of devotion to spiritual practice, and this focus is clear and strong in the work of Maritain.[43] Here is where insights into the natural and supernatural and the theological virtue of charity played a key role in the relationship between religion and politics. This was because of the problem of sin – what today we would speak of with words like ideology, bias, domination, corruption, and self-interest. Human life is forever finite, and finitude is not simply a matter of limitation, it is also a problem of bias and corruption. Sin harms and distorts our ability to reason and act. Yet while this corrupting influence is strong, it never pronounces the final word, and this is because, beyond the virtues we can achieve through our moral practice, we are also able to receive theological virtues like charity by opening ourselves to transformative experiences through prayer and the sacraments. The theological virtues, mediated through religious practice, can break the hold of this corruption and restore reason's basic orientation to truth and value. What this means is that moral, social, and political life require devotion, not simply to ethical and rational development, but also to the religious development that is required to undo the corrosive effects of sin and renew the powers of reason and responsibility that are our proper nature.

While politics is the work of natural reason, still religious virtues are needed to exercise their empowering and healing effects on reason. Traditionally, this was interpreted to require Catholic institutions acting directly in the sphere of politics. But on this issue, the Catholic authors who influenced Shriver were "Personalist."[44] Maritain examined the contemporary historical context of democratic pluralism and argued that presently religions must exercise their influence through the interiority of persons as citizens.[45] The place where the theological virtues of charity, hope and faith do their work is the hearts of persons, and this means that the primary focus must now be on interiority and liberty. Religious institutions influence political life, but indirectly through the interior life of "the believer as citizen."[46] Religion is essential for political life because politics calls for human reason acting at its best, and this requires a spiritual formation for undoing the distorting effects of sin and elevating reason to its proper capacities. But the locus of this interaction of religion and reason is now understood to be the heart and conscience of persons. With the recognition of freedom, democratic pluralism, and religious liberty, the importance of religion for politics is not diminished, rather the analysis shifts to focus on interiority – the place where spirituality does its work. In democracies, religious institutions operate directly to cultivate the hearts of citizens through various channels, and indirectly in the public sphere through the work of believers as persons and citizens.[47]

We argue that this framework, influenced as it was by Maritain, helps explain Shriver's religious vocation to politics in the speeches of his early years of public life. His was a traditional Catholic faith, yet he remained open and committed to the compatibility and relevance of this faith for public life in American pluralist society. Indeed, as early as January 1937, when Shriver took over as chair of the editorial board of the *Yale Daily News*, he declared that the upcoming year's publications would be guided by five principles: they would be Christian, Democratist, Aristotelian, American, and Optimistic.[48] Shriver's biographer notes that his parents frequently sent copies of *Commonweal* magazine for Sarge and his friends, and the issues were read and debated avidly in the halls and residences of Yale.[49] *Commonweal* editors celebrate the influence of Maritain and Dorothy Day in the magazine's history, and the name of Maritain shows up frequently in Shriver's speeches of the Chicago years. Both traditional and liberal influences from American Catholic social ethics are clear in the speeches of his early public life. Shriver took these influences into novel directions,[50] and we argue that he lived out a vision of religion and politics that both reflects and calls for a deeper understanding of the "turn to interiority" that is central to his vocation to public life.

Religion, Schools, and the "Wall of Separation"

Shriver's vision of religion and politics may appear plausible to some whose convictions have not been tainted by bitter liberal-conservative disputes that gained momentum in the decades following his public life in Chicago. Today, however, this sense of plausibility does not seem widespread, and one of the reasons is the way public imagination came to be galvanized by the image of a "wall of separation" between church and state. The image arose during the middle of the twentieth century as a result of a series of court challenges related to the role of religion in schools.[51] Could local tax money be used for bus transportation for parochial school students? Could public schools start the school day with a prayer? The result was a growing conviction that not only must political and religious institutions remain separate, they must never be seen to collaborate in any way. Shriver remained convinced that such collaboration remained not only permissible but essential for political life. Still, public imagination did not keep up with Shriver.

The roots of the issues go back to colonial times. With the Constitution in 1789 and the Bill of Rights in 1791, the legal and political framework was established for specific forms of distinctions and relations between religion and politics. Thomas Jefferson led the way with a perspective that affirmed that genuine religious conviction is a matter of conscience, not coercion, and people are answerable to their god and to themselves, not to the government, for the integrity of their religious beliefs. His focus was on religious coercion, and the core of the issue was conscience. Yet colonial Americans assumed that the exercise of conscience could be expected to yield visible forms of religious influence on political life. Shriver shared this perspective.

When the states ratified the Bill of Rights in 1791, these constitutional amendments applied only to the newly formed federal government, not to the states. Developments in Constitutional law over the next 150 years, however, coupled with expansions in the ranges of programs and services offered by both churches and governments, combined to bring state and local policies within the ambit of the First Amendment and the jurisdiction of the Supreme Court. [52]

A major development occurred in 1868, when Congress adopted the Fourteenth Amendment. This Amendment guaranteed all US citizens the right to due process and equal protection under the law, requiring the states, for the first time, to meet the same due process and equal protection standards that the Fifth Amendment imposed on the federal government. Almost 60 years later, in a series of decisions beginning in 1925, the Supreme Court began interpreting the "due process clause" of the Fourteenth Amendment in a way that held states progressively more accountable for the rest of the legal protections guaranteed to Americans by the Bill of Rights. In 1940, the Supreme Court ruled that the religion clauses of the First Amendment applied to the states as well as to the federal government, and like Congress, state legislatures could "make no law respecting an establishment of religion or restricting the free exercise thereof."[53] With this decision, the Supreme Court took on the role of arbiter and interpreter of religion and politics in America.[54]

In the years following, a series of local disputes arose that led to Supreme Court Justice Hugo Black's historic 1947 ruling, *Everson v. Board of Education.* It was a ruling that marked a dramatic shift in public thinking about religion and politics. If colonial Americans had few doubts about religion's relations to politics, Americans after Justice Black would now be plagued with doubts about any and all forms of religion's relations to politics.

The disputes arose as a result of changes in forms of institutional involvements by churches and local governments in delivering and funding educational programs and services for citizens. Over the years, both churches and governments had expanded their respective institutional capacities and missions. By 1947 churches were in the business of running schools and local governments were in the business of collecting taxes, setting school policy, and regulating public transportation. The result was a proliferation of novel opportunities for collaboration between religious and political institutions. In Ewing, New Jersey, these institutional developments converged in a Board of Education decision that used tax revenues to reimburse parents for the cost of sending their children to school on public transportation. The policy reimbursed public school parents and Catholic school parents alike, a scope of action that upset Mr. Everson, a local taxpayer who filed suit to challenge the right of the Board to reimburse parents sending their children to Catholic schools.

The Court's decision in *Everson v. Board of Education* was both mundane and momentous. On the one hand, the court ruled on a dispute over school transportation policy in Ewing, New Jersey by affirming the policy already in place: the school board can continue to reimburse both public school and Catholic school parents for the cost of sending their children to school on public transportation. On the other hand, in making the decision the way it did, the court set forth an interpretive framework it would use to rule on all subsequent First Amendment cases – thereby shaping the images influencing public thought about religion and politics today.

Justice Hugo Black wrote for the majority in *Everson v. Board of Education*.[55] In so doing, he made it clear his principal concern was to prevent a recurrence of the "turmoil, civil strife and persecution" that characterized religiously motivated conflict in the colonial period.[56] Justice Black shared Thomas Jefferson's focus on the problems of oppressive alliances of religious and political institutions; alliances that resulted in coercion, discrimination, and oppression. The challenge he faced, however, was different from the one confronting Jefferson. In colonial America, Jefferson faced the challenge of conflict and strife caused by laws that made religious affiliation a determining factor in a citizen's liberty and political standing in the community. Justice Black's focus was on avoiding even the smallest perception of influence resulting from the distribution of public funds when religious and political institutions collaborate in delivering public goods.

While his decision provided some clarity on religion-politics relations, in the course of formulating his decision, Justice Black used language that would galvanize public imagination around images of "neutrality" and a "wall of separation." What Black allowed was for state money to be used to provide public goods delivered in a relationship of collaboration with religious institutions. This form of relation was to be permitted as long as it involved the state in the delivery of social goods like transportation, and this relation was judged acceptable even when the transportation was to religious schools. His language, however, appealed to the idea of neutrality in this relation.[57]

For Black, the normative relation between church and state is the relation of institutional neutrality. His reasoning aimed at preventing discrimination on religious grounds and the direct involvement of state in the sphere of religious teaching or practice. But for Black, even the smallest amount of funding provided in support of programs or practices that could be construed as explicitly religious could threaten this neutrality. In his view, the decision to fund a religious activity or institution created an unconstitutional relation between church and state.

> No taxes in any amount, large or small, can be levied to support any religious activities or institutions, whatever they may be called, or whatever form they may adopt to teach or practice religion.[58]

The content of Black's ruling focused on precise forms of institutional relations in the delivery of public goods. But the image he used shifted the focus to cast doubt upon all but the most remote forms of institutional collaboration. To accentuate the stakes in the case, Black conclude by evoking the image of a wall.

> The First Amendment has erected a wall between church and state. That wall must be kept high and impregnable. We could not approve the slightest breach. New Jersey has not breached it here.[59]

The image of a wall between church and state metaphorically conveyed Black's interpretation of the First Amendment.[60] Clearly, his interpretation was motivated by a sincere respect for the rights of religious belief and a deep concern to prevent a recurrence of the religiously motivated conflict that once oppressed and divided colonial America. His language, however, created new images that moved beyond the substance of his carefully formulated decision. Black's image cast doubts on any and all forms of religion-politics relations. In the years immediately following 1947, no Supreme Court Justice disputed the "wall" interpretation. Disagreements turned on where to locate the wall separating church and state, but the wall as the guiding image was not challenged. In 1952, the court's decision allowed New York City schools to grant release time to students for attending voluntary, privately funded religious education classes off school property. The private source of funding and physical location of classes defined the location of the wall, and release time, in the court's judgement, did not breach the wall. But no dissenting voices questioned the principle of neutrality or the image of a wall.[61]

Shriver's Vision: Religious Resources for Guarding Diversity

Sargent Shriver's early speeches reveal significant insights into healthy religion-politics relations that were becoming obscured by a public imagination galvanized by the image of a wall of separation. Shriver accepted the principles of institutional distinction and liberty of conscience. But his focus was on important resources that religion brings to politics; resources that politics needs to do the very work of making good on these principles. His was a traditional Catholic faith practice and a traditional Catholic theology and philosophy. But he showed how these resources could nurture and bolster an American pluralist commitment to democracy, liberty, diversity, and social justice.

Interesting for our purposes is the role of Shriver's Catholic tradition in promoting a public education system that takes seriously its social and political obligations to religious and cultural diversity. His faith was deeply Catholic and his practice profoundly conservative, yet his Catholic God never ceased to be big enough to welcome the diverse cultural and religious beliefs and expressions that Shriver encountered in his public life at home and abroad. In his address to the Conference on School Administration and Educational Leadership at Northwestern University, July 9, 1957, Shriver provides a vision of diversity that would come to fruition four years later in the Peace Corps. He outlined an ideal for American schools that would prepare American children to become:

profound leaders of world culture, truly exceptional students today, truly great leaders for tomorrow, men and women distinguished by their understanding of and consequent love for all mankind whatever the color of skin, the sound of language, the background of mind.[62]

He proposes a program that would put them to work as ambassadors of America abroad, a proposition that would come to realization with the Peace Corps:

> Tomorrow they will be called upon to speak for America, to explain America, to excite enthusiasm for our American way of life. To do this they must be able to speak the language and understand the mind of the audiences they will be addressing – not only in California but in Calcutta, too.[63]

Shriver outlines the rationale behind his vision:

> The purpose of studying other cultures ... is based on the belief there is no need for all men and all cultures to follow identical paths. It expresses the conviction that practical good fellowship and foreign relations need not be based upon uniformity in politics, doctrine, or culture. On the contrary, it seeks through education to bring men together on terms of equality and understanding for the good of human society as a whole.[64]

Seven months later, in his address to the Illinois State Normal University, February 7, 1958, Shriver provides evidence of his profound respect for the "shrinking planet," the "unity of humankind" that was beginning to influence political life on the planet, and the great religious traditions that have shaped the diverse cultures of world:

> Instead of concentrating almost wholly on teaching Anglo-Saxon culture in our high schools and colleges, I suggest that we start to offer courses in the seven great world cultures, six of which are now vying for space on our ever-diminishing globe. The cultures I suggest are these: The Moslem Culture; The Hindu or Indian Culture; The Chinese or Japanese Culture; African Culture; Hebrew Culture; Christian Culture; and by way of background and perspective, the Classical Cultures of Greece and Rome.[65]

Later that same month, Shriver offered this vision for the cultural and religious diversity of humanity:

> Instead of criticizing each race, or nation, let us try to imagine the human race as a great orchestra composed of many, different instruments but all playing together to create the perfect music of a glorious symphony. There is room, there is even need, in any orchestra for violins, pianos, trumpets and drums. So is there need in human life for Jew and Gentile, Negro and White Man, Moslem and Hindu, for out of these differences will come a more beautiful song that alone any one race, or group could sing.[66]

Shriver's exposure to cultural and religious diversity came early in life. In 1934, when he was nineteen, finishing his years at Canterbury Catholic prep school in New Milford, Connecticut, Shriver accepted an invitation to participate in Donald Watt's "Experiment in International Living." It was a project that would give young people from diverse nations and cultures an opportunity to live with each other in families across Europe, South America, and India. The premise was that early exposure to cultural diversity would cultivate a widespread capacity among citizens of the world for "international cooperation and global fellowship."[67] On two occasions in later years, in 1936 and 1939, Shriver was invited back to Europe through the "Experiment" project of Watt, and he would spend considerable time in pre-war Germany. These experiences galvanized both his appreciation of cultural and religious diversity and his understanding of the threats of war that were brewing in Europe at the time. Shriver's letters home during this last venture reveal his growing appreciation of the political challenges of navigating diversity.[68]

We suggest, however, that deeper roots of Shriver's commitment to diversity lie in traditional elements of his Catholic faith. To be sure, his openness to diversity places him squarely within the community of secular Americans. But his rationale for embracing this value may seem rather odd. His basis for respecting diversity is his religious faith with its foundations in natural law, the nature-supernature distinction, and the theological virtue of charity.

Between July 1957 and February 1958, Shriver delivered three speeches as President of the Chicago Board of Education to audiences of secular and religiously diverse educators gathered in public conferences and meetings at Northwestern University, Champaign Community Schools, and Illinois State Normal University, all public institutions. In all three speeches he presents his argument for the overall framework of an "Education for the Future," and then he offers a vision of what this longer-term future will be and what it will need to achieve, given the dramatic global and cultural transformations he observed in his time. In all three speeches he begins the final section of his speech with remarks similar to the following:

> Now I'd like to conclude with a few remarks about education for the more distant future - the future world of 1980 and 1990 and the world of the 21st Century, now only 43 years away.
>
> In my judgment the number one problem in these years to come will be this:
>
> How can all of us – white, black, yellow and brown people – of different nations and different cultures – live together in peace?[69]

This challenge of peace is formulated with the assumption that such a peace as unity-in-diversity is indeed possible and it is followed by an analysis of statistics on population growth, the shrinking size of the planet, and the cultural and economic requirements for a widespread understanding of the diverse cultures and religious traditions that will now be living closely together in this new global unity. Shriver concludes this analysis with a proposal for a curriculum educating young Americans on diverse religions and cultures for this new unity context.[70] Then he offers his argument for what he believes this curriculum would achieve:

> If in the United States by the time of the 21st Century we could perfect an education of the type I describe, we could begin to prove three most important points:
>
> First, we could demonstrate that we know that our neighbor is the man to whom we show understanding, mercy and compassion, not solely the one who does us good.
>
> Second: we could demonstrate our faith in the natural and supernatural unity of mankind, of all races, creeds and social conditions.
>
> Third: We could show that the U.S. is the proper leader of a united world based on knowledge and love as compared to a Soviet world based on fear and hate.[71]

On October 7, 1958, in his address to the Annual Convention Banquet of the Illinois Association of Secondary School Principals, at the University of Illinois, Urbana, Shriver makes his thinking on the unity-in-diversity of humanity clear:

> The point is simple though elusive. There are needs which are basic to humanity, irrespective of time, place or culture – needs like the need for mastering language, understanding one's religion, enjoying music, performing in an art ... You are best qualified because only you educators know, or should know, both the timeless, basic, intellectual needs of every man, and, his transient, passing needs as an individual in a particular town, village or community ... How can these local, transient needs of a particular time and community be covered in our program of studies along with the essential, timeless, trans-historical needs of all human beings at all times in all places? ... The needs that pertain to a man as a human being, which transcend time and place, the needs which will help to make him a good man and a good citizen, should be known to the true educator. It is his job, his primary job, to discover these needs, to explain them with clarity, and to defend them with eloquence.[72]

Finally, Shriver turns to his secular and religiously diverse audiences and tells them that "A great man has written these words":

> "It is not from outward pressure, it is not from the sword that deliverance comes to nations; the sword cannot breed peace, it can only impose terms of peace. The forces that are to renew the earth must proceed from within, from the spirit … The re-education of mankind must be above all things spiritual … [it] must be actuated by justice and crowned by charity."[73]

The quote is from a popular translation of the October 1939 Encyclical of Pope Pius XII, *Summi pontificatus*, delivered on the eve of the outbreak of World War II, subtitled "On the Unity of Human Society," and sometimes referred to as "Darkness Over the Earth."[74] The Encyclical is explicit in focusing on the natural law foundations of a universal human nature and the religious foundations of a charity that heals and perfects the pursuit of natural justice. Shriver's argument is that the diversity of human cultures, states, and religions only serves to accentuate an underlying unity that has both natural and supernatural foundations.[75] These foundations have their basis in fact, but they also present a moral and spiritual imperative that is both possible and urgent, to educate ourselves in justice, and to pursue a path of social and political life informed by the theological virtue of charity.

We argue that, for Shriver, the traditional Catholic doctrine of natural law – the universal structure of human reason and human nature – established the philosophical and political foundation for his commitment to diversity. Furthermore, we argue that his commitment to the theological virtue of charity – the virtue that constantly renews and enables this natural law to do its work in service of humankind – grounded his openness to the religious and spiritual traditions of the world. Shriver's Catholic faith was traditional, but his faith was in a God that was clearly a single God who created humans with a commonly shared intelligence that enables them to speak together, live together, share their lives together, navigate difficulties together, and build a world peace through dialogue together. Shriver's God of tradition was big enough to welcome the diverse forms of worship that are expressed through the world's great religions.

Most important is the way Shriver signals the importance of religious resources in grounding and dynamizing a public commitment to the political project of preserving diversity, preventing religious discrimination, and halting religiously motivated conflict. If popular images evoked a conviction that guarding diversity required a wall of separation between church and state, Shriver remained confident that such a wall was neither necessary nor helpful. In fact, it would deprive citizens of the tools for achieving the very objectives of diversity. Politics in a democracy is a high calling for citizens, and Shriver's faith provided him with resources for a life committed to living out this calling.

The Campaign Against Racism

The most dramatic and compelling demonstration of Shriver's faith-based commitment to justice, diversity, and the unity of the human family was the leadership he exercised in the Chicago Catholic community's campaign against racial discrimination. From his earliest years as President of the Chicago Board of Education (1955) to the end of his term when he left to join Kennedy's presidential campaign (1959), Shriver's commitment to civil rights figures prominently in his speeches. Between 1956 and 1959, four of his speeches focus entirely on the problem of racism,[76] five others deal with racism as part of the broader range of challenges to education in Chicago,[77] and others allude to problems of racial and religious discrimination as part of his concern for peace and unity-amidst-diversity at home and abroad.[78]

Early in his childhood in Westminster near Baltimore, Shriver had played baseball with African American children.[79] But his real initiation into race relations came in Chicago in the 1950s as activists called for the desegregation of Chicago's school system. In the two decades following the outbreak of World War II, more than six million African Americans were forced to leave the South to travel to Northern states in search of employment.[80] The preferred destination in this migration was the city of Chicago, and Chicago's South Side became famous as the "capital of Black America." At one point in the decade, over two thousand Black immigrants arrived weekly in the city.

Generally speaking, the American Catholic bishops of the 1950s were not known for their leadership in the campaign against racism in the US. But Chicago was a different story. Prominent Catholics like Samuel Cardinal Stritch, Archbishop of Chicago played leadership roles in the battle against racial discrimination, and it took little persuasion to convince Shriver to join the team. He became a member of the Catholic Interracial Council (CIC), he became chairman of its school committee, he was elected president of CIC in 1955, and he remained actively involved in the civil rights movement all the way through his public life as President of the Chicago Board of Education. One of the first goals of CIC was to grapple with the racism that existed within the Catholic Church itself, and a chief vehicle for this was the focus on Catholic high schools. All schools accepted the principle of racial integration, but high tuition costs created effective racial segregation. Shriver's first step was to establish a scholarship program for African American students that would level the playing field and allow Black children into previously all-white schools. The effects were significant, and the program launched a trend towards desegregation that would be followed in other American cities. Other programs to combat youth delinquency in Chicago had noticeable impacts on race-based poverty, and some became pilots for Job Corps, the prime program of Shriver's War on Poverty ten years later.

The influence of Shriver's work for racial justice was felt in diverse forms in the years to come.[81] Throughout the 1950s he influenced the mobilization of Catholic participation in civil rights activities including the historic civil rights marches at Montgomery and Selma, Alabama in March 1965.[82] In 1958, the CIC presented him with the James J. Hoey Award for Interracial Justice.[83] And in the same year, as a result of Shriver's work with the National Catholic Conference for Interracial Justice (NCCIJ), the American bishops issued a pastoral letter against racism titled "Discrimination and the Christian Conscience."[84]

The most dramatic result of Shriver's work against racism, however, was its impact on the presidential campaign of John F. Kennedy. Shriver was given charge over the Civil Rights Division of Kennedy's campaign, and he began work in the fall of 1959, drawing on the contacts and resources he had developed during his Chicago years, engaging the support of prominent civil rights leaders, and confronting blatant racism in campaign primaries in poor white districts of West Virginia.[85] In 1960 the Democratic Party had little history of involvement in Civil Rights, and in the decades after the Civil War, African American voters had traditionally supported the Republican Party.[86] Shriver's biographer notes that at the outset of the campaign, "The inner circle at Kennedy's headquarters considered the Civil Rights Division to be only a marginally important assignment."[87] But as the campaign progressed, everyone involved came to appreciate that Kennedy needed the support of African Americans to win the election. To gain this support he had to get serious in making the promise of civil rights legislation a program priority.[88]

The event that proved noteworthy in shaping the direction of the November 1960 presidential election campaign was Kennedy's phone call to Coretta Scott King, the pregnant wife of Rev. Martin Luther King, Jr.[89] On October 19, Coretta's husband led a group of activists into a famous restaurant in Atlanta Georgia and demanded to be served. When asked to leave, King refused, and he and his fellow protesters were arrested for trespassing. The event prompted other similar occupations in the days following. What complicated matters was that several months earlier, King had been arrested and put on probation for a trumped-up motor vehicle charge. Now a De Kalb County judge ruled that the restaurant charge put King in violation of probation and he sentenced

King to six months of hard labor in prison. The sentence was outrageous and Coretta feared King would be killed in prison. King's supporters called on both Kennedy and Nixon to intervene. But intervening posed problems for the Democrats. They needed the votes of African Americans, but they also needed the support of Southern Democrats who had a notorious history of racism.

One of Shriver's close colleagues in the Kennedy campaign was Harris Wofford, a Notre Dame University Law professor, well known for his activism in civil rights.[90] Wofford had become friends with the Kings and he suggested to Shriver that Kennedy make a direct and personal gesture to Coretta, a phone call expressing sympathy and support. Shriver agreed and he rushed to meet Kennedy at his motel near O'Hare International airport in Chicago. Within minutes he managed to convince Kennedy to make the call then and there, and Kennedy placed the call.

The first reaction in the Kennedy inner circle was negative. They feared that once word got out, the intervention would alienate Southern Democrats and lose the election for Kennedy. But events proved otherwise. King's father was present when Coretta received the call, and he and Coretta announced publicly that Kennedy's gesture of personal compassion was decisive in determining their political allegiance. Bobby Kennedy, formerly opposed to Shriver's actions, reconsidered, and contacted the De Kalb judge directly, calling him to release King by sundown. On October 28, ten days before the election, King was released from prison. Shriver worked vigorously to publicize the events, and when results were tallied on election day, the Democrats reported historic gains in support from African Americans. Their voter turnout was the highest reported in history, and exit polls showed more than 70 per cent support from African American voters.[91] Clearly the call to Coretta King was not the sole factor in securing success for Kennedy. But the Civil Rights Division under Shriver played an impressive role in shifting directions, both in the campaign and in the subsequent policies and programs of the nation's new president. Three years later, in 1963, Shriver was given the honor of presenting Rev. Martin Luther King Jr. with the Chicago Catholic Interracial Council's John F. Kennedy Award for improving race relations.[92]

Shriver's actions speak volumes. But his words provide evidence of the meanings behind the actions. In the anti-racism campaign, it is clear that the meanings flow, once again, from his religious vocation to public life. His speeches never cease to frame the campaign as a spiritual calling which he lived personally and called others to live:

Everyone who professes to believe in the Fatherhood of God, and the brotherhood of man, and certainly one who lives the tenets of Catholicism, has the source of inspiration and strength and the impelling motives to help his fellow man. In the last analysis, the solution to this problem is a spiritual one, the putting of Christ's principles to work.

In putting these principles to work, there is no place like home, right here in Chicago. The opportunities here are great, the need is even greater. In this hour of decision involving matters of worldwide importance, let us remember once again the thought of His Eminence, our own distinguished Cardinal: "Christ was sent, and He sent His Church, and His Church in turns sends us."[93]

Shriver concludes his address to the Annual Convention Banquet of the Illinois Association of Secondary School Principals, University of Illinois, Urbana, October 7, 1958, with the following words:

Finally, let me mention, very briefly, the situation involving integration in our schools. Our state laws are very clear on this point. All of you know those laws, probably by heart. 95%, so to speak, follow these laws, adhere to them and support them completely. But a small percentage of our schools are not living up to the letter or the spirit of those laws, and we are all suffering from this dereliction on the part of the very few ... May I urge you, one and all, to rededicate yourselves to the Judaeo-Christian principles of charity and justice with regard to this important question of contemporary American life. I hope we shall get action; I look forward to effective action. But, in the meanwhile, let us all make sure we each are doing what we can to assure justice and equality in educational opportunity to all persons of all races, and of all creeds ... And in most of the world today, we see this age-old pattern still in operation. In India the caste system imprisons millions within their occupational and cultural group; in Russia, no one may change his job or status without government approval; in China, men are shackled to their jobs with little hope of liberation.

Two great forces have worked for two thousand years to change this ancient pattern; - religion and education, - especially liberal education, so named because it liberated man, opened his mind to a full view of society, and gave him hope and light to guide his children into a full participation in the life of mankind.

Today, as in the past, it should be our ambition to extend this education universally. It is not our purpose to prepare students only for induction into the existing communities of Pittsburgh, Chicago, Champaign, Detroit or Little Rock. On the contrary, it is our purpose, the purpose of true education, to enfranchise man into the great, human community of free men and free spirits, of all times and all places. Let us not deny admission to this great community because of preconceived notions about intellectual capacity based on I.Q. tests and the other paraphernalia of behavior scientists. Let us prove that our famous American know-how can accomplish what the Russians are proving themselves afraid to try, namely, the production of more and more boys and girls, fully educated, fully alive to all the glories of culture and civilization, fully aware of their responsibilities, each to each, and all to all, in our American democracy.

In this task of surpassing importance and great challenge, you educators of Illinois must be the leaders. May God bless all your efforts. May He crown them and you with laurel wreaths of victory.[94]

On race relations, we observe a framework similar to that in Shriver's comments on religion and politics, diversity, and the unity of the human family. His tone is one of charity and good will, he issues the call as a personal appeal to interiority, he frames the issue in terms of a global vision of the nature-based unity of humankind, he calls for justice through both reason and charity, and he situates the entire project within the cosmic drama of Divine blessing.

The Turn to Interiority

We argue that Sargent Shriver's commitment to diversity and social justice were grounded in his faith convictions about the universality of reason and natural law, the natural-supernatural distinction, and the supernatural gift of charity. Shriver was able to hold onto central convictions from his religious tradition, not by glossing over, compromising, or relativizing conflicting values, but by appreciating the convictions of all sides and understanding how core values of some can actually bolster those of others. In later years, the Catholic natural law tradition and its understanding of charity were subjected to considerable criticism, and these criticisms, together with the responses they evoked, played a role in widening gaps between conservative and liberal Catholics. In the fourth chapter, we develop a fuller discussion of the arguments in these conversations. Our present purpose, however, is to offer a sketch of the early years of Sargent Shriver's religious vocation to political life. And we conclude this chapter with a feature that signals an important development that was underway during this period, "the turn to interiority." Shriver not only lived out his religious tradition, he also anticipated developments that would reshape this tradition in directions, we argue, that are central for navigating the turbulent waters of religion-politics conversations today.

In the conclusion of his April 17, 1957, address to the Chicago Teachers Historical Association, Shriver situates the challenge of American education within the dark drama of international politics and the Cold War. His response to this drama, though, was not what you would expect. Instead of calling for the traditional weapons of battle, Shriver argues that the victory in this drama is to be won in the "hearts" of citizens. The center of this drama is interiority, the human mind, heart, and soul:

> If the U.S.A. is to fulfill its possibilities for world leadership, it will do so not because we are healthy, have pearly white teeth, drive longer and lower automobiles on smoother and smoother super-highways, but because in this day and generation we put our dollars to work where work is needed – in the minds, hearts, and souls of young America.
>
> Here in Illinois, it is said, we are located in the "Heart of America." It is, perhaps, our special responsibility to make known the true nature of that heart, – a heart dedicated to the enlightenment of man's mind and the inspiration of his soul.[95]

We observe the same reflections in two earlier speeches, where Shriver speaks about core issues of world politics as challenges that can only be met by addressing "minds" and "hearts."[96] Then, the following year, in his April 27, 1958, address, "Men, Money and Missions in the Far East," delivered to the Fourth Degree Exemplification and Banquet of the Knights of Columbus, Rockford, Illinois, Shriver offers the following "final thought for this evening."

> If we have failed in America, our failure has been to produce great hearts rather than great minds. We have failed to turn out enough men and women with profound faith, conviction and courage.[97]

Five months later, Shriver offers the following remarks:

> may I suggest that the test of good education is whether it will make people want to do, and enjoy, and make, and contemplate, the things most worthy of them. If education does not create a need for the best in life, if it does not open new vistas for the mind and the soul, new ambitions, then we are stuck in an undemocratic, rigid, caste society.[98]

Whenever he articulates the vision behind his commitment to public life, Shriver takes the turn to interiority. His turn is not outward, to the institutional forms of social life or the objects of human experience and achievement, but inward to the habits of heart and mind that are the basis for physical, social, economic, and political life. Shriver's commitment to diversity and social justice is rooted in his traditional faith in the supernatural, natural law, and charity. But his was a tradition in transition. The transition was from a static, mechanistic, extrinsic vision of transcendence, nature, and charity to one rooted in the spiritual interiority of women and men.

In April 1957, the same month that Shriver delivered his address to the Chicago Teachers Historical Association, Bernard Lonergan published *Insight: A Study of Human Understanding*, a work that articulates a method that grounds this turn to interiority at the center of the transition in Catholic tradition. The method was inspired by Lonergan's own study of Thomas Aquinas. But it was developed through his careful examination of interiority; an examination of the operations of understanding that are at work in life, scholarship, and the methods of the natural and human sciences. His discovery was that we not only have an interior life of "minds" and "hearts," we can also turn our attention to the examination of this interior life in a type of science that is no less methodical, no less disciplined than the best of the empirical sciences.

Our day-to-day living involves performing operations of meaning and valuing, yet reflecting methodically on these operations can yield an extraordinary discovery. We can discover that the familiar operations of wondering, questioning, understanding, and verifying reveal a pattern and a direction towards self-transcendence. Through these operations we move out of ourselves into an engagement with the world, and there is a structure or pattern at work in this movement. This pattern provides a norm or criterion for distinguishing between development and its opposite, decline. This is not a mechanical idea of development, chugging along as mindless law. Nor is it an extrinsic norm of "human nature" whose outward form is frozen in a particular age or culture. Rather it is a patterned inclination that is present and discernible in all of our lives and it can be chosen or refused as grounds for our decisions and actions. This insight into interiority provides a basis for a whole new way of retrieving and transposing core insights from Catholic tradition on natural law and charity.

Shriver does not appeal explicitly to Lonergan. Yet we argue his work reflects a transition to interiority that was and still is underway in his faith tradition. It is a transformation that retains the traditional commitment to truth, value, family, community, fidelity, and charity, but transposes this tradition from a static extrinsic theory to an interior principle discernible in the operations of wondering, questioning, understanding, verifying, and deciding of women and men from all traditions. The transposition allows the basic features of traditional faith to open up to social justice and religious diversity without losing integrity or objectivity. We suggest that this transformation can be observed at work in Shriver's

November 30, 1956 address to the Mary McDowell Settlement House. At the center of his concluding remarks we find the turn to interiority that we argue marks the core of this transformation:

> At the beginning of this talk I described my admiration for the remarkable work achieved in this neighborhood. Your record in developing participation in your programs by members of various racial and religious groups is an inspiration to all other sections of the city. You have taken many of the steps necessary to create a genuine community, a community which is something more than a mere neighborhood with rows of houses contained within specific geographical limits.
>
> A genuine community is formed only when the individuals are present, not only physically, but also spiritually – strictly speaking, when they humbly acknowledge their mutual interdependence on one another. Then a true community comes into being, when along with the physical nature there is formed a vital community spirit in which true democratic action can take place. Buildings may be destroyed, or even devastation take place. But as long as we have a genuine community spirit, we can rebuild and recreate. We can even form indestructible communities – communities based on the primacy of the spirit, the mind, and the ideals of man.[99]

Concluding Remarks

If the "wall of separation" evokes an image about religion and politics that, by the end of the 1950s, was coming to dominate public habits of thought and feeling, then Sargent Shriver's image of "communities based on the primacy of the spirit" reveals a more profound dimension to religion-politics relations whose import needs to be retrieved today. For Shriver, thinking adequately about religion and politics could not be achieved by focusing on simplistic images about institutional separation. Rather, it requires probing deeper to discern the spiritual forces that work diversely to dynamize the political involvements of women and men who dedicate their lives to the service of others in bringing peace and justice to families, neighborhoods, and global nations and cultures. Politics needs religion to do its work. In fact, it was Shriver's tradition that provided the dynamism and rationale for the very commitment to diversity that marked his life's work as a politician. His was a truly religious vocation to public life. In the chapters that follow, we develop the method of interiority to explain Shriver and to help work out more careful, more nuanced insights for distinguishing and relating religion and politics in the service of peace.

Chapter Three

Shriver on Spirituality and Politics, 1961–1964

The Chicago period of Shriver's early public life extends from his election as Board of Education President in October 1955 until October 1959 when he stepped down to join John F. Kennedy's campaign for the 1960 US presidency. In the decade prior, Shriver had worked for Jack's father, Joseph P. Kennedy, co-managing the famous Chicago Merchandise Mart, and during these years he was active in Chicago politics and in Kennedy family life. With his marriage to Eunice Kennedy, Jack's sister in May 1953, Shriver joined the Kennedy family and found in Eunice a true partner in his spiritual vocation to public life. Following Kennedy's inauguration on January 20, 1961, Shriver was tasked to begin a new phase of his vocation, designing and launching the program that would fulfill one of Kennedy's most important campaign promises, the Peace Corps. He completed the design work within a month, and on March 4, 1961, he was appointed first director of the Peace Corps. He would remain in this role until February 1, 1964, just months after the Kennedy assassination, when the new President, Lyndon Johnson, would name him to head up his new program, the War on Poverty.

Reading through the speeches of the Peace Corps years, what is striking is the difference in language from the Chicago years. Religious language is everywhere in the Chicago speeches of the 1950s. Whether his audience is religious or secular, Shriver never ceases to draw on religious imagery, cite religious authors, and appeal to religious values in support of his arguments. Three weeks after his appointment to the Peace Corps, however, his speech to the New York Herald Tribune Youth Forum (March 24, 1961) sets a new tone that would be followed time and again in the next three years.[1] He uses little or no religious language, he cites no religious authors, and he makes no reference to explicit religious values to support his arguments. It would not be difficult to conclude from this that Shriver understood his move to the Peace Corps as a shift in life – a move to a fully secular role, no longer informed by his religious faith, no longer dynamized by the spiritual vocation that played such a dominant role in the Chicago years.

Nothing could be further from the truth. To be sure, the change in language is significant. Our argument in this chapter, however, is that the change arises from a broadening and deepening of his understanding of things spiritual and a sharpening of his insights into relations between spirituality and politics. Shriver never leaves his Catholic faith tradition behind. But his turn to interiority points to developments in this tradition that, we believe, explain Shriver's work and provide a framework for navigating contemporary divisions in American public life.

Shriver's Vocation and the Peace Corps Years

While most of Shriver's speeches between 1961 and 1964 follow the general pattern of secularized language set by the New York Herald Tribune Youth Forum speech, a few speeches delivered to religious audiences during this period provide indications that his public life remained a truly spiritual vocation rooted in his Catholic faith. On June 4, 1961, Shriver delivered the commencement address to Notre Dame University, and he frames the new project, the Peace Corps, within a cosmic religious drama of the unity of the human family that echoes his vision of the Chicago years:

> they will be sent to work and work hard alongside other human beings in need of what we and we alone can give them – hope, skill, and a knowledge of the dignity of man under the Fatherhood of God ... There is a world-wide struggle going on. A revolution. All men are trying to achieve human dignity and a common identity. You and I are part of that struggle, for no matter whether a man be Jew, Buddhist, Moslem, Hindu, Communist or Christian, he has been born of woman like every other man alive, he is living on this small spinning planet like every other man alive; he needs food, shelter and spiritual comfort like every other man alive; and he will die the death like every other man alive. And if there is a destiny after death, the community of our experience here on this earth indicates that life hereafter will be common to all.[2]

Three days later, in his commencement address to De Paul University, Shriver situates the Peace Corps within a similar grand-scale religious-historical narrative:

> Since that day Abraham set out from his city founded "on blood and fear and injustice," searching for a city "whose builder and founder is God" men

have longed for a new order. Plato wrote about it in his Republic. Ghandi saw it in the "Kingdom of Ruma." Sir Thomas More yearned for it in Utopia. The Hebrew prophets peered into the future for the day when nations would beat their swords into plough-shares.

Today the longing is epidemic for a new order in which justice and peace prevail and all men share a better life. The Peace Corps is a small part of the effort needed to achieve that order.[3]

One year later, in his June 2, 1962, commencement speech to St. Louis University, Shriver uses the explicit language of "vocation" in speaking about the Peace Corps and its projects.[4] And the year following, in the January 15, 1963, Speech at the National Conference on Religion and Race in Chicago, he refers to the role his Catholic faith plays in both the Chicago years and in the Peace Corps:

My only credentials for speaking to you are my experience here in Chicago with the Interracial Council, my work with the Peace Corps, and a layman's strong interest in making faith personally meaningful in a disturbing world.[5]

The 1963 Religion and Race Conference Speech reveals a lot about how Shriver understood the Peace Corps in spiritual terms. He refers to the role of religious faith in the abolition of the Slave Trade and the mid-twentieth-century campaign against racism.[6] He questions whether racial equality can be won without the dynamism of a religious faith that evokes personal responsibility for action against injustice.[7] He speaks about the challenge of "religious laissez faire," a sort of spiritual illness resulting in the failure of religions to mobilize action in service of racial justice and peace.[8] And he speaks about "tithing" as the religiously mandated dedication of one's time to the pursuit of justice:

If such a program intended finally to bury religious laissez faire in racial problems were instituted, it would encourage each member of the congregation to pledge a tithe of their time to removing racial barriers at work, at play, at worship.

I wonder why an appeal requesting every church member to give a tithe of time has not been made already. Just a few Sundays ago in a Catholic weekly newspaper, The Sunday Visitor, the whole front page was devoted to this subject of tithing, but the discussion was focused primarily on the financial aspect of tithing ... But isn't it easier to give a tithe of your money than a tithe of your time? Isn't the time you give yourself more important than the money?

Let me be more specific.

The Peace Corps has shown what Americans will do when they are challenged by a high purpose. They respond enthusiastically no matter what the personal cost.[9]

We observe similar language when he cites the encyclical *Mater et magistra* of Pope John XXIII in the February 24, 1963, speech to the Chicago Knights of Columbus[10] and in the June 12, 1963, commencement address to Fordham University.[11] Two decades later, when Shriver reflects back on the early years of the Peace Corps, he speaks of the project as a cooperation with God in the struggle for peace.[12] Clearly, in all these texts, Shriver is reflecting something of his own religious vocation that continues to dynamize his commitment to justice and peace throughout the Peace Corps years.

The speeches of 1961 to 1963 offer evidence that Shriver never ceased thinking of his public life as a spiritual vocation. The strongest statement, however, is to be found two decades later, in his 1983 Dedication of the US Catholic Bishops Pastoral letter, "The Challenge of Peace." The text is striking in what it reveals about Shriver, the personal faith that sustained him throughout his entire life, the traditional religious symbols that marked his self-understanding, and the supernatural drama that set the context of meaning for his life of service to the human family. We argue that this cosmic religious vision of service never ceased governing Shriver's public life and work as a vocation. The text is worth reproducing in its entirety:

With humility and love we dedicate this Pastoral Proclamation to all human beings living on the land mass of the American continent north of the Equator. All of us would die, be poisoned, or maimed immediately or soon after the beginning of a general, unrestrained nuclear weapons war. Thus we have all become equal in a new way in our plight and in our prospects.

In this predicament we beseech the Virgin Mary, Mother of Jesus, whom we adore as God made man, to take all of us under her maternal cloak and shield us, each and every one, from the fire, the heat, the pressure, the vapors, the stench of the holocaust.

We pray for the day when her spirit and mantle and power will replace the nuclear umbrella as protection for our dear friends on the continent of Europe, birthplace of our civilization.

We invoke her benign care and intervention on behalf of the millions of Orthodox and Uniate Christians, covenant Jews, holy men and women of Islam in the Soviet Union, who like us worship the God of Abraham, Isaac, and Jacob.

We implore God our Father to protect all who look upon us as their ene-
mies, to lighten their burdens and drive away their fears, so that together
with us they may join in affirming our common dependence on one
another, our need for one another, our finitude, our weakness, our ignorance, our brevity of life, our love for our planet with its wonders of creation
which we all share. Make us children in gentleness, tender with one another
as a mother with child, quick to calm fear, ready for peace.

Finally, we rededicate our land and its inhabitants to Mary, the Immac-
ulate Conception. Our predecessors, the Catholic Bishops of the United
States, chose that title and established our commitment to her in 1846. May
she and all the saints in heaven, those known and unknown, those who have
died within our fold and those whom God in his mercy and wisdom has
taken to Himself, pray for us struggling mortals upon whose frail and transi-
tory hearts and minds the future of so much of humankind now depends.[13]

The "Wall of Separation"

While Shriver was developing a political career and a political institution,
the Peace Corps, based on his tradition's call for religion's authentic role
in shaping the form and content of a dedication to peace in political
life, the American Supreme Court was reinforcing a public imagination
that would undermine the very plausibility of this role. The interpretive
framework provided by Justice Black's "wall of separation" in *Everson v.
Board of Education* left the court blind to resources necessary for gaining
clarity and precision on religion-politics relations when deeper issues
related to religious experience and human conscience would be at stake.
In the early 1960s, during the years when Shriver was developing the
Peace Corps, and when the court faced the challenge of ruling on a set
of disputes over prayer in public schools, the limitations of the images
of "the wall" became manifest, both in the decisions it made and the
backlash it evoked.

In agreeing to hear *Abington v. Schempp* (1963), the court combined
two nearly identical cases, one originating in Pennsylvania, the other in
Maryland. In Pennsylvania, the Schempp family challenged an Abington
School District policy that provided for a teacher or student to read ten
or more verses of the Bible over the public address system, without commentary, at the beginning of each school day. The policy also called for
all students to stand and recite the Lord's Prayer together, following the
reading. In Maryland, the Murray family challenged a Baltimore School
Board Policy that called for beginning each school day with the reading of a chapter in the Bible (without commentary) or the recitation of
the Lord's Prayer. Both policies provided students and teachers with the

option not to participate, if they so chose. The States of Pennsylvania and Maryland defended the policies, with 18 other states filing "friends of the court" briefs in support.[14] After hearing arguments, the court ruled by an eight-to-one majority in favour of the Schempp and the Murray families, and against the States of Pennsylvania and Maryland. Justice Tom Clark wrote the majority opinion, Justice Potter Stewart offered the lone dissent.

In bringing their cases before the court, both the Schempp and Murray families argued that they could not, in good conscience, allow their children to comply with the roles and tasks required by the policies of religious exercises at their schools. For their part, the Schempp family objected that, as Unitarians, "a literal reading of the Bible [purveyed specific religious doctrines] which were contrary to the religious beliefs which they held, and to their family teaching."[15] For theirs, the Murray family objected that, as atheists, the school policy "threatened their religious liberty by placing a premium on belief as against non-belief and subjecting their freedom of conscience to the rule of the majority."[16]

Both families also contended that the policies stigmatized their children. Mr. Schempp declared that he did not feel comfortable asking to have his children excused from the exercises, because "he [believed] that the children's relationship with their teachers would be adversely affected."[17] The Murray family asserted that to be excused from the religious exercises would "render sinister, alien and suspect the beliefs and ideals [of the Murray children], promoting doubt and question of their morality, good citizenship and good faith."[18] Both families argued that the school policies violated their First Amendment rights to the free exercise of their religion.

In writing for the majority, Justice Clark did not focus directly on the Free Exercise Clause of the First Amendment. He did not ask whether and how the schools' policies on reading scripture and reciting prayers protected or failed to protect the rights of the Schempp and Murray families to the free exercise of their respective religions. Rather, following the precedent set by Justice Black in *Everson v. Board of Education,* he focused on what he took to be the more fundamental issue, the fact that in creating the policies, the school administrators violated the Establishment Clause by co-mingling the interests of the state (educating children) with the interests of religion (conducting religious exercises). For Justice Clark, the issue, once again, was the wall separating institutions.

As Justice Clark pointed out, for 20 years the court had consistently (and with virtual unanimity) ruled that the State must remain neutral with regard to religion, pursue only secular objectives, and "neither advance nor inhibit religion" in its laws and policies:

The Establishment Clause has been directly considered by this Court eight times in the past score of years and, with only one Justice dissenting on the point [i.e., Justice Stewart], it has consistently held that ... to withstand the strictures of the Establishment Clause there must be a secular legislative purpose and a primary effect that neither advances nor inhibits religion.[19]

Clark found that the school policy in this case failed on both counts. He argued that school policies calling for Bible reading and prayer recitation had a religious, not a secular purpose, and their primary effect was to advance the Christian religion.

According to Justice Clark, two lessons from the history of religiously motivated conflict in colonial America underscored the legitimacy and importance of his ruling. First, on the religious side, "bitter experience" taught Americans that the power of the State has no legitimate role in the cultivation of religious belief and practice. Indeed, for Clark, religion does have an "exalted" place in American society precisely because Americans rely on "the home, the church and the individual heart and mind" – not the government – to develop their religious beliefs and commitments:

The place of religion in our society is an exalted one, achieved through a long tradition of reliance on the home, the church and the inviolable citadel of the individual heart and mind. We have come to recognize through bitter experience that it is not within the power of government to invade that citadel, whether its purpose or effect be to aid or oppose, to advance or retard.[20]

Second, on the political side, he spoke of an ever-present danger that powerful groups seek to advance their own interests by "fusing" the functions of government with the interests of religion. Justice Clark agreed with Justice Black that to prevent these problematic alliances the State must maintain its neutrality:

The wholesome "neutrality" of which this Court's cases speak stems from a recognition of the teachings of history that powerful sects or groups might bring about a fusion of governmental and religious functions to the end that official support of the State or Federal Government would be placed behind the tenets of one or of all orthodoxies.[21]

What Clark missed in his analysis, however, was the role of religious education in cultivating and sustaining the very commitment to peace that overcomes the conflicts at the root of the "bitter experience" of the past. What he also missed was the fact that a diverse proliferation of institutional involvements in delivering public goods has now created a situation in which public (government) funds can be used to pay for education that reaches "the home, the church and the inviolable citadel of the individual heart and mind." The novel situation calls for novel analytic tools. What prevailed, however, was not nuanced understanding, but simplistic images.

To prevent the misuse of government power in the name of religion, Justice Clark ruled against the States and overturned the school policies. He ruled that "the [religious] exercises and the law requiring them are in violation of the Establishment Clause."[22] His immediate goal was to enforce the mandate of the Establishment Clause and roll back the "fusion of governmental and religious functions" created by school officials in Pennsylvania and Maryland. The effect of his ruling, however, was to reinforce the public image of a "wall of separation" that would remove religious belief and practice from the political arena. Shriver's vision, we argue, reveals a deeper dimension to religion-politics relations. While politics needs to remain vigilant in guarding appropriate institutional distinctions, religion has a vital role to play in animating and guiding politics in its dedication to justice and peace.

Political Backlash

Despite its high ideals and Supreme Court precedents, Justice Clark's decision did not go down well with the parents, teachers, school administrators, and public officials who favoured scripture readings and the recitation of the Lord's Prayer in schools. Justice Clark's ruling in *Abington v. Schempp* precipitated a backlash of resentment and resistance that continues to this day. In parts of the country, many schools simply refused to comply with the ruling.[23] In Congress, a group of Senators and Representatives moved quickly with proposals to amend the Constitution,[24] and such proposals continued to emerge, including the effort in 1994, spear-headed by Speaker of the House, Newt Gingrich, to permit voluntary prayer in schools.[25]

Soon, detractors began to refer to *Abington v. Schempp* as "the day they kicked God out of school," and resistance to *Abington v. Schempp* motivated conservative Christians to mobilize politically. During the Presidential campaigns of 1980 and 1984, political organizers distributed a "Moral Report Card" to evangelical churches nationwide. This report card "graded" candidates for Congress, Senate, and the Presidency on key moral issues. The issue at the top of the grading list was "Prayer in Schools."[26]

On the local level, schools continued to develop policies involving prayer and to pursue litigation that challenged the scope of the ruling in *Abington v. Schempp*. In *Wallace v. Jafree* (1985), the court banned silent meditation for religious purposes, and in *Lee v. Weisman* (1992), the court banned prayer at public school graduation ceremonies. In the ensuing decades, the conflict deepened and wedge issues multiplied to include abortion, same sex marriage, teaching evolution in schools, displaying the Ten Commandments in local courthouses, and now government health care insurance programs.

One of the issues in the backlash was the apparent contradiction between the equivalent status between belief and non-belief implied in the ruling and the inequality that seemed to be created by the exclusion of prayer from schools.[27] Justice Stewart and other critics argued that non-belief is a religiously protected stance and so must be treated equally as a religion alongside traditional religions. They were outraged that the ruling, focused as it was on institutional separation, actually gave preferential treatment to secular or atheist belief traditions in schools. If both command protection under the First Amendment, then both must be accorded equal treatment. How can we speak of "neutrality" when the ruling of *Abington v. Schempp* served to mask a bias in favour of secular belief traditions?

As the backlash grew, the emotional and symbolic cloud surrounding Clark's decision darkened and threatened. His judgement became experienced as contentious rather than peaceable, hostile to traditional religion rather than respectful of it. The message they heard was that only the religion of secularism is permitted in schools. *Abington v. Schempp* was experienced as demeaning and condescending. It was interpreted as casting doubt on civic motives, as questioning religious integrity, as a slap in the face, as an affront to God.

Justice Clark's decision only served to evoke the ire of its opponents. Critics of *Abington v. Schempp* overlooked or minimized crucial distinctions between religious belief and political allegiance. Support for the ban on school prayer came to be characterized as rejection of religion, even rejection of God. The school prayer issue came to be judged as the measure of religious fidelity. As the range of wedge issues multiplied and report cards displayed simplistic versions of candidates' stances in political campaigns, efforts to gain clarity on the deeper reasoning behind the issues became obscured. As education became the battleground over religious freedom, it became more and more difficult to provide educators with reliable tools for both preserving and transforming religious convictions from past ages. In each case, simplistic slogans replaced careful understanding and significant insights were obscured by images that became markers for institutional allegiances.

With *Abington v. Schempp* and the backlash it provoked, we witness the reign of an approach to religion and politics that focuses on simplistic, extrinsic institutional markers and fails to consider the deeper elements, rooted in interiority, that are necessary for working out precise forms of religions' involvements in concrete contexts of political life. Authentic religion has a crucial role to play in dynamizing politics. A simplistic form of religious imagination can be observed in both the Supreme Court's interpretation of the Establishment Clause and the arguments of communities of Americans opposed to the ruling. Over the ensuing decades, the conflict has grown in scope and power to a degree that now polarizes America. Moving beyond this polarization requires a return to a careful analysis that can both distinguish and relate religion and politics in diverse contexts. Most important, it requires recognizing that politics needs religion to do its work.

The situation becomes all the more urgent as governments and religious groups become more and more diversely involved in providing and funding public goods of all kinds to diverse groups of citizens whose diverse religious liberties must be protected. We suggest the direction forward in this pursuit requires understanding the precise characteristics of the spheres of public goods involved in the case and the precise characteristics of diverse forms of religious belief and non-belief of the parties. It requires understanding the diverse forms of institutional involvements in the case. But it also requires precise criteria for establishing value priorities when spheres of value conflict. We suggest that moving in these directions requires the turn to interiority that can be observed in words and deeds of Shriver's Peace Corps years.

Differentiating and Relating Spirituality and Politics: What Shriver Said

Through the years of Chicago politics and the years of the Peace Corps, Shriver's speeches and political programs reveal a deeper dimension to religion-politics relations than was being articulated in the simplistic images of institutional separation of the Supreme Court decisions. He lived his public life as a spiritual vocation of service to human dignity, and he understood this life as a participation in a cosmic drama of human history, unfolding within the broader mystery of Divine love. Yet, Shriver's linking of spirituality and politics did not result in an undifferentiated fusion of the two. Quite the contrary. During the Peace Corps years, Shriver developed some carefully nuanced insights into how the spheres of religion and politics need to be both distinguished and related.

The June 12, 1963, commencement address at Fordham University is devoted to the elaboration of some of these insights. He opens with a reference to Pope John XXIII as a "Pope of Reconciliation," and then tells his audience he will "focus his principle of reconciliation on one of the most troublesome questions of our society: the relationship of Church and State."[28] He follows with a brief historical background explaining the need for differentiating spirituality and politics:

> There was a time in the West when Christ's admonition to keep distinct our obligations to God and Caesar was neglected; when religion fought for control of the State, and the State for control of religion; when differences of belief were fought out on the battlefield. There was a time, too, when the poor and oppressed found that the Church was aligned with the rich and the powerful against them.
>
> From this flowed the erection of legal barriers between Church and State and the rise of anticlericalism. We must remember that our own First Amendment has as its primary purpose, not only the protection of the State against religion, but the protection of religion against the State.[29]

The next section of the address takes the differentiation for granted, but moves on to explore how the two spheres need to be related. He invites his audience to reflect on contemporary events to recognize that between then and now, conditions have shifted. This shift calls for new insights that go beyond the old, to ask how the two remain different but are related; they work together in service of human dignity and welfare:

> It was an outstanding Jew, Justice Felix Frankfurter, who helped give the answer. "Religion is outside the sphere of political government," he wrote, "but this does not mean that all matters on which religious organizations … may pronounce are outside the sphere of Government … Much that is the concern of temporal authority affects the spiritual interests of men."
>
> And it was my deputy, Bill Moyers, a Southern Baptist, trained as a minister of his church, who suggested that I reaffirm to you today his belief as well as mine that separation of Church and State does not mean the divorce of spiritual values from secular affairs.[30]

He explores how, precisely, they are to work together:

> Legal separation is an important principle. Equally important is the need for cooperation and common effort in attacking social problems. For the State to deprive itself of the support of religious belief and organization is to enter the battle for social justice without our strongest weapon: the

spiritual beliefs from which social action springs. And without the cooperation of Church and State, of belief and power, our efforts will be doomed
to failure.[31]

Shriver's main argument is that politics needs spirituality to do its work.
Earlier the same year, at the January Speech to the Religion and Race
Conference, he develops this idea. The Conference was a major inter-
religious event, widely covered by the press. It brought together over
700 Catholic, Protestant, and Jewish religious leaders for three days,
both to commemorate the one hundredth anniversary of the Eman-
cipation Proclamation, and to focus the moral and political force of
religion on the problem of racial justice in the United States. Abraham Heschel opened the conference, Martin Luther King spoke on
the final day, and Shriver headlined day two. What comes out clearly
in Shriver's address is his singular ability to live out his convictions by
speaking seamlessly as both a government official and a man of profound faith and spiritual acuity. He begins by accepting the traditional
separation of church and state, but rejects the idea that religion has no
role to play in politics.

> Justice for men is a common objective of religion and government and the
> exclusive domain of neither.
>   I hope the traditional American regard for the separation of church and
> state will never be interpreted as an excuse for either to preempt - or ignore -
> the vigorous pursuit of human dignity and freedom which are the legiti-
> mate concern of both church and state.[32]

As in the Fordham address, Shriver's argument is that politics needs religion to do its work:

> But laws and government are, at best, coarse and inefficient instruments
> for remolding social institutions or illuminating the dark places of the
> human heart. They can deal only with the broadest and most obvious
> problems: ... They can call for the highest standards of moral conduct, but
> those standards are only tortuously and imperceptibly imposed on a com-
> munity which does not accept them, ... For even though law can compel
> and even educate, in the last analysis the rule of law depends upon a legal
> order which embodies the convictions, desires and judgments of the men
> it governs.
>   If we recognize that laws alone are inadequate, that legislatures and pres-
> idents cannot impose moral convictions, then we must look to those institu-
> tions whose task it is to teach moral values, to restate eternal principles in

terms of today's conflicts, and to conform the daily conduct of men to the guiding values of justice, of love and of compassion. Pre-eminent among those institutions is religion and the church.[33]

What is interesting is the vision of religion underlying Shriver's analysis. Recurring throughout these texts and throughout the entire speech are a series of words denoting the sphere of human experience that is the proper domain of religion: "heart," "convictions," "desires," judgments," "moral convictions," "moral values," "eternal principles," "guiding values," "justice," "love," "compassion." This is the realm of human interiority. Shriver's assumption is that while politics involves institutions, laws, and mechanisms for making and implementing decisions for achieving public goods like justice and peace, these instruments of politics cannot do their work without the interior convictions, values, and virtues that must be cultivated and sustained by religions. His assumption is that religion and politics are two distinguishable spheres or levels of human living, but they do not work separately or autonomously. Rather, he seems to assume that while politics might be considered a particular field of human experience, religion or spirituality is actually an inner realm of all human persons that exerts its influence in all fields of human experience. Moreover, his assumption is that for politics to achieve its goals, this inner spiritual realm of persons must be kept healthy and well-developed by whatever religious or secular belief tradition we belong to. Politics needs spiritually healthy citizens.

Shriver does not approach issues of religion and politics by thinking about religions primarily in terms of traditions and institutions. His focus is not on external manifestations but on the sphere of interiority where values, feelings, and virtues are cultivated. This realm of interiority is personal, but it is not private. On the contrary, interiority does the work of influencing all sectors or fields of human life. Moreover, what is striking is Shriver is convinced that for social and political life to achieve its goals, this sphere of interiority of persons must be healthy. We gain some insight into his standards for discerning what this means when we observe his reflections on some of the obstacles to achieving racial justice in America.

I find it alarming, therefore, when the Government looks to the religious community for its share of the task and encounters, too often, a bland philosophy of laissez faire.

As a layman, for example, I wonder why I can go to church 52 times a year and not hear one sermon on the practical problems of race relations ... I wonder, furthermore, why each minister, rabbi, and priest does not map a specific program for his congregation – a program that will produce concrete gains over the next twelve months. Such a program could do many things ... If such a program intended finally to bury religious laissez faire in racial problems were instituted, it would encourage each member of the congregation to pledge a tithe of their time to removing racial barriers at work, at play, at worship.[34]

Shriver's vision of spirituality and politics, as open and inclusive as it is, remains critical. It contains central criteria for discerning spiritual wellness and differentiating between religion that harms and religion that heals. He reveals his understanding of these criteria when he invites us "to conform the daily conduct of men to the guiding values of justice, of love and of compassion."[35] Shriver shares with conservatives the concern for the relevance of religion for politics, and he shares with liberals the focus on peace and justice as central to the work of politics. But his guiding vision is centered on "love and compassion." These are the central criteria for discerning how this is to be achieved. From his earliest years of public life, Shriver's message to women and men of America is that their central vocation as citizens is to the love and compassion that dynamize and inform the pursuit of justice and peace.

Throughout his speeches, the prime obstacle in the struggle against racism in America is an interior attitude, a state of conviction, that renders citizens inactive, unconcerned, indifferent in the face of the ravages of racial injustice. This inner state Shriver considers as something like a disease of the soul. It is a distinctly spiritual form of illness. In fact, he considers this inner spiritual illness to be so important that he places it front and center in the opening paragraph of his address. He recounts a passage from an essay by James Baldwin in which he and two African American friends were refused service in the lounge of Chicago's O'Hare airport. None of the white people around them lifted a finger to help. When one of them finally turned to a young white man asking why he did not help, his response was: "'I lost my conscience a long time ago.'"[36] Shriver launches his speech with this focus on the religious task of re-awakening conscience so that politics can achieve the goals of justice.

The purpose of this meeting is to re-awaken that conscience – to direct the immense power of religion to shaping the conduct and thoughts of men toward their brothers in a manner consistent with the compassion and love on which our spiritual tradition rests.[37]

From Charity to Spirituality and Compassion

In the Chicago speeches of 1955–9, Shriver speaks of the dynamism animating the pursuit of peace and justice as the theological virtue of charity. His language is explicitly religious and Catholic. With this language, he draws on a traditional Catholic framework for distinguishing and relating the natural and the supernatural. He understands justice and peace as natural virtues, framed within a Thomist natural law theory of politics. He understands that our natural capacities for the discernment and actuation of virtues and values are universally human but corruptible by sin. Yet he knows that sin never pronounces the final word, for beyond our natural capacities, we can also receive the supernatural virtue of charity, transforming us, dynamizing, healing, and elevating our natural capacities for justice and peace.

In the speeches of the Peace Corps years, he shifts away from this traditional Catholic theological language of charity. To be sure, it is not difficult to understand why. He is now a US government public servant, speaking to audiences from diverse religious and secular belief traditions, about a program that crosses religious and cultural boundaries. Our question, however, is how he understands his work with the Peace Corps. We have argued that, in the Peace Corps years, Shriver does not lose the conviction that his work of public service is a truly religious or spiritual vocation, rooted in his Catholic faith. And we have outlined core elements of his understanding of the relationship between spirituality and politics. Our question now is whether this spiritual self-understanding can be discerned in the more "secularized" language. Can we find in the new language continuity with elements of his earlier religious framework with its focus on charity? If so, then how does it shape his thinking about the Peace Corps? How does he navigate the transition in language while retaining and developing the substance?

In his March 24, 1961, speech to the New York Herald Tribune Youth Forum, Shriver's language begins to reveal how he will speak publicly about the US government program that he designed and launched as an expression of his personal spiritual vocation to public life. He refers to Ghandi and speaks of "the belief that dedicated and disciplined individuals can illuminate the shared dream of the human heart."[38] He speaks about "the second American revolution," and "the belief in the power of individual moral conscience to re-make the world."[39] He outlines the four principles basic to the Peace Corps and speaks of them as "fundamental human beliefs ... at the moral heart of the universe."[40] He frames his description of Peace Corps volunteers in the same language of interiority that he uses two years later in his Fordham and Chicago Religion and Race Conference Speeches on spirituality and politics:

> And it is because the men and women of the Peace Corps are the inheritors of these beliefs, because they have absorbed them in the schoolrooms and churches, on the farms and cities of our country, that they have been able to cross barriers of language and culture, religious faith and social structure, to touch the deep chord of common hope and principle which belongs to all men.[41]

A few months later, he delivers two speeches to educators gathered in Atlantic City, New Jersey, and Nashville, Tennessee, and speaks about "the Peace Corps mission," its advanced teaching methods that are able "to turn out a 'whole' person,"[42] and its "exciting revolutionary philosophy" that "can remind us of the spirit of freedom and revolution that ignited our own revolution."[43] In Nashville, in July 1961, Shriver concludes with the language of service in "the cause of world peace."[44] At Salem College, West Virginia, he expands on this idea of service in his opening remarks: "In speaking to you men and women of Salem College, I want to set forth ... the doctrine of the demanding life, the life of sacrifice and service."[45] Later in the same speech, he offers a fuller account of the demanding life of service of Peace Corps volunteers:

> A Peace Corps Volunteer, therefore, is really a "rare bird." He is unique. He goes to a foreign country to work within that country's system; he helps fill their needs as they see them; he speaks their language; he lives in the way they live and under their laws; he does not try to change their religion; he does not seek to make a profit from conducting business in their country; he does not interfere in their political or military affairs.[46]

One month later, he restates this doctrine of other-oriented service at Springfield College, Massachusetts:

> I am proposing a new conception of citizenship in a Democracy. I believe that all citizens, young and old, should give a significant part of their lives to the voluntary service of their country and their fellow man, especially those most in need.
>
> That's what the Peace Corps stands for.[47]

Always the salesman, Shriver sprinkles his speeches with the language of American patriotism. What is interesting, however, is his interpretation of what this patriotism entails. For Shriver, true patriotism is service to others in need, not simply at home, but in all corners of the world, on their terms, in their languages, freely given as an act of self-sacrifice and generosity. This is remarkable. We argue that in these texts, we are observing the transposition of core elements from the Catholic doctrine of natural justice and supernatural charity into a broad-based vision of spirituality, grounding and animating a demanding life of service to justice and peace, on behalf of universal humanity.

In Nashville he begins using the language of "spirit" and "spirituality" in reference to the Peace Corps,[48] and in October 1961, June 1962, May 1963, and June 1963, he delivers five speeches to diverse audiences that return to this language of "spirit" and "spiritual values."[49] In these texts, Shriver reveals a great deal about how he understands "spirituality." He speaks of the Peace Corps as "a two-way street."[50]

> Our nation and our Volunteers will get as much out of the Peace Corps as we put into it ... There are new heroes of freedom and new statesmen of liberty in each emerging nation of the world ... Our Volunteers can share with these people our knowledge of how to build and to prosper in a world torn between freedom and slavery. But these people, in turn can remind us of the spirit of freedom and revolution that ignited our own revolution.
>
> To be completely frank about it, our own revolution has only begun. Progress in the area of human development – the heart of any revolution – may have been ignored as we have grown financially fat, spiritually soft, and morally callous. Our revolution of the human spirit has turned prematurely gray. Our young people need to see the spark of freedom burning in the hearts and minds of their counterparts overseas. This fresh understanding, this fresh reminder, related to our own traditions, will help to tear down the barriers of ignorance on both sides of the ocean.[51]

The Peace Corps is structured so that volunteers not only bring something to their work, they also receive something from it. Moreover, this something is essential for the accomplishment of their work. It is a transformative experience arising from personal encounter with their international partners. This something is spiritual transformation. And Shriver understands this spiritual transformation as a healing and enabling response to a spiritual illness that has crept into American and world society. In three speeches he evokes the image of "a spiritual woman associate of Ghandi" named Ashadevi, who offers a challenge to Peace Corps volunteers.[52] She speaks of a "valuelessness spreading in the world."[53] Elsewhere Shriver speaks of a moral and spiritual illness that has set into American life.

The years following the Korean War were gray years for American youth. Pundits commented that the new American seemed to be "a guy with an empty mind, a hollow heart, and a full belly." Cries of "Soft" were in the air. "Did not one-third of the Americans in North Korean prison camps collaborate with the enemy? Did not another third die?" The sign of the new generation became a question mark.[54]

He speaks of this illness as a "spiritual flabbiness" that corrupts and compromises the person's capacity for vigorous moral action on behalf of global peace and justice.[55] He evokes the criticism that Americans are "too flabby in body, too flaccid in spirit" to respond adequately to the challenges posed by the Peace Corps.[56] We suggest that Shriver understands "spirituality," not simply as moral action, but as something broader and deeper; a state or capacity of the whole person that arises from transformative experience. The effect of the transformation is to heal us from an infliction or illness – a "hollow heart" – that renders us impotent in the face of the great moral challenges of our age.

We observe here central elements of the traditional Catholic doctrine of sin and grace, now expressed in the language of interiority. In his February 24, 1963, speech to the Chicago Knights of Columbus, Shriver reveals explicit links between these ideas and the traditional Catholic framework as he addresses an audience familiar with the language of his tradition. On three occasions he makes explicit reference to love and the theological virtue of "charity."[57] He frames his address as a challenge to his Catholic audience for failing to accept Cardinal Cushing's invitation to contribute to a project allied with the aims and ideals of the Peace Corps.[58] He cites the papal encyclical, *Mater et magistra*, reminding his audience that they have a special responsibility to the world's poor "since they are members of the Mystical Body of Christ."[59] Then he explains that dedication to the values of natural justice is not simply about doing good for others, it is also about their own spiritual transformation:

> You will not only help Latin America, you will help yourself. You and your children will have an opportunity to broaden your horizons through learning in a direct and immediate way – of the problems and life of people in other lands.
>
> You also will benefit through contact with the flourishing culture, the deep spiritual values, and the firmly rooted tradition of individual human dignity in Latin America. For we have much to learn in the way of the mind and spirit from our brothers in Latin America who have kept alive their deep beliefs despite an adversity which is almost beyond our capacity to imagine.

> With this program ... We can capture that spirit of individual sacrifice
> and meaningful effort which, by bringing us closer to other men, brings us
> closer to God.[60]

In his June 1962 commencement speech to St. Louis University,
Shriver uses the language of "generosity" to speak about this spiritual
transformation and the role of the Peace Corps in effecting a "migration" in the American spirit towards peace and service to others. But
we believe the term that best captures the spirit of charity in his new
language of interiority is "compassion." In the opening paragraphs of
his January 1963 Speech to the Chicago Religion and Race Conference,
Shriver articulates the core component in the relationship between spirituality and justice:

> The purpose of this meeting is to re-awaken that conscience – to direct the
> immense power of religion to shaping the conduct and thoughts of men
> toward their brothers in a manner consistent with the compassion and love
> on which our spiritual tradition rests.[61]

Again, in setting forth the challenge of cultivating the "convictions,
desires and judgments" of the people who must implement State programs on behalf of justice and peace, he speaks of religion in terms of
the "guiding values of justice, of love and of compassion."[62] Five months
later, at Fordham University, he speaks of the transformative capacity
of "compassion" to "dissolve obstacles of race or belief anywhere in the
world."[63] Finally, one year later, in his Remarks at the Dedication of the
Vatican Pavilion at the New York World's Fair, April 19, 1964, Shriver
reveals most fully his understanding of the direct link between charity
and compassion.

> To achieve the peace that goes beyond treaties, that goes beyond ideolo-
> gies, a peace that binds hearts and creates a true community, we need the
> world of art to lift our spirits – we need the world of religion to give us a
> better standard than the things we see around us. Here is that standard, in
> the sorrowing mother, holding what was failure as the world goes, but which
> proved to be the greatest success of all time. It was successful because, as
> the Pieta reveals, it was a life of compassion. Michelangelo captured that
> compassion, which is what we need to see and what we need to understand
> if the world is ever to know true peace.
>   For the saints and sages of the great religions have always agreed that a
> peace that passes understanding can be reached only by compassion. This is
> the ideal that must illuminate, from the very center, all our efforts to bring

a better life to our world, within our own country, or in the farthest reaches of the planet. And even in the deepest privacy of our lives in the prayer that each of us makes in his own tongue and by the dictates of his own heart, there will be no solitude so absolute that it would exclude this compassion.

Just as this masterpiece has crossed the Atlantic undamaged, unmarred – no ocean can be wide enough to exclude the compassion that presides in this Pavilion, the silence of Michelangelo's Pieta. It is only with that compassion that man can look upon man – through the mask of many colors, through the vestments of many religions, through the dust of poverty, or through the disfigurement of disease – and recognize his brother.[64]

In these texts we find a transposition of core elements from the traditional Catholic language of nature and grace to the broader language of peace, justice, compassion, and spiritual transformation. We use the term "transposition" because we argue that central elements of the traditional doctrine remain. Most important is the centrality of the theological virtue of charity, the Divine gift that effects a transformation of horizons from apathy or self-interest to generosity and compassion. What the new language does is evoke the shift to interiority by placing the accent on the spiritual transformation of the whole person. And in so doing, the language gains its power to speak to women and men from diverse secular and religious belief traditions about a transformative spiritual experience open to all.

Spirituality, Politics, and the Peace Corps: What Shriver Did

On October 13, 1960 – immediately following a Presidential debate with Richard Nixon – Jack Kennedy flew to Ann Arbor to address a campaign rally at the University of Michigan. Swept up by the enthusiasm of the 10,000 chanting students waiting for him when he arrived on campus at 2:00 a.m., Kennedy began to engage the crowd with extemporaneous remarks: "How many of you would be willing to spend your days working [as teachers, doctors, and engineers] in Ghana?" he shouted out. When the crowd roared back its affirmation, Kennedy responded: "On your willingness to contribute part of your life to this country, I think will depend the answer whether we as a free society can compete [in the cold war world.]"[65]

Three weeks later, and just one week before Election Day, Kennedy gave this idea a political life of its own in a speech at the Cow Palace in San Francisco. Borrowing the name from national service introduced into Congress earlier that year by Hubert Humphrey, Kennedy proposed the creation of "a 'Peace Corps' of talented young men and women willing and able to serve their country – well qualified through vigorous standards; well-trained in the language, skills, and customs they will need to know." On January 21, 1961, the day following his Inauguration, President Kennedy assigned Sargent Shriver the task of developing the Peace Corps. At that point in time, it did not exist, and nothing like it had ever been tried.[66]

In a speech delivered in Bangkok, Thailand, Sargent Shriver speaks directly to the practical, transformative purpose of the Peace Corps. He explains to his audience at Chulalongkorn University that the mission of Peace Corps volunteers is to build peace with other people by joining them in service to human welfare and dignity:

> [the volunteer] goes overseas not merely as a willing and a skilled worker – but as a representative, a living example, of the most powerful idea of all: the idea that free and committed men and women can cross, even transcend, boundaries of culture and language, of alien tradition and great disparities of wealth, of old hostilities and new nationalisms, to meet with other men and women on the common ground of service to human welfare and human dignity.[67]

Obviously, Peace Corps volunteers "go overseas as willing and skilled workers." Any successful endeavor requires this. What is interesting is Shriver's account of what happens to both them and their international partners when they engage in implementing the principles and policies of the Peace Corps. The result is a change in them. They are enabled, with the result that they now begin to achieve what previously they could not. They "can cross, even transcend, boundaries of culture and language, of alien tradition and great disparities of wealth, of old hostilities and new nationalisms." What effects this transformation is a personal sacrifice of "service to human welfare and human dignity." The policies and practices of the Peace Corps, focused as they are on service to human welfare and human dignity, not only presuppose spiritual transformation, they effect it by cooperating with the gift of Spirit. For Shriver, the notions of human welfare and human dignity are not abstract ideals or empty slogans. They are institutionalized principles for concrete action and for the organizational structures that facilitate and direct concrete actions. Their implementation, he believes, results in a change in social situations that is grounded in the spiritual transformation of persons.

To be sure, the method of peacebuilding of the Peace Corps flies in the face of the so-called "realism" of power politics. As a witty, but scathing editorial in the *Wall Street Journal* expressed at the time: "Who but the very young themselves can really believe that an Africa aflame with violence will have its fires quenched because some Harvard boy or Vassar girl lives in a mud hut and speaks Swahili?"[68] Yet Shriver and his staff were themselves concerned about the hard realities reflected in this line of criticism. From the outset, they sought to ground the peacebuilding values and activities of the Peace Corps in hardheaded pragmatism and realistic administration. In an article published in *Foreign Affairs* in 1963, Shriver reflects back on early Peace Corps efforts to realize this vision:

> Of course, youthful enthusiasm and noble purposes were not enough. They had to be combined with hardheaded pragmatism and realistic administration. In the early days of the Peace Corps, we were looking for a formula for practical idealism.[69]

In building the organization, Shriver and his staff consciously developed program policies and procedures oriented towards facilitating experiences in which both volunteers and their international partners would be changed by their work. They structured Peace Corps service assignments to maximize the possibilities for the transformative experiences of cross-cultural understanding and personal growth. In a speech to the Commonwealth Club of California, Shriver described this "formula for practical idealism":

> The rules are few and simple. First, learn the language of the people with whom you work. Second, make up your mind that the work of developing nations is worth the price of personal sacrifice. Third, anchor yourself in the customs and traditions of the country where you are serving. Fourth, take your standard of living down near enough to the local level to make it possible to mix freely and easily with the people – get down to eye level with them. Fifth, believe in the power of personal integrity, humility and determination.[70]

These "simple rules" channel the skills and energy of the volunteers, put the core values of the program into action, and concretely structure the way volunteers treat the people they meet in their host countries. This set of practical program guidelines – learn the language, commit personally to development work, embrace local customs, live at or near local standards of living, cultivate personal integrity, humility, and determination – establishes patterns of actions of Peace Corps volunteers and host country nationals, and these patterns have the effect of transforming personal relations by transforming persons. By putting themselves in service to the welfare and dignity of others, volunteers level the barriers and hierarchies created by economic, social, and cultural difference and open up possibilities for new ways of meeting on "common ground."

As Shriver makes clear, the policies and programs of Peace Corps volunteers do not aim at proselytizing, or promoting "political theories, economic systems, or religious creeds":

> Nor do our Volunteers go overseas as the salesmen of a particular political theory, or economic system, or religious creed. They go to work with people – not to employ them, use them, or advise them. They do what the country they go to wants them to do – not what we think is best. They live among the people, sharing their homes, eating their food, talking their language, living under their laws – not in special compounds with special privileges.[71]

Practicing what the program preaches, the Peace Corps developed a policy of posting volunteers in their service assignments without primary regard for their race, ethnic background, gender, or religion. Predictably, this policy attracted its share of critics and skeptics. Shriver was fond of drawing attention to these critics in his speeches:

> Yet at every step of the way we were met with the warnings of the timid. "Don't send Negroes to Africa," we were warned, "the Africans will think you are condescending." "You can't send Jews to Tunisia and Morocco." "You can't send Protestants to the Catholic country of Colombia." "You can't send Puerto Ricans to Latin America because 'they' look on Puerto Rico as an American colony." We refused to heed any of these warnings. And they all proved untrue-the folklore of "experts" who had never got to the level of the people.[72]

All these warnings "proved untrue," Shriver goes on to say, because "compassion and service" break down the barriers of race, belief, and culture:

> The fact is that compassion and service can dissolve obstacles of race or belief anywhere in the world. People are hungry for contact, for fellowship, for the breaking down of barriers.[73]

For Shriver, the central principle of the Peace Corps's programs and procedures is "compassion and service." What we observe here is the language of interiority that he uses to transpose the traditional religious language of charity. We argue that this language is not accidental. Shriver's focus is the experience of spiritual transformation that is both presupposed and facilitated by the Peace Corps. Engaging in Peace

Corps programs and activities, participants and nationals experience the transformations that can "dissolve obstacles of race or belief anywhere in the world." He structured the programs of the Peace Corps so participants everywhere could encounter others in actions of "compassion and service."

Shriver's belief – a belief that proved itself time and again – was that these actions would indeed result in "breaking down barriers." The reason he believed this was because he believed that all humans everywhere "are hungry for contact, for fellowship, for the breaking down of barriers." We argue that Shriver believed that all members of the human family, in all our wondrous diversity, share the dynamism of this hunger at our very core. It is a moral hunger for justice, but it is more than this. It is also a hunger for a broader and deeper state of ourselves as persons that both enables the discernment of peace and justice and mobilizes us to action towards peace and justice in a specific manner – out of compassion for them and in self-sacrificing service to them as persons. It is a hunger for transformative experience that open possibilities for justice and peace where previously they were closed by domination, self-interest, apathy, or tyranny – what previously we would have called "sin." It is the hunger for transcendence, and it is the "nature" of all of us.

Concluding Remarks

From the outset, our question in this book has been how to navigate the distinctions and relations between religion and politics. Our focus is on how to rise above past histories that have poisoned these distinctions and relations with the bitter effects of conservative-liberal and religious-secular divisions in society and in our belief traditions. Our chosen strategy is to explore the words and deeds of a major American political figure whose accomplishments have done not a little to achieve this goal, Sargent Shriver.

We focus on the early years of his public life and divide these into two periods, the first in Chicago as President of the Board of Education, 1955–9, and the second in Washington as Director of the Peace Corps, 1961–4. Our method is to examine his speeches in these two periods and to draw on relevant background material to explain how he understood and lived a rather distinctive approach to religion and politics – an approach we believe is as relevant today as it was then.

What we find is a transition in language in the speeches from the first period to the second. In the first, Shriver's language is explicitly religious, traditionally Catholic. It reveals how he understood his public life as a religious vocation, rooted in his Catholic faith tradition, with its conservative framework of nature-supernature, natural law, and the theological virtue of charity. Yet, the language of this period also reveals a commitment to diversity, social justice, and openness to world religions. Typically, these two sets of ideas have been at the center of conservative-liberal and religious-secular social divisions. Oddly enough, he seems to appeal to the resources of the conservative framework to makes sense of the liberal convictions. Our argument is that during this period Shriver is already marking a distinctive turn in his appropriation of the traditional resources, a turn we call the shift to interiority.

In the second period, Shriver shifts to a language that is less explicitly religious more explicitly what we might call public or secular. With a few exceptions, his speeches are less reliant on religious terms, they cite fewer religious authors, and appeal to fewer religious values and principles. Yet at times, particularly in his addresses to religious audiences, he does reveal how he continues to understand his public life and work as a religious vocation, in continuity with his vocation of the Chicago years. More important, the analysis reveals how the newly chosen language of spirituality and compassion is Shriver's way of advancing and deepening the transition to interiority begun in the earlier period. We argue that the transition is actually a transposition, a shift that retains the core elements of the traditional Catholic framework, but now transposes them into a broader and deeper philosophy of the human person. In the next chapter, we draw on the work of Bernard Lonergan to explain this transposition, how it works, and how it provides resources for present and future efforts to do as Shriver did, transcend the divisions that hamper our ability to think wisely on matters of religion and politics.

In the first period, the traditional Catholic framework of nature and grace provided tools for Shriver to understand the need for the separation of the institutions of church and state. Politics belongs to the realm of the natural, the human, the things that are to be understood and managed by human intelligence and responsibility. Yet Shriver's Catholic tradition also reminded him of the relevance of sin – what we would now speak of as self-interest, corruption, ideology, domination, and oppression. And because of his faith tradition, Shriver remained an optimist – not a naive optimist committed to the perfectability of humanity, but a wise optimist convinced that, beyond morality and sin, we can also expect to encounter the Divine gift of charity. The properly supernatural character of charity as Divine gift grounds a clear distinction between nature and grace, and this is the key to understanding the proper distinction between politics and religion. Politics belongs to the realm of nature and humanity. Charity, on the other hand, belongs to the realm of the supernatural, and this is the proper domain of religion.

Shriver reveals a departure from traditional Catholic language for interpreting this relation when he takes the turn to interiority. Older Catholic authorities appealed to the nature-grace distinction to argue for the intrusion of Church authority in politics and culture. Their argument was that only this intrusion can ensure that grace is dispensed sufficiently to hold back the tidal wave of sin and liberate natural reason to work properly in politics. What Shriver discovered is that while religious institutions must do the work of healing and elevating human reason, they do so diversely, and they do so within the interiority of conscience. To be sure, not all traditions and not every stream of any tradition does this adequately. We must remain vigilant and interiority provides tools for remaining critically discerning. All this requires respect for the institutional separation of church and state that guarantees liberty of conscience. Only a free conscience can accept the gift of charity. Politics does indeed need religion, but it needs it to work in the interior life of conscience of citizens and public leaders. Religious institutions must be free to do this work of cultivating interiority, and political institutions must be free to mobilize this interiority in the service of justice and peace.

More striking, however, is Shriver's belief that tools from Catholic tradition can explain how this transformative work of charity works through diverse traditions to dynamize the commitment to peace and justice in the lives of people everywhere, on behalf of universal humanity. Shriver's natural law was a truly universal understanding of the interiority of persons. And his Catholic God was the God of universal humanity, operating in all cultures and traditions, through the gift of charity that transforms interiority from apathy and hate to responsibility, compassion, and service as self-sacrificing love.

Our argument is that the distinctive appropriation of the tools of Catholic tradition in the Chicago years – an appropriation rooted in interiority – set the groundwork for the transposition to the more open, more universal language of compassion and spirituality in the Peace Corps years. What is dramatically new about the second period, however, is how this transposed vision left its mark on the very structure of the Peace Corps itself. Peace is not only a work accomplished in the public life of politics of a person motivated by religious faith. We argue it is an incarnation of the very spirituality of this vocation. Shriver saw the Peace Corps as establishing the institutional conditions for facilitating the spiritually transformative experiences that he understood as the work of the Divine gift of charity.

At some point along the way, Shriver shifted out of the classicist way of thinking about the realms of the natural and the supernatural as different spheres of "stuff." Instead, he seems to have adopted a framework for understanding the interiority of persons as dynamized by a hunger for transcendence. He knew this interiority can be distorted or harmed. But he also knew we are open to spiritually transformative experiences that can shift us from indifference or hate to engagement and love. This, he believed, is the way the Divine gift of charity works. And, in true fidelity to the Catholic doctrine of cooperative grace, he structured the Peace Corps to do just that.

To this point, our focus has been on Shriver, his speeches, and their interpretation. Our effort has been to understand the speeches and to provide the evidential base for lines of ideas operative in his public expressions. While Shriver's theological and philosophical understanding is far more subtle than would be expected normally from a public leader, there does remain important work to do in explaining how his insights remain valid, not only in his time, but in present and future times. The challenges of religion and politics are not going away. This is because they are a feature of a massive historical shift that is taking place. In the next chapter, we provide a framework, rooted in the work of Lonergan, for understanding and navigating this shift wisely. Those familiar with Lonergan will know that our presentation is brief. Yet we believe that linking our understandings of Lonergan and Shriver can help understand the significance of both. Most important, we hope we can provide insights for living more graciously, more compassionately, the conflicts of the present and future.

Chapter Four

Explaining What Shriver Did

Sargent Shriver carried his religious vocation into politics in a way that found resonance in the hearts of women and men from diverse secular and religious belief traditions. His vocation, rooted in his traditional Catholic faith, was his own ministry to peace and justice, but it was also an open engagement with the people of America and the world. The speeches of his early career bear witness to this vocation. And the political programs he built mark the fruition of this life of service to charity and justice in a culturally and religiously diverse world. This diversity, he believed, could be trusted to yield the common human resources for the pursuit of peace and unity among women and men everywhere.

Shriver was a liberal American, committed to diversity and to the distinction between religion and politics that was essential for guarding this diversity. Yet his liberal values were bolstered by a conservative Catholic belief in objective moral values, and he was committed to the relations between religion and politics that were essential for fostering these values. He championed the values of family, church, school, hard work, liberty, self-sacrifice, the natural law, religious fidelity, the sacredness of life, prayer, and the sacraments, the splendor of Catholic Church tradition, and the amazing work of the Holy Spirit transforming history and society through the religious gift of charity. Shriver's life and work brought together core values of both conservatives and liberals and provide insights into diverse forms of concrete religion-politics distinctions and relations. What is most impressive, however, is the way he transposed core principles from his traditional Catholic faith into the Peace Corps, a political program that would touch the hearts of all. In this chapter, we explore resources on religion and politics from his tradition, both past and present, that explain how he could do this and how we can continue doing this in present and future years.

Religion and Politics: Shriver's Catholic Tradition

Shriver's Catholic tradition provided him with sophisticated resources for navigating the boundary between religion and politics. The first of these is the very distinction itself, and it finds expression in St. Augustine's fifth-century treatise on The City of God and the City of Man. An older heritage goes back further to ancient empires, Hebrew prophets, and Greek philosophers.[1] Historians tell us that religion has always influenced politics. In fact, for millennia, there was no clear distinction between the two. This was not simply because of the ideas held by ancient leaders and sages, but because of the very structure of human consciousness.[2] Politics invariably engages our convictions about things of ultimate concern, things that bring us to the edge of life, death, and eternity. Consequently, we have always needed to know that our political convictions reflect a broader sense of ultimate order and truth. We need to know whether we are squandering our lives or sacrificing our children foolishly following the programs and campaigns of political leaders. This means relating politics to ultimate convictions. We seek some sort of coherence between the political programs that make demands on our lives and the beliefs we hold about ultimate meaning and transcendent value.

The problem is that sages also discovered something that has become glaringly clear in our time; not all ideas about ultimate values are good for us. In fact, even when they are good for us, not all applications to politics are good for us. What emerged in Jewish, Greek, Christian, and Islamic traditions was an immense enterprise of careful intellectual analysis that sought to differentiate between religion that harms and religion that heals. This is theology. Within this, an important task was the work of demarcating the boundaries of religion and politics.

Theologians discovered that politics is a this-worldly affair. It is finite, it is fallible, it is limited. Our religious convictions, on the other hand, make claims about ultimates; about all of life, all of history, all of the cosmos, all of the universe, transcendence, and life beyond. In some way or another, our ultimate claims point beyond the limitations of politics and history, and this means that there can never be full coherence between politics and ultimate meanings. God's name cannot be known and the Kingdom of God is not of this world. In the early centuries of the Christian churches, this came to be formulated as a demarcation between the City of God and the human city, and it translated into a distinction between church and state. Church institutions are responsible for religious meanings and the symbolic world associated with the City of God. Their task is reflecting on ultimates and distinguishing between religion that harms and religion that heals. To do their work properly they can never come under the control of the state. Politics, on the other hand, belongs to the human city. It must accept some sort of guidance from religion, but can never claim to realize fully the aspirations of religious ultimacy. This lies beyond politics.

Disasters arise when state authorities attempt to realize ultimate aspirations in political programs. The wars of religion of past centuries and the totalitarianisms of the twentieth century provide ample evidence of this. In fact, the horrors of the twentieth century reveal that fanaticism is no less destructive when its political programs promote ultimate aspirations clothed in secular garb. Scholars have shown that modern day secular traditions can be rather prone to this problem because they borrow ultimate aspirations from religious traditions and import them into secular programs, forgetting the careful work done by theologians cautioning against the perils of neglecting the distinction.[3] The problem is that ultimate aspirations can never be of this world. Human life is not perfectible by politics. This is the truth that has been taught to us by totalitarianism. We thought we could retreat from totalitarianism by rejecting religion. But we have discovered our ultimate aspirations forever crop up in new philosophies and secular belief traditions that function like religions. Shriver's Catholic tradition taught him the value of vigilance in attending to the role of ultimates in politics.

This is doubly important because legitimate influences can and must flow from religion to politics. Politics needs guidance and is forever shaped by ideals whose roots lie in religious traditions: ideals about the dignity of persons, the goodness of the universe, the pursuit of justice, freedom, peace, rights, and the common good. This means navigating the boundary between religion and politics remains a complex affair. Theologians and philosophers are forever charged with the task of differentiating between religion that harms and religion that heals, while politicians and political philosophers remain forever charged with the task of navigating the tension between ultimate aspirations and political limitations. Clearly, this is serious business.

Through the ages, Catholic theologians developed an impressive body of critical tools to help guide this work of distinguishing and relating religion and politics. In his 1956 address to the Chicago YMCA "Youth Citizenship Luncheon," Sargent Shriver drew on a range of Catholic principles to inspire his public audience with a vision of excellence, public service, and devotion to others. His appeal was to ideas about the nobility of politics, the common good, the just wage, and the sociality of the human person.[4] These ideas had considerable public appeal. Yet they have roots in the Catholic theology and philosophy of past centuries that came to be articulated in novel ways in a series of nineteenth and twentieth-century documents by Catholic popes, bishops, philosophers, and theologians.

Two of these documents, *Rerum novarum* and *Quadragesimo anno*, were issued in 1891 and 1931 by popes Leo XIII and Pius XI, and they played an important role in Shriver's early public life. They offer scathing criticisms of the evils of nineteenth-century industrial capitalism, they call for justice for workers, and they criticize political, social, and economic ideas enshrined in extreme forms of Marxist communism and liberal individualism. During the 1950s and 60s, Catholic theology was being transformed by influences that would shape the entire Catholic world at the Second Vatican Council, and one of the authors living in America whose "personalist" ideas influenced this transformation in social and political thought was Jacques Maritain.[5] Maritain's work had a dramatic effect on Shriver.[6] Yet, as we will observe, Shriver's work reveals guidance from these sources as well as an original practical intelligence of his own that would take this guidance into novel directions.

At the core of this body of ideas on religion and politics in the Catholic tradition lie three sets of ideas that provided resources for distinguishing and relating the worlds of religion and politics: the natural-supernatural distinction, the natural law, and the theological virtue of charity. All three of these achieved their most influential forms of expression in the Middle Ages, most notably in the work of Thomas Aquinas. But by the mid-twentieth century, they were being transformed by influences from science, history, and philosophy.

The first of these, the natural-supernatural distinction, was an insight that demarcated the boundaries of a realm of human experience, distinct from the supernatural, that was properly knowable by human reason.[7] The realm of the natural was judged proportionate to human understanding and this meant that the work of understanding the world was a worthy task. The supernatural, by contrast, remained the proper realm of ultimates or absolutes and must be tagged transcendent mystery, ever important in our lives, but ever beyond our ability to capture and formulate in concepts and theories.[8] It is this realm of transcendent mystery that is the domain of religion. Politics, on the other hand, belongs to the realm of the natural, and gaining knowledge and values relevant to political programs remains something we can and must do if we are to live together responsibly.

The natural-supernatural distinction provided the basis for distinguishing religion and politics. In Shriver's tradition, politics belongs to the realm of the natural, and this has important implications. Because politics is natural, it does not belong, first and foremost, to the realm of religious mystery. It is properly knowable by human understanding. But because it belongs to the natural, politics can never claim to realize ultimate aspirations. The Catholic tradition reminds us to remain wary of the fanaticisms that arise when we seek perfection in this world through the pursuit of technology, wealth, military might, or even liberty.[9] Perfection does not belong to this life. We aspire to great things in politics, but we must learn to accept that achievements will always fall short of ultimate aspirations. In theology, this is known as eschatology. Our ideas about salvation, redemption, and ultimate fulfilment belong to a realm that, in some mysterious way, lies beyond history.[10] We have developed a symbolic world around ideas of the glory of God's final victory over evil, and these symbols have exerted a massive influence on the Western world through art and culture. But theologians remind us that these symbols can never be formulated as political programs. Politics is a fallible, natural affair, and can never be charged with ultimate expectations that belong to the realm of the supernatural.

What politics can do is receive guidance from religious ideas. And the avenue for this guidance was provided by the second idea from Catholic tradition, the natural law.[11] Based on an understanding of the human person rooted in the philosophy of Aristotle, natural law provided a framework that helped pave the way for the moral and legal insights of international law. Jacques Maritain went so far as to argue that natural law provided the hidden or implicit grounds for agreement on international treaties on human rights.[12] Given the diversity of cultures, traditions, and religions, who could imagine that humanity could formulate norms for international rights and relations that could command the assent of all? Yet, in some measure, this was achieved, and Catholic popes and scholars argued that natural law provided a framework and resources for applying reason towards the pursuit of peace, justice, and the common good in political relations.[13]

Examples of the guidance provided by natural law for politics abound. Human reason can examine human persons and discern an inclination that directs us to use our rational faculties to order lower biological faculties towards the goods of our higher nature.[14] Yet we seldom do this on our own, most often we do it together with others in ordered patterns of social and political life in which we secure the common good.[15] Reason can examine social living and discern patterns of communal order through which we secure elements of biological life – elements like food, shelter, and security. But reason can also operate creatively to devise new patterns for social life that groups can pursue in common to secure new types of goods.[16] In both cases, understanding these patterns yields norms that guide politics towards the pursuit of higher intellectual and spiritual levels of human personhood.[17] Maritain argued that natural law provided both the basis for the right to self-government and the norms governing directions for this self-government.[18] He argued it yields insights into truths about social order that grounded a radical critique of totalitarianism. He came to believe that democracy was one of the best expressions of these truths.[19] And his insights on natural law and property rights provided norms for policies on economic justice that sought to avoid the extremes of both unbridled capitalism and totalitarian communism.[20]

What is interesting about natural law is that, although it belongs to Roman Catholic tradition and has been articulated and promoted by religious authorities, it is not properly religious; it does not belong to the order of the supernatural.[21] It belongs to the natural, which for humans is the order of human reason. It therefore carries the features of finitude and limitation that distinguish the natural from the supernatural. This means that the natural law does have a proper role to play in politics. Yet Catholic tradition has always understood the natural law to be shaped or influenced by principles rooted in the properly religious dimension of transcendent mystery. Religion is not only distinguished from politics, it is also related. And we observe this influence at work in Maritain's analysis of relations between the person and the common good.[22]

In the Thomist Catholic tradition, persons are understood to be oriented to God, and this means that the highest good of persons is properly religious. It is the ultimate end or goal of all persons' life to find our highest fulfilment in unity with God. This means that no political order can make a higher claim on citizens or stand in the way of their religious aspirations, and it means that the political order must create conditions that serve and support persons in living their lives in light of this highest destiny. For Maritain, this framework gave rise to insights into human dignity and human liberty that found expression in a range of political values and policies.[23] He believed these values and policies were best realized in open democracies. Yet he also recognized that, because democracies belong to the natural, they require pluralism and their programs and policies must be articulated in the language of reason, not the language of faith.[24] Religion influences political reason, but because political reason belongs to the order of the natural, not the supernatural, it must find expression in the language appropriate to this sphere.

We can observe here an example of how religion, while institutionally distinct from politics, could still be understood to influence politics. Because the orders of the natural and supernatural remain distinguished, the proper content of the natural law remained open to human reason and subject to the scrutiny normally offered in political analysis and debate. Yet because religion and politics are related, insights into the human person gained from a religious horizon can influence the substance of political values and policies. Maritain was convinced that American democratic institutions of his time provided a good illustration of how the two orders could be lived out in appropriate forms of distinctions and relations. Sargent Shriver was influenced deeply by these ideas. References to natural law principles and ideals can be found scattered throughout the speeches of his early public life. Yet, he was able to articulate these insights to diverse audiences, in languages appropriate to each.

Most compelling for Shriver, however, was his conviction that human nature alone could never tell the whole story about human life. Beyond the work we do on our own, he was convinced that we participate in the deeper and broader life of the Mystical Body of Christ, and this opens us to the work of the Holy Spirit whose gift of charity supports and enhances our efforts to achieve public goods.[25] This brings us to the third resource from Catholic tradition, perhaps the most important influence on Shriver's vocation to public life, the theological virtue of charity.[26] In the theology of Thomas Aquinas, charity properly understood is not principally the duty to give money to the poor. It is not a moral obligation to do justice. In fact, it is not first and foremost something we do to others. Rather, it is something God does to us. It is a gift we receive in grace. Charity is the transformation of our habits and our willingness that comes from God's most precious gift to us, the personal experience of Divine love. Charity is one of those curious moments when we are changed in our habits and expectations because of our encounter with transcendence. The experience of charity is all-embracing love, and it shapes our hearts and minds, enabling and disposing us to make our own lives a loving gift of service to others. Properly speaking, charity has its origins in the realm of the supernatural. Yet, its result is a transformation of our lives, a joyful devotion to others that can find expression in countless projects and programs of natural life.

Through the centuries, Catholic schools and hospitals have been launched and sustained by women and men whose selfless devotion to others has been dynamized by the virtue of charity. One of the compelling influences in Shriver's early life was the example set by Dorothy Day's Catholic Worker program. During his teenage years in New York and in his university years at Yale, Shriver was impressed by the women and men who devoted themselves tirelessly to sustaining the lives of the poor and homeless on the streets of New York. This touched him deeply.[27] The force of charity is not the force of obligation, and its appeal is not the appeal of argument. Rather, even when it comes to us by example, its ground is an encounter with a Divine Other whose gift is a life of love. Its effect is to change us, to inspire us, to dispose and enable us to feel, care, and desire to do the same.

Charity has had a profound influence on political life, but its influence is never direct. It does not translate directly into natural virtues like justice and can frequently challenges ideas about justice.[28] Its effect is not first and foremost to issue concrete obligations. Rather, it works by transforming us as persons in our habits and dispositions. It enhances our capacity to deliberate and decide, and it does so by changing our habits of feeling and willing. Still, its results can be discerned as a shift of direction in our decisions, and this remains true in political life. In previous chapters, we explored how the theological virtue of charity influenced Shriver by providing his life with a sense of purpose, direction, vocation. For Shriver, all his work was a form of prayer.[29] We suggest this vocation lent a distinctive shape and direction to his early public life, and in particular, to what is arguably his most compelling achievement, the Peace Corps.

Coming to Terms with Diversity

Shriver's Catholicism was a muscular faith, and its foremost muscle was intellectual. The natural-supernatural distinction grounded the distinction between religion and politics, and it established a realm of the natural where we could have confidence in reason's ability to understand the world. The natural law tradition assigned a profound dignity to the work of human reason in politics, and it opened avenues whereby religion could influence politics without harming the integrity of reason. The theological virtue of charity meant that sin and evil never pronounced the final word on human reason; we can dedicate ourselves to intellectual and practical work in politics with the expectation of transformative experiences that continually liberate and renew our hearts and minds.

In past centuries, the natural law tradition provided the framework for articulating and integrating these three sets of insights in Catholic moral theology. More recently, however, natural law did not retain its vitality. More important, it was not able to retain support among broad ranges of Catholic theologians whose work focused on the concrete diversity that was found in the careful study of historical ages and cultural contexts. The issue that galvanized divisions among Roman Catholics and cast a shadow over natural law ethics in North America was contraception. The 1968 papal encyclical *Humanae vitae*, issued by Paul VI, appealed to a natural law ethical framework to reaffirm the traditional Catholic condemnation of artificial contraception. What was troublesome, however, was that it did so while affirming a new theology of marriage, centered on conjugal love, that reflected a new cultural and historical context for ethical reflection.[30] Critics argued that the methodology, employed properly within the new historical, cultural, and theological framework, should open doors for novel moral alternatives.[31] They accused natural law proponents of "physicalism," an over-emphasis on the physical structure of ethical acts.[32] But the encyclical's defenders held firm,[33] and the result was a widespread loss of confidence in the natural law framework among Catholic theologians in North America. By 1977, Charles Curran, one of America's most popular and influential Catholic moral theologians, had taken distance from the natural law approach, opting instead for his own relationality-responsibility model.[34]

Critics argued that the natural law had become somewhat mechanical and sterile.[35] It was not renewed by important developments that had occurred in the historical sciences.[36] More problematic was their claim that it enshrined culturally limited meanings into principles it proclaimed as universal. Our consciousness of historicity is a consciousness of diversity. It stands opposed to an earlier form of consciousness, called classicism, whose horizon does not envision significant historical change or cultural diversity. Classicism takes the flourishing of a particular culture as the norm for human development. What we discovered in the West between the eighteenth and nineteenth centuries was the diversity of cultures and the diversity of paths that human development had taken. What crowned this discovery was the diversity we found within the West's own historical past. The result was an invitation to think in new ways when exploring and formulating ethical principles to guide social and political life. Catholic theologians working within the natural law framework struggled to take up this invitation, but fell short of expectations.[37]

The result was that natural law's influence waned among North American Catholics. And with it, so too did the framework for distinguishing the natural and supernatural and relating the two in terms of the theological virtue of charity. The first of these to be abandoned was the strong distinction between the natural and the supernatural. In his 1987 historical study of Catholic moral theology, John Mahoney traced the influence, extending until Pius XII in 1950, of an extreme interpretation that tended to emphasize reason's capacity, when functioning properly, to do all the work required by ethics. Grace, in this view, supplied only a remedial corrective for reason's tendency to succumb to sin. The result was a view of natural law (particularly when interpreted by church authorities) as virtually equivalent to Divine law. This left theologians wondering what ideas about the supernatural added any positive substance to ethics. Indeed, it seemed to preclude the possibility of any distinguishing content that would flow to ethics from a life of Christian faith.[38] Catholic theologians working in this stream found it difficult to articulate what, if anything, might constitute a properly or distinctively Christian ethic.[39] Mahoney observed that many Catholics found this troubling, and he turned to Karl Rahner's idea of the "supernatural existential" for an alternate interpretation that seemed to diminish the nature-supernature distinction by enhancing the supernatural dimension of the natural.[40]

Another historical factor, coming from exactly the opposite direction, was the legacy of an older heritage that exaggerated the natural-supernatural distinction and devalued the import of natural knowledge of the world. Mahoney argued that Jansenism, with its excessive preoccupation with sin, had left a profound mark upon Catholic tradition, and reaction against it made its own contribution to advance the turn away from the language of nature and supernature. A truly "Christian" ethic, in this light, was a higher spiritual aspiration inspired by the gospel, that invited Christians to devalue the natural world of humanity and reason, to leave it behind, and to be preoccupied only with the afterlife.[41] Nature, in this analysis, never amounted to much more than fallen nature, and the natural law provided only a limited ethic, forever subject to the constraints of a sinfulness that defined the lot of humanity. The alternative, provided by an exclusivist Catholic faith, was to look elsewhere, either to a life beyond death or to religious orders. As lay Catholics grew weary of being hammered by this devaluation of their lot in life this side of eternity, they began to look elsewhere. Their focus turned to theological currents that, in Charles Taylor's language, added a higher dignity to "ordinary life."[42] These included currents that found spiritual significance in the lives of friends and colleagues of other faith traditions. Again, Mahoney turned to Rahner for an interpretive framework that spiritualized our understanding of the natural world and opened doors for an "anonymous Christianity" that might be present in the lives of women and men of other faiths.[43] These arguments, however, seemed to purchase their conclusions by diminishing the significance of the natural-supernatural distinction.

As the languages of nature-supernature and the natural law diminished in significance, the theological virtue of charity no longer seemed necessary for explaining the religious component of Christian life. In its place, Catholic theologians turned to a range of biblical and historical themes, accessible to natural reason, that provided interpretive schemes for imaging moral life. Mahoney assembles a range of such images that provide ordinary life examples that offer direction for moral life in terms other than law: invitation and attraction; call and response; narrative;

pilgrimage; co-creation; beauty and wonder; aesthetic discernment; and mystical life.[44] These alternatives reflect an approach that regards religion as a resource available to reason to adherents of a tradition who accepted its symbols and texts. This became a widespread understanding of the role of religion in ethics. Yet it was a far cry from Shriver's spectacular vision of a God entering life and transforming habits and inclinations with an infusion of supernatural charity. In a world where science provided the context for understanding everything and where the natural-supernatural and the natural law had faded from view, it seemed increasingly difficult to imagine how charity so understood could be articulated in any language that could be considered remotely public.

The analysis of Charles Curran provides a good indication of an explanation. The reasons for the shift away from the language of charity as supernatural virtue can be found in the very context in which the church was challenged to speak. The word he used to define this context was "inclusive." The church is called to be "inclusive in membership," "inclusive in its concerns," "inclusive of other realities," and "inclusive of different levels."[45] In other words, to be properly catholic, theological ethics in the Catholic tradition must meet the challenge of diversity. To do this it needs to find alternative approaches that envision Christian faith as operating through channels that can be articulated in diverse languages to broad publics. Christian language must meet the challenge of speaking across diversity.

One can imagine that conservative critics would object vigorously to this analysis, and this they did. They took issue with the methods of scholars allied with Curran, and they held fast to the language of natural law. Leading the way were John Finnis, Germain Grisez, Joseph Boyle, and William May. Their focus was on moral objectivity. *Humanae vitae*, they argued, remained valid precisely because it held to a moral framework that refused to sacrifice objectivity in the name of anything resembling diversity. Ethics, Finnis argued, "is identification of and participation in the true human good."[46] The trajectory expressed by the works of Curran and his colleagues, focused as it was on a consequentialist or proportionalist calculus of experience-based (and thus historically or culturally contingent) notions of benefit or harm, led away from this goal, and could only result in emptying the world of its objective moral character and robbing moral reason of its proper object.[47]

What was interesting was the way the critics framed their analysis. Finnis argued that natural law could no longer rest on a foundation provided by a metaphysical account of nature, human or otherwise. Nature, understood as scientific or anthropological fact, could no longer be imagined to provide a proper basis for moral "oughts." G.E. Moore had

shown how a moral "ought" could never be derived from a factual "is."
No appeal to factual data on human desire or inclination, cultural consensus, or mere historical change could ever, on its own, provide grounds
for a compelling moral argument. This meant that a New Natural Law
was now required, a natural law whose grounds would be different from
that attributed to older Thomist or Aristotelian accounts.

Finnis' approach was to engage in an interesting self-reflective examination of human reasoning.[48] His argument was that a turn to interiority
of his own revealed an understanding of moral reasoning as an enterprise that moved beyond data on the facts of experience to discover
and affirm an intelligibility whose character is irreducibly and properly
moral. His discovery led him to conclude that the normal exercise of
this reasoning yielded ordered wholes whose ethical character could
never be broken out into experiential components that were ethically
normative on their own. Rather, it was the entire intelligible whole that
was grasped in practical reason that presented the moral valence and
thus the proper object of ethical reasoning and willing. His method led
from a self-reflective analysis of practical reason to an examination of
the intelligible objects of this reason. The result was the elaboration of a
set of basic, underived, and incommensurable goods whose intelligible
moral "natures" were grasped and affirmed in the practical reasoning
of ethics.[49]

The effect of these arguments was to place the natural law squarely
on the side of conservative opponents to diversity. But they had another
effect, and this was to introduce divisions among conservative theologians who opposed Curran's claim to diversity as the primary challenge
to Catholic theology. Janet Smith, an ardent defender of *Humanae vitae*,
took issue with the vision of natural law proposed by Finnis, Grisez,
Boyle, and May. She argued that, by stepping away from a metaphysical
understanding of nature and grounding the method in a phenomenology of practical reason, they had robbed it of its proper foundations.[50]
She argued for a return to older Catholic approaches to natural law. But
in so doing she provided further evidence to support the argument for
diversity. Diversity exists not only among alternatives to natural law, it
exists within natural law itself.[51] For his part, Sargent Shriver remained
committed to the challenge of diversity. Yet he refused to give up on
natural law.

In the decades following *Humanae vitae*, the task of meeting the challenge of diversity was taken up by philosophers of the public square:
figures like John Rawls, Charles Taylor, Alasdair MacIntyre, Hans Georg
Gadamer, Paul Ricoeur, and Jürgen Habermas. Their work gave rise
to ideas that commanded attention in circles of Catholic theologians

working at the frontiers of religion and politics.[52] Early on, David Hollen-bach recognized that Catholic social thought, based as it was in natural law, had produced an array of wonderful ideas that remained relevant for political life. But it needed to reinterpret its roots in conversation with these philosophical ideas as they were being articulated and debated in the public square.[53] His critical engagement with the work of John Court-ney Murray focused on the limitations of the older natural law frame-work for this work, and he drew on David Tracy to propose an alternative model for a fundamental political theology that could navigate between the particularity of Christian tradition and the universals claimed in a pluralist American public philosophy. In his judgement, an appeal to natural law that jumped too quickly to endorse a particular image of universal reason threatened to leave unchallenged an extant public phi-losophy, based on a deformed idea of reason, that failed to discern the presence of the spiritual within public life. For Hollenbach, Murray had done a fine job of distinguishing the institutions of religion and politics and justifying religious liberty, but he had not gone far enough in work-ing out how the two need to relate in order for the spirit to continually renew the vitality of public life.

Hollenbach's call for a fundamental political theology was insightful. During the 1980s and 90s, he contributed significantly to developing this political theology in America, both in his own writings and his work with US Catholic bishops on documents that challenged American public policies on nuclear disarmament and economic justice.[54] What this work revealed, however, was the magnitude of the task. Public debate, par-ticularly in an increasingly polarized political environment, demanded frameworks that could meet the demands of both liberals who sought this public engagement and conservatives who criticized it for betraying the foundations of objectivity of their traditions.[55] Political philosophers recognized that for democracy to function at all, some basis for agree-ment was needed in order for politics to navigate the dramatic differ-ences that polarized democratic life.

Two of the dominant philosophical voices in these conversations, John Rawls and Jürgen Habermas, proposed solutions that carved out lines of distinction between a properly public realm that required common con-sent and a non-public realm where members of belief traditions could articulate their convictions to each other in languages and symbols of their choosing. A political theology as envisioned by Hollenbach could contribute to discourse in the public realm, but to do so it needed to speak in a language that reached across diversity. Their task was to work out the philosophical fundamentals for this language. If the natural law could not do this work, something else had to take its place.

For Rawls, the philosophical fundamentals were provided by a device that he called "the original position under the veil of ignorance."[56] Invoking this device yielded principles of justice that stressed liberty, equality, and the protection of vulnerable minorities. For Habermas, they were provided by a discourse ethic that was based on a social scientific study of universal principals that could be discerned in the structure of discourse itself.[57] And, like Rawls, his focus was on the protection of vulnerable minorities from domination and exclusion in the discourses that decided their fate. In both cases, the results were frameworks for discourse in the public realm that distinguished between languages appropriate for discourse within traditions and norms appropriate for public discourse across traditions. An interesting feature of both theories was the recognition that some appeal to universals was required for public discourse to function in democracies. If the natural law was not adequate, then something had to replace it. Equally interesting was their agreement that secular belief traditions function like religions in providing "comprehensive doctrines" that make ultimate or comprehensive claims that invariably stamp their imprint on politics. Like Hollenbach, their works, particularly late in life, recognized the historical influence of religion on politics and sought to work out inclusive frameworks for assessing these influences.

Needless to say, the proposals of Rawls and Habermas drew their own criticisms. Central among these was the charge that the universals they proposed were excessively "procedural." They pertained to the procedures for democratic discourse but could not provide direction on the substance of any of the issues. For deliberation to be democratic, it must be governed by norms that have sufficient universality to command the free agreement of all. But both philosophers drew the line between the norms governing the procedures of public discourse and those governing the content of the issues and traditions debated by parties. In their view, the first can be universalized while the second must be left open to difference and diversity.

The problem, of course, is when politics actually functions, parties in the deliberation focus resolutely on the issues. This is precisely where guidance is required. Charles Taylor argued that a theory of democratic deliberation cannot do an end-run around the content of issues or the substance of belief traditions. Rather, working through the issues requires a dialectical retrieval of elements from our traditions and an authentic interpersonal engagement in which "we have been transformed by the study of the other."[58] This transformation involves the emergence into consciousness of new elements that at first are strange and unfamiliar. It gives rise to broader horizons, new frameworks for understanding, and new standards for evaluation and judgement.[59] Taylor's argument recalls David Hollenbach's proposal for a fundamental political theology.[60] And in his 2002 effort at a dialectical retrieval of the "common good" tradition in Christian ethics, Hollenbach cites Taylor when he proposes this transformative engagement with others across traditions as *learning*.[61]

This focus on learning brings us back to Shriver and the natural law. If the natural law was about anything, it was about the universal human structure of learning and how this is transformed by charity. Shriver was aware of the contemporary challenges to natural law presented by diversity. Yet, he also knew that efforts to reach across traditions required a common learning framework for navigating diversity, even as insights flowing from this learning sought expression in the languages of diverse interlocutors. With Taylor, he knew we could not do an end-run around the content of issues or the substance of traditions. He also knew that his own tradition's formidable contributions to the work of distinguishing and relating religion and politics needed to be transposed to meet the demands of our time. He shared the commitment to objectivity that was the concern of his conservative colleagues who refused to give up on natural law. And he had an intimate knowledge of the transformative spiritual experiences that preserved objectivity even as they ushered in horizons that validated the objectivity of new moral insights. Most important, he was personally aware of the transformative experiences that arrived as gift from the encounter with transcendent love. Such was his life.

We argue that these conversations and the task of explaining Shriver signal the need for deeper reflections on the transformative process of learning that is central to the proposal of Taylor and Hollenbach. In his 1981 study of debates between political philosophers Gadamer and Habermas (debates whose issues arise again in Hollenbach's conversation with Alasdair MacIntyre[62]) Frederick Lawrence finds that the turn to interiority and self-knowledge are central to both Habermas's critique of ideology and Gadamer's integral hermeneutics.[63] In the case of Habermas, the norms governing emancipatory discourse are to be discovered in a self-reflective analysis of our engagement in discourse.[64] In the case of Gadamer, the enterprise of critique, that provides for the self-correction of traditions in the hermeneutic circle of belief and immanently generated knowledge, only arises in a self-knowledge that reflects communally on the social process of learning.[65] Indeed, R.J. Snell finds that John Finnis' own efforts to renew the natural law tradition were launched by a self-reflective analysis of practical reason.[66] Both Lawrence and Snell argue that the direction signaled by these authors is carried forward by Lonergan's turn to interiority.[67]

Transposing the Tradition: Diversity and Interiority

Of all the authors who have sought to develop a self-reflective method-ology of interiority for transposing core elements of Catholic tradition to meet both conservative demands for objectivity and liberal demands for diversity, the most thoroughgoing has been Bernard Lonergan.[68] His most comprehensive contribution to this method was his 1957 study of human understanding, *Insight: A Study of Human Understanding*. His question was about the very operations of consciousness that are at work in the transposition to diversity and historicity. His argument was that the methods of the natural and human sciences can be extended and transposed to the study of interiority. He offered this method as a route towards retrieving and transposing core insights from the natural law tradition into a framework adequate for historical consciousness; a framework that retrieved the nature-supernature distinction and related the two via transformative spiritual encounters with transcendence. Most important, he offered his work as a method that can ground objectivity, yet can be undertaken by women and men of diverse traditions.

Bernard Lonergan understood the importance of historical and cul-tural diversity. But he also understood the problems it posed. We experi-ence a dramatic shift in horizons with historical consciousness. On its own, however, this shift does not furnish resources for navigating respon-sibly the diverse cultures and ages. In fact, it creates a problem that can challenge the very foundations of responsible life. Finnis understood this. Without a compass for navigating diversity, this new consciousness lands us in relativism and the loss of objectivity.[69] Historical conscious-ness leaves us open to diversity but does not help us differentiate between wholesome and destructive forms of diversity. In *The Ethics of Authenticity*, Charles Taylor develops a penetrating analysis of the problems of relativ-ism arising within the Modern pursuit of authenticity.[70]

For Lonergan, the move to historical consciousness is not a one-step affair, it requires taking two steps. It requires moving into relativism, but through it and beyond it to interiority. This is because the shift to histo-ricity and diversity, if it is not to lose the critical controls necessary for navigating life responsibly, must understand the very transformation it has undergone. It must transpose the critical controls formerly rooted in classical ethics onto a new foundation that is grounded in this newly achieved understanding.

Understanding diversity requires the transposition to interiority that investigates this shift in structure. The key insight is that studying diver-sity requires something more than attending to its products, it requires attending to the interior operations that give rise to its products, the operations of human meaning. It requires attending to a normative pattern that we can all observe and discover in these operations. Doing this properly requires a method for examining, understanding, and appropriating our own operations of meaning.

The method was inspired by Lonergan's own study of Aquinas. But it was developed through his careful examination of the operations of understanding at work in the natural and human sciences. His discovery was that gaining knowledge is not a single act, it is a cluster of diverse operations that are grouped together on diverse levels, each higher level transforming and developing the products of operations on the lower levels. Knowledge is not simply a passive affair of receiving information, it is also the active pursuit of knowledge by attending to the data of experience. It involves the creative work of human minds asking questions and gaining insights that yield and transform human meaning. Knowing is not simply a matter of experience, it is also a matter of questions and insights that go beyond experience. But achieving knowledge does not stop there. It requires a third step in which we reflect on our insights and make judgements on whether our insights can be verified in an appeal to the data. Finally, we do not rest with knowledge of the world, we also turn our minds to the operations that discern, affirm, and decide on values that build on knowledge of the world to change the world.

It was the insight into the cumulative structure of these operations that was central to Lonergan's method of interiority. Our day-to-day life involves performing operations of meaning, yet reflecting critically on these operations can yield an extraordinary discovery, the discovery of a self-transcending dynamism that can be discerned in our every engagement with daily life. There is a pattern at work in these operations, and this pattern provides a norm or criterion for distinguishing between development and its opposite, decline.[71] This is not a mechanical idea of development, chugging along as mindless law. Rather it is a patterned exigence or inclination that is present and discernible in our lives but can be chosen or refused as grounds for our decisions and actions. This insight into self-transcendence provides a criterion for navigating the perils of difference and diversity without losing our way.

This insight reveals how the natural law can be transposed into a method and framework that takes seriously the achievements of historical consciousness without falling prey to relativism.[72] The method of interiority does not abandon the older Catholic insights into human nature and ethical responsibility. But neither does it retreat from historicity and diversity to take refuge in a classicist past. The core of the older tradition was its link between a normative orientation discernible in nature and operative in human persons who make judgements of value. Lonergan's turn to the method of interiority keeps this link, but transposes it into a framework that can be far more attentive to diversity because its grounds are the very operations at work at the core of diversity itself. The doorway into this framework is a method that can be performed by anyone, the method of investigating and appropriating the normative structure operative in her own consciousness.

A historically conscious transposition of the natural law places ethics, politics, and even spirituality on a new footing within a broader framework that is grounded in the methodical turn to interiority. Two of the central ingredients of this transposed framework are the structure of the human good and the scale of values. The first, the structure of the human good, arises when we implement the self-reflective turn to interiority to examine operations of meaning engaged in questioning and deliberating about values. We can discover that values are not solid objective bullets, nor are they merely individual desires or convictions. Rather they have an internal structure in which higher-order skills and social patterns of cooperation are developed and implemented to yield hosts of particular goods arising in personal and social life. These skills and patterns of the human good have their basis in experiences and desires of particular goods, but are not reducible to experiences and desires. Rather they entail ordered patterns of higher level aspirations and obligations that are apprehended in feelings, grasped in insights, and affirmed in judgements. Completing the transposition to interiority involves understanding and appropriating the dynamism of self-transcendence that carries us through the successively higher levels of the human good. Doing this reveals that there is indeed an objectivity to values, and the ground of this objectivity is the authenticity with which we live out the dynamism of self-transcendence in our experiencing, understanding, judging, and deciding.

Our value judgements affirm that these personal skills and social patterns either do or do not promote progress and reverse decline in human living. Value is a dynamic notion that expresses relations of self-transcendence unfolding among pasts, presents, and futures that come into being as instances of the structure of the human good emerge and operate in diverse historical ages and cultural contexts. Our value judgements reflect an internal normativity operative both within the human good structure of the value and within the self-transcending consciousness of the person valuing. Indeed, it is the correlation of these two that is affirmed in the value judgements.

But there is another criterion at work in value judgements, the scale of values, and this is the second central ingredient of the framework that arises with the transposition to interiority.[73] Values do not operate in isolation, rather they operate together in ordered patterns in which higher values fulfill conditions for the emergence and survival of values on lower levels of the scale. We seek vital values like food and shelter. But these vital values are delivered within ordered patterns of relations of an economy that operate on a higher, social level of the scale. Further analysis reveals that complex economies cannot operate anywhere, rather, they require skills, convictions, dispositions, and habits that are only formed in cultures whose patterns of cultivation are supplied by successively higher levels of the scale. These higher levels of value related to cultural aspirations and the intrinsic worth of persons are themselves either nourished or eroded by "habits of the heart" pertaining to convictions about ultimacy. When we make value judgements, we judge both the internal structure of a value and its location in relation to other levels of the scale. What we can discern in the transposition to interiority is the dynamism of self-transcendence that is operative in our consciousness, in the structure of the human good, and in the relations among the levels of the scale of values.

Most interesting for our purposes are the religious, spiritual, or ultimate values on the highest level on the scale. The method of interiority opens us to a broader framework for relating politics and spirituality. Lonergan's analysis of religion in *Insight* retains the basic structure of the older Catholic tradition. Evil corrupts our reasoning abilities. Charity enters our lives in the form of transformative experiences of love that break the hold of this corruption restoring reason's abilities. Consequently, social and political life requires devotion, not simply to moral and rational development, but to the spiritual development that is continually undoing the corrupting effects of sin and renewing our powers of intelligence and responsibility. With the transposition to interiority, however, the tradition is now opened to recognize the transformative experiences of love on the highest level of the scale of values that occur in the lives of women and men of diverse religious and secular belief traditions. It was this openness that characterized Shriver's life and work, and we suggest that Lonergan's framework provides tools for understanding and replicating the best of his life's work.

As Lonergan probed further in his reflexive investigation of the cognitional operations of the natural and human sciences, he discovered a spiritual dimension to the sciences that is often overlooked in arguments about religion and politics, the unrestricted character of the questioning itself. The questioning of the sciences does not admit restrictions. This would be unscientific. The questioning of science intends the total intelligibility not only of this universe but of any other universe that might ever be discovered by any possible science, natural, human, or otherwise.

In fact, our questioning always heads beyond this limit, and this means that it forever takes us beyond knowledge to mystery; both the actual mystery beyond any extant science and the ultimate mystery beyond all possible science.[74] When we pay careful attention and examine the interior texture of this questioning, we discover that it reveals a horizon that connects us to the mystery of transcendence. Authentic questioning opens us to this horizon, and in a manner so subtle as to escape notice, it also links us existentially to this horizon beyond. We seem forever locked in a state of engagement with ultimate mystery in a way that requires us to admit that ultimate mystery is transcendent mystery. Most important, this engagement is operative in the very act of unrestricted questioning that is fundamental to science.

Lonergan's approach was to reflect empirically and critically on this unrestricted questioning. What is it about? What does it tell us about ourselves and the universe? His effort was to take seriously the unrestricted character of the questioning of women and men of diverse religious and secular belief traditions. But his effort was to deal with these questions by focusing resolutely on what we actually *do* when we reach towards ultimates and are connected to transcendent mystery in unrestricted questioning.

His observation was that questioning about ultimates evokes experiences of awe and wonder, and the turn to interiority can give rise to empirically rigorous methods of examining these experiences.[75] Women and men from diverse religious and secular belief traditions speak about such experiences and it is not unusual for self-proclaimed atheists or agnostics to talk about awe and wonder. The fact is that women and men from diverse traditions can reflect on these experiences together. This reflection can become empirically disciplined through the appropriation of self-reflexive methods that focus on the experience of questioning at the heart of awe and wonder.

But Lonergan also observed that women and men experience transformations in their patterns of engagement with ultimate mystery: from despair to hope; from hatred to love; from anger to joy; from suspicion to trust. These transformative experiences occur and have been communicated in literature and celebrated through the ages in ritual, music, painting, sculpture, and dance. Moreover, people from diverse traditions can relate to each other's experiences and appreciate their transformative power in enriching human life. The traditions of expression are diverse, but the transformative experiences themselves can be studied together in a human science whose focus and methods can be shared by all.

The discovery in this reflexive study of interiority is that the study of transcendence does not have to be pre-scientific, beyond rational scrutiny. Neither does it have to remain locked within the confines of individual traditions. Self-reflective methods can be applied rigorously to the operations of interiority, and their practice can reveal horizons of transcendent mystery, operating on the highest level of the scale of values, that connect with the authentic questioning of the sciences. They can reveal an engagement with mystery that evokes transformative experiences that enrich human living. Prophets, sages, and philosophers of past ages were not wrong in their focus on religion; we do live in a world whose ultimate proportions are indeed loving mystery. And contemporary encounters with transcendence can indeed be found in both religious and secular belief traditions. We can discover something important about ourselves by attending to the structure of our meaningful engagement with mystery.

Politics is called to recognize it has always received guidance from religion and continues to do so even as ultimate convictions come clothed in secular garb. There remains a legitimate human science that transposes empirical methods for the study of interiority, and this human science reveals the significance of spirituality and transcendent mystery for personal and social life. In fact, the mobilization of this method of interiority can be helpful, even necessary, for politics. It can provide tools for differentiating between religion that harms and religion that heals. It can ferret out instances when ultimate claims, clothed in the garb of secular language, begin operating destructively in politics. It can help when religions add their authority to natural values that have not been transposed successfully to new historical or cultural contexts. It can help assess when influences from both religious and secular traditions prove positive for political life. And it can help women and men from diverse traditions mobilize the convictions, attitudes, and values required to live out the demanding obligations of democratic life. Sargent Shriver was guided by these convictions. We argue that the turn to interiority explains why these convictions make sense.

Interiority and Conflict: The Insight Approach

Shriver's speeches and programs reveal this attention to the spiritual experiences that renew and liberate politics. He drew on his tradition to understand and appreciate the role of charity as the transformative experience of compassion in politics. Yet his appeal to tradition was not a slavish or mechanical replication of exterior forms. He turned to interiority to transpose the traditional Catholic categories of natural law and charity into a broader method for "spiritualizing" politics. Most important, he understood how transformative spiritual experiences play a vital role in building peace at home and abroad.

Lonergan's methodical turn to interiority, we suggest, provides a breadth and depth that captures the heart of Shriver's words and actions. In the years since Shriver's early public life and the launch of the Peace Corps, scholars have drawn on this method to advance the study of peace and conflict, and this body of theory and practice offers resources for explaining Shriver's achievements and advancing his legacy. Notable in this scholarship is the body of theory and practice that has come to be known as the Insight approach to conflict.

The publication that marked the launch of the Insight approach was *Transforming Conflict through Insight,* by Cheryl Picard and Kenneth Melchin. The focus of this text is conflict mediation, mostly in interpersonal and small group contexts. Picard's second book, *Practicing Insight Mediation,* offers resources for teaching and learning mediation skills. The Insight approach, however, has not remained limited to interpersonal mediation, and by the time *Transforming Conflict* appeared in print, Picard and Melchin had been joined by a group of scholars dedicated to applying Lonergan's work to the study of conflict in diverse contexts. James Price, Andrea Bartoli, Derek Melchin, Marnie Jull, and Megan Price have all made distinctive contributions to the Insight approach.[76] As this book goes to press, the team of scholars and practitioners working in this area of application is growing.[77]

Needless to say, the Insight approach to conflict is not the only area of application of Lonergan's work. Scattered through the 43 years of issues of *Lonergan Workshop* and *Method: Journal of Lonergan Studies,* readers can find countless examples of scholars drawing on Lonergan to advance their respective disciplines. As these studies became more practice- and profession-focused, scholarly journals like *The Lonergan Review* and *Theoforum* began dedicating special issues to "Applications of Lonergan."[78] The fields influenced by these applications are wide-ranging: Psychology, Business, Education, Economics, Political Studies, Interfaith Dialogue, Healthcare Ethics, History, Public Service Ethics, Feminist Studies, Religion and Science, Art, Urban Studies, Mathematics, Research Ethics, Philosophy, and Theology. The list goes on.

Given our focus on religion, politics, and the Peace Corps, we draw on resources from the Insight approach to conflict to advance our understanding of Shriver. The Insight approach was not developed by Lonergan himself. It can be said, however, that fundamental insights from Lonergan remain central to this body of work, and the self-reflexive method of self-appropriation remains a guiding thread running through applications to the field of conflict. In addition, sections from

Lonergan's published texts have offered clear lines of guidance in developing aspects of the Insight approach, notably those focusing on the role of spirituality in creating conditions for the transformative experiences that are central to building peace.[79] We follow these lines in developing our explanation of Shriver's achievements.

Studies of conflict frequently signal the importance of transformative moments when parties in conflict shift directions, opening avenues for constructive dialogue. In past decades, practitioners of mediation and conflict resolution have sought to replicate these moments by devising strategies for intervention in conflict. Often, however, these efforts falter, and conflict analysts frequently point to flaws in theory as reasons for the limited success of practice. More recently, Price and Bartoli have highlighted how a notable group of approaches explore the role of human meaning and intentionality in the construction of conflict and in creating conditions for the transformative moments that open spaces for dialogue and resolution. They locate the Insight approach within this group.[80]

In *Transforming Conflict,* Picard and Melchin draw on the method of Lonergan to understand the interpersonal dynamics of meaning at work in conflict and mediation. In contrast to other approaches, their work examines the role of *learning* in conflict. There is significant learning going on in the interpersonal schemes of gestures and responses of conflict and its resolution. Conflicts involve the back-and-forth exchange of meaning, and conflict emerges in this scheme when parties begin learning that the meanings of others threaten their own cares and concerns. The experience of threat-to-care has the effect of radically narrowing and focusing the learning of parties.

A central ingredient in constructive dialogue is the curiosity that engages parties in the other's world of meaning. We are curious about others, and our questioning leads us along paths that provide entry into their worlds of experience. When we are successful in following these paths, we catch glimpses of another's world, not simply as we would have thought it to be, but more and more as they experience and interpret it. Our insights transform us. We learn new things about them, and often this reveals novel insights into our own lives. All of this changes, however, when we feel threatened. When threats emerge, the openness previously operative in questioning shifts and our learning begins channeling along narrow pathways marked by defence and attack. To be sure, our curiosity is not gone and our learning does not stop. But there is a change in the path of learning in conflict; our curiosity is pressed into service responding aggressively and defensively to threats-to-cares.

Derek Melchin examines this learning at work in the construction of conflict.[81] The experience of threat-to-care seems to have a narrative structure that is apprehended rapidly in the form of feeling. Probing feelings reveals that they intend cares or values. Often the values may not have achieved explicit formulation, yet they remain operative as meaning-saturated feelings that dynamize action. When cares are threatened, value narratives are evoked that draw on past experience to anticipate future dire consequences that would follow on present action if threats were realized. The result is the channeling of curiosity to mobilize strategies of attack-defence.

Notable in all this is the party's certainty about the intentions of others. A leading scholar and practitioner who explores this role of certainty in conflicts is Andrea Bartoli.[82] The narrowing of learning gives rise to a certainty that expectations embedded in threat-narratives provide the truth governing future events. This certainty emerges quickly in conflict, and it stamps both parties' experiences with its own clarity and focus, a clarity and focus that radically constricts curiosity. The effect is that, without significant self-awareness and practiced methods, most of us have little reflexive ability or felt need to open ourselves to curiosity once this certainty is implanted in conflict.

Picard and Melchin ask whether explaining successful interventions in conflict might explore how mediators shift parties out of certainty and onto paths that re-open curiosity.[83] They discover that successful mediators can and do facilitate transformative experiences that give rise to these shifts. They explain the shifts as a de-linking of threats-to-cares, a dismantling of certainty, and an opening of the broader curiosity about the meanings and intentions of others.

Mediator strategies include lines of questioning that invite parties to deepen insights into the threats-to-cares that lie at the heart of the positions they hold.[84] Their effort is to facilitate parties' probing of feelings that dynamize their interpretations of their own actions and those of others in conflict. This deepening often involves some interesting learning, not only of others, but of ourselves. The upshot of successful deepening is an experience of a subtle but profound shift in parties' engagement in the conflict. Insight mediators explain this shift as a de-linking of threats-to-cares. As plausible cares are expressed and novel avenues for futures opened, parties begin asking questions. Most important, their curiosity starts probing beyond the narrow confines previously governed by threats-to-cares. Often the transformative experiences are emotionally compelling. Parties discover paths for understanding past, present, and future events in ways that de-link from prior constraints that hampered learning in the dialogue scheme. Free to explore on their own, parties often take charge of the directions opened up in the dialogue, and mediators often find their work all but finished once the transformative experiences emerge in the process.

We suggest that two observations are in order here to link this discussion of the Insight approach to our exploration of resources on religion and politics from Shriver's Catholic tradition. The first is the understanding of conflict that is operative here. The Insight approach offers a transposed form of what, in older Catholic tradition, would have been called a "natural law" analysis of conflict. The insights into the "nature" of conflict provide normative grounds for mediator interventions that curb harm and promote healing in conflict. In addition, the older natural law approach has been transposed via the turn to interiority. Conflict is understood as a dynamic scheme of operations of human meaning and learning that are explored in the self-reflexive method of interiority proposed by Lonergan.

The second observation is that the significant moment in healing conflict is a transformative experience that shifts parties from certainty to curiosity and from fear and aggression to openness and engagement with others. We suggest that this experience shares characteristics with the spiritual transformation we have been exploring as central and vital in Shriver's vision of politics. Shriver understood such transformative experiences in the language of charity from his Catholic tradition, and in later years he transposed this to the broader, more inclusive language of compassion. We suggest there is indeed a spiritual component to the transformation operative in conflict. Recently, Insight analysts have begun asking about the role of spiritual values and traditions in creating conditions for enabling or facilitating these experiences that de-link threats-to-cares and opening parties in conflict to constructive dialogue.[85] In the next chapter, we explore how these resources help explain the Peace Corps.

The Insight approach to conflict, we argue, offers a contemporary example of the transposition, via interiority, of traditional Catholic ideas of natural law and charity that guided Shriver in his early years of public life in Chicago and the Peace Corps. Advancing the Shriver legacy requires explaining his achievements, not only as he understood them, but with the best resources of our time. We have drawn on Lonergan and Lonergan scholars to show how the turn to interiority can be implemented in a methodically disciplined investigation of the acts of meaning at work in our daily engagements with others in social and political life. Exploring conflict and peace through this method brings us to the deepest core of our engagements in political life, and it brings us face-to-face with transformative experiences encountered by all of us, regardless

of our diverse belief traditions. We suggest this direction is worth following in our efforts both to explain Shriver and to advance his legacy.

Religion and Politics Revisited

In light of directions provided by Shriver's speeches and programs, and
in light of our turn to Lonergan to explain these directions, we suggest the question of religion and politics needs to be recast. We have
encountered enormous difficulties wrestling with religion and politics,
and engaging badly with these difficulties has harmed us. We suggest this
is because it is actually a different kind of problem than we had thought.
It is not first and foremost a problem about institutions, although institutions invariably get involved. It is a problem involving traditional religions, but not in the way we had thought. Secular belief traditions now
make comprehensive claims that influence politics in similar ways, and
we need clarity on how both are called to do this responsibly. It is not a
problem of choosing between diversity and objectivity because objectivity must be gained amidst diversity. Most important, it is not a problem
of either separating or combining religion and politics, we must do both,
and our task is learning how to do them well.

Our portrait of Shriver points to resources from his Catholic tradition
that influenced how he navigated the frontiers of religion and politics.
The nature-supernature distinction provided grounds for distinguishing
religion and politics as different spheres of experience and therefore
different spheres of institutional competence. The natural law provided
a philosophical framework for distinguishing and relating these spheres
and a method for gaining insights into values relevant for political life.
It provided methods and criteria for affirming legitimate influences that
can and should flow from religion to politics and for flagging problematic values and practices that have their origins in religious beliefs. The
theological virtue of charity, the most important for Shriver, provided
insights into transformative encounters with transcendence that enrich
the lives of citizens and leaders in ways that prove most valuable for
politics.

In his early years, the framework that explained all this for Shriver
was the philosophical tradition of natural law, most likely as it was interpreted by one of his favourite authors, Jacques Maritain. As he faced the
challenge of diversity during the Peace Corps years, however, he came to
understand something that John Rawls discovered two decades later, that
the philosophy of his tradition would not provide an adequate language
for speaking across diversity to engage women and men from a variety
of religious and secular belief traditions. Like Rawls, Shriver responded

by transposing this framework. What he developed was not theoretical, it was practical, it was incarnated in his policies and programs, notably those of the Peace Corps. Our challenge today is explaining what he did.

Shriver's experience in politics challenged him to speak and work with wide ranges of citizens at home and abroad. Yet he did this by following a path that was different from those taken by many of his Catholic colleagues, he never gave up on the three central ingredients from Catholic tradition that shaped his thought and action. Instead, he transposed them. Rather than speaking about the natural law, he spoke about interiority and conscience. Rather than speaking about the supernatural, he spoke about the spiritual. Rather than speaking about the theological virtue of charity, he spoke about compassion.

Still, the basic architecture that defined his policies and programs remained. His thinking about religion and politics remained based, not only in the institutional distinction that was central to Jefferson's analysis, but also in the turn to interiority and conscience that marked the later legacy of Jefferson's novel achievement. Religion and politics are separate institutional spheres because they are different spheres of human interiority. Religion is the sphere of ultimate or comprehensive values, higher than politics; the sphere whose openness signals our orientation to transcendent mystery. Politics, on the other hand, remains the sphere of this-worldly knowledge and values, ever fallible, yet ever worthy of our lives. For Shriver, the most important relations flowing from religion to politics were the transformative experiences that arise in encounters with transcendent mystery; experiences that shift us from hatred to love, from despair to hope, from apathy to engagement. He knew that, more than anything, citizens and leaders in politics need these transcendent experiences, they need the habits of compassion that arise from them, and they need the belief traditions that nourish and celebrate them.

Explaining Shriver's achievements requires a philosophy, and like Rawls and Habermas, we argue that meeting the challenge of diversity without compromising objectivity requires a philosophy that is not based on principles or propositions, but on a method that can be implemented by women and men everywhere. Lonergan's method of interiority provides this. The method involves attending to our operations of experiencing, understanding, judging, and deciding as we perform them in everyday life. The focus of the method, however, is not on the meanings we understand, judge, and decide, but on the operations we invoke that bring forth these meanings.

The most interesting observation we make in the method is that the operations themselves assemble cumulatively, and in the pattern or path expressed by this assembly we can discern a trajectory, an orientation in ourselves we can notice and attend to. This trajectory is not a mechanical cause, rather it is an inclination or exigence we can choose either to accept or refuse. Following its path provides a normative basis for discernment, deliberation, and judgement in politics. It is the basis for the notion of integrity. We can choose to be persons of integrity, or not. This norm is not extrinsic, it is intrinsic. This is why the language of conscience, integrity, and authenticity remains compelling, even amidst the scandals that rock politics. Understanding the basis in interiority for this normativity provides important resources for politics, resources that can speak across diverse traditions without compromising objectivity. Objectivity, properly understood, is the authenticity operative in persons who choose integrity.

Implementing the method of interiority gives rise to insights into the operations of consciousness, the dynamism of self-transcendence operative in the cumulative assembly of these operations, the structure of the human good that is reflected in our judgements of value, and a scale of values that can be discerned, not simply in the ordered pattern unfolding among the values we affirm, but also in the feelings we invoke in our engagement in social-political life. The result of all this is a philosophy, we argue, that can do the work needed to explain what Shriver achieved in transposing the natural law.

Most important is what the method provides for ideas about spiritual experience that Shriver built into the policies and procedures of the Peace Corps. Spiritual experience is not simply another field of experience like computers, cars, sports, or business. It is not simply a domain of life we can decide to experience, or not. Rather, it is an ultimate or comprehensive sphere that arises in all fields of experience. It arises without our invitation, and in one way or another is present in all of us as the horizon of ultimacy that pervades all our experiencing and understanding. Beliefs about ultimacy insinuate themselves into all our assumptions about what we are doing in our life decisions, particularly in politics. They provide the highest, most comprehensive level of the scale of values operative in our feelings and decisions.

What the method reveals is that we actually do have transformative spiritual experiences that shape the beliefs and values we hold about ultimacy. This happens to all of us and it happens often enough. The challenge is gaining a language and framework for noticing these experiences, for understanding them, judging their worth, and integrating them deliberately into the other judgements and decisions we make as citizens in political life. The centrally important task in navigating the religion-politics frontier for Shriver was this. He knew these experiences were spiritual, regardless of how they might be understood diversely by citizens. And he knew they were fundamental, universal, and crucial for politics. Of course, he knew his older language of natural law could not engage citizens in thinking adequately about these experiences. He adopted another language, yet this newer language did not jettison the older framework, it transposed it. And we suggest Lonergan's method of interiority articulates what he achieved in his practical transposition.

What, then of current debates about religion and politics? When we examine historical issues that have exacerbated divisions between conservatives and liberals, we can observe that many involve influences that flow to politics from the spiritual, ultimate, or religious level of the scale of values. The word that expresses this relation of influence between the religious and political levels of the scale of values is "sublation." Spiritual or comprehensive values sublate political values. They take up political values into wider, more comprehensive horizons, they evaluate them within these horizons, and they provide an additional depth, breadth, and intensity of meaning that is imputed, either positively or negatively, to the meanings that the values would otherwise hold on the purely political level.

So, for example, Christian spiritual values about persons created in the image of God influenced ethical values about the dignity of persons, and this exerted a tremendous influence in the lives of women and men involved in the political work of bringing about the abolition of slavery in the nineteenth century. They did their work again in the battle against racism that engaged Shriver in the 1960s. And they continue to do so in ongoing efforts to redress the legacy of racism in our time. In each case, spiritual values sublate political values. What is important to observe, however, is that in these cases, while the spiritual values influenced the people engaged in politics, the issues themselves remained issues on the ethical and political levels of the scale. They had to be evaluated on their own terms as person values and justice values, not religious values. There is a relation of influence, but the influence does not obliterate the differentiation between criteria appropriate to different levels of the scale of values.

Religious leaders are invited to remain vigilant in attending not simply to the relations but also to the distinctions that are operative when spiritual values sublate political values. This is important when religious leaders lend their authority on behalf of social and ethical values associated with war, economics, contraception, and abortion. Democracies need women and men willing to engage vigorously in debates on these issues, and religious values play important roles in political processes associated with the issues. What remains important, however, is that the values themselves are not values on the properly religious level of the scale, they are on the lower levels that fall within the sphere of ethical and political deliberations. When religious representatives claim exemptions from rulings related to these values, the merits of the case must be decided on the basis of criteria and arguments appropriate to that level.

In similar but reciprocal ways, women and men from secular belief traditions are invited to remain vigilant in attending not simply to the distinctions but also to the relations that are operative when spiritual values sublate political values. This is particularly important when popular culture has not developed habits of careful attention to claims and assumptions about ultimate or comprehensive values – values on the highest level of the scale – within secular belief traditions. These values exercise their influence on arguments on lower levels of the scale and careful attention needs to be paid to these influences, particularly when they frame discussions in ways that conceal their influence.

This is especially important in institutions of public education. Teaching science in schools can easily lead to occasions when women and men from secular belief traditions reveal the influence of comprehensive values, but fail to help students understand and appreciate that the conversation has moved from the natural to the religious level of the scale of values. In subtle ways, teaching in all subject areas opens doors to discussions about religious, spiritual, or comprehensive values. Teachers need to be taught to explain to students how the classroom frequently becomes a forum for instruction on religious or comprehensive values. Clearly, this has implications for issues related to public funding and religious education. Understood in these terms, schools can never escape the business of religious instruction. The challenge is doing this responsibly, in ways that deal adequately with the challenge of diversity.

Concluding Remarks

In order to assure that politics remains vigilant in attending to both distinctions and relations that must be navigated responsibly at the frontiers of religion, it is essential that political charters and constitutions include explicit recognition of the higher spiritual or comprehensive level of values to which politics is accountable. In the past, this was done by invoking language associated with particular religious traditions. As the diversity of secular and religious belief traditions multiply, language associate exclusively with one tradition or group of traditions becomes difficult to justify. What can be justified, however, is a philosophical language, rooted in a method of interiority accessible to all, that recognizes the significance of the religious or comprehensive level of the scale of values and its import for politics. We suggest that Shriver's example and our explanation of his life's work point the way forward.

In the next chapter, we turn our attention to the analysis of one of Shriver's most successful achievements, the Peace Corps, as an illustration of the method at work. Our focus is the turn to interiority and how this reveals both an openness to diversity and a transposition of critical tools from Shriver's tradition for navigating diversity. In particular, we explore the role of interiority in the insight approach to conflict and how this offers both an explanation of Shriver's achievements and future direction for advancing the Shriver legacy.

Most important in our analysis is the way the method provides a framework for insights into the role of spirituality in mobilizing and transforming values that are essential for political life. We explore how Shriver's work with the Peace Corps draws attention to the transformative experiences that renew and liberate politics. We show how he drew on his tradition to understand and appreciate the role of charity or compassion in politics. But we also show how he turned to interiority to transpose this traditional Catholic category into a broader method for spiritualizing politics in the Peace Corps. Finally, we show how the Insight approach to conflict helps us understand Shriver's work and provides guidance for meeting diverse challenges arising at the intersection between politics and religion in present and future decades.

Chapter Five

Religion, Politics, and the Peace Corps

In November 1960, just one week before the election that would name John F. Kennedy the thirty-fifth President of the United States, Kennedy delivered a speech at the Cow Palace in San Francisco in which he proposed to create a "Peace Corps" of talented young women and men who would serve their country abroad.[1] At that point, it was not exactly clear what this service would involve. But in the early weeks of 1961, following Kennedy's inauguration, Sargent Shriver set to work organizing the Peace Corps, planning what this service would be, and launching the institutional framework in which it would be delivered. Shriver's decision was that Peace Corps volunteers would be trained at the highest standards in diverse areas of skill as well as in the languages and customs of their host countries, and they would live among the women and men who hosted them, in conditions shared by them, on terms specified by them, performing community, technical, educational, medical, family, and other services needed and requested by them, all free of charge. They would not be saleswomen or salesmen. They would not promote political, economic, or religious doctrines. They would work with the people, not employ them. They would listen to the people, not preach to them. They would perform services as the people requested. They would live with them, eat their food, obey their laws, and share their lives.[2]

In the intervening years, we have become familiar with the Peace Corps. But to understand the achievement it was requires stepping back and examining how its programs and policies were structured to promote its goals. We argue that this structure involves the implementation of values – both natural values and spiritual values – that have their origins in Shriver's religious vocation to public life. Most notable in this, we argue, are the natural and spiritual values that can be understood as transposed versions of the natural law and the theological virtue of charity from Shriver's Catholic faith tradition. We have traced the influence of these values in the speeches of Shriver's early public life in Chicago and his first three years as Director of the Peace Corps. And we have shown how Shriver made the transposition from a narrow faith tradition to a broader application to public life via a turn to interiority whose fullest elaboration can be found in the philosophy of Lonergan.

Our goal in this chapter is to show how Shriver's spiritual values shaped the structure of policies and programs of the Peace Corps. Our focus is on the role spirituality plays in Peace Corps programs so that actions of volunteers create conditions for the transformative experiences that are central to resolving conflicts and building peace. Throughout the analysis, we draw on Lonergan and the Insight approach to peace and conflict, based in his work, to explain Shriver's achievements. And we offer Shriver's Peace Corps as an example worth following in present and future efforts at bridging conservative and liberal divides in differentiating and relating religion and politics.

The Peace Corps

Three years after the launch of the Peace Corps, it had gained considerable international recognition, and Shriver explained to his audience in Bangkok, Thailand, his rationale for organizing the Peace Corps as he did. The mission of the Peace Corps, he explained, is to promote peace in a world bristling with violent conflict, and it achieves this mission by joining volunteers with people of other nations in programs of service to human welfare and dignity. The Peace Corps achieves its goals by putting into practice "the most powerful idea of all":

> . . . the idea that free and committed men and women can cross, even transcend, boundaries of culture and language, of alien tradition and great disparities of wealth, of old hostilities and new nationalisms, to meet with other men and women on the common ground of service to human welfare and human dignity.[3]

It would not be difficult to imagine, only sixteen years after World War II and more than a decade of living under the Cold War threat of nuclear annihilation, that Shriver's program would have attracted some criticism from political "realists." Indeed, the idea still seems rather naive today. To be sure, criticism did follow, particularly in the early weeks and months.[4] Shriver's response was that he and his staff were not indifferent to the hard "realities" reflected in this line of criticism. In its own way, he argued, the program does reflect a certain hardheaded realism. In an article published in Foreign Affairs in 1963, Shriver reflects back on the early years of the Peace Corps.

> Of course, youthful enthusiasm and noble purposes were not enough. They had to be combined with hard-headed pragmatism and realistic administration. In the early days of the Peace Corps we were looking for a formula for practical idealism.[5]

Eighteen months later, Shriver explains what he means by "realistic administration" by offering an example of how the Peace Corps does its work. At a speech delivered to a Poverty Conference in Tucson, Arizona, January 25, 1965, Shriver, now Director of both the Peace Corps and the War on Poverty, recounts a story about a difficult Peace Corps experience in Panama. Shriver's Arizona audience had just lived through the long, hot summer of race riots of 1964 in America, when "angry mobs of citizens roamed the streets, defying policemen, looting, and rioting and injuring innocent bystanders." Shriver's story is about a conflict in Panama in January 1964, involving Peace Corps volunteers, some local villagers, and "marauding bands" of angry, vengeful Panamanians.

> Last January, in Panama, anti-American riots broke out. At that time, Peace Corps Volunteers were stationed all over Panama. We feared for their safety. Latin American "experts" advised us to withdraw all Peace Corps Volunteers from the country – or at least order them to the "safety" of the Canal Zone. We rejected that advice – the advice of the experts. We had gone to Panama for one purpose – to work – to work for and with the Panamanians. And we decided to stick it out! Orders were dispatched to every Volunteer – "stay put – don't leave your villages."
>
> And then we held our breath – and sweated: For three days we heard nothing.[6]

Sargent Shriver and his staff at Peace Corps headquarters in Washington, DC confronted a crisis. They had Peace Corps volunteers stationed all over Panama. The country was and still is strategically important to the United States. The Panama Canal is a short cut for American ships – merchant and military – across Panama between the Atlantic and the Pacific Oceans, a strategic alternative to the long journey by sea around Tierra del Fuego at the tip of South America. The United States built the Panama Canal under President Theodore Roosevelt, and in 1964, US troops continued to guard and patrol the land on both sides of it. In January, violent, anti-American, anti-colonialist riots erupted through the country. As Director of the Peace Corps, what should Shriver do? Pull the volunteers out – or tell them to stay put in their villages?

Shriver describes the dilemma. On the one hand, he and his colleagues feared for the safety of the volunteers. Indeed, experts at the State Department were deeply concerned, and advised the Peace Corps to pull out all volunteers immediately, "or at least order them to the 'safety' of the Canal Zone." On the other hand, Shriver and his colleagues were deeply committed to the efficacy of the values and policies of the Peace Corps – to build peace through selfless service to human welfare and dignity. As Shriver expresses it, the volunteers were posted to Panama "for one purpose: to work for and with Panamanians." In the end the decision was clear: "Stay put. Don't leave your villages." For three days, they heard nothing. They held their breath. They sweated.

> And then the cables started coming through – they told how the Peace Corps Volunteers, those white North Americans, those "imperialists," those "gringos," had been protected by the Panamanians, hidden, when necessary, in Panamanian homes. And, then, the New York Times came out with the incredible story: Not one single Peace Corps Volunteer had been injured. Only in the "safety" of the Canal Zone, surrounded by the armed might of U.S. military forces, had anyone been hurt. In the rural villages, in every town, where Peace Corps Volunteers lived, the villagers had repulsed every marauding band searching for North American victims, and hidden the Volunteers in their own homes.[7]

For Shriver, the story is not finished. He returns the attention of his audience from the riots in Panama to the riots in the United States. He confronts them with some questions and a conflict of their own:

> From that incident, we can learn a lesson. If we think back to the long, hot summer of 1964, last August and September – in Philadelphia, in Rochester, in Harlem, in Brooklyn, angry mobs of citizens roamed the streets, defying policemen, looting, and rioting and injuring innocent bystanders. Do you think that the inhabitants of those neighborhoods – many of them as poor as the villagers in Panama – do you think they would have offered protection to the teachers, the welfare investigators, the social workers, the building inspectors? Do you think they would have taken those "professionals" into their homes – the very professionals who are dedicated to helping the poor, to serving the people in those neighborhoods? And if not, why not?[8]

Shriver's answer to these questions is clear. Most inhabitants of those urban neighborhoods – unlike the inhabitants of the Panamanian

villages – would not have offered protection to the teachers, social workers, building inspectors, and welfare investigators who were working
in the community to help them. Why not? Not because Panamanians
are inherently better people than the residents of Philadelphia, Roch-
ester, Harlem, and Brooklyn. Not because Peace Corps volunteers are
themselves inherently better people than American-based teachers,
social workers, building inspectors, and welfare investigators. Rather, it
is because the Peace Corps is organized differently to achieve its goals
differently. The government's approach to the social problems of race
and poverty is based on organizational methods that are not sufficiently
"realistic." They do not understand the realities of violence and conflict
at the heart of poverty and racism. For Shriver, a true and effective realism requires understanding that peace is built by the selfless pursuit of
personal relations in service of human welfare and dignity. Nothing else
will do.

How the Peace Corps Works

In his biography of Shriver, Scott Stossel tells us that, from the outset, a
range of organizational features stamped the Peace Corps with its distinctive character.[9] The first was the sense of urgency and scale that marked
its planning and inception. Influenced as he was by a draft paper titled
The Towering Task, by William Josephson and Warren Wiggins, two veterans of the American foreign policy bureaucracy, Shriver made an early
decision to launch the Peace Corps rapidly, not as a small trial project,
but on a "big, bold scale."[10] The Peace Corps would be launched by an
executive order from the president on March 1, 1961, less than six weeks
after Shriver was named to head up the project. By September 22 of
the same year it would receive $40 million in funding for its first year of
operation.[11] And by the fall of 1962, the program would have 5,000 volunteers in the field, with approval from Congress for $59 million to add
another 5,000 in the upcoming year.[12] This attitude of "big and bold"
continued to influence the organizational shape of the Peace Corps, in
large measure because it reflected Shriver's commitment to the high
ideals of welfare and dignity enshrined in its goals and an awareness
that only a highly visible project could command the funds required to
achieve them.

A second feature was the role of free discussion and debate in the
design, launch, and administration of the Peace Corps. Shriver had
learned from his father-in-law, Joseph P. Kennedy, the value of listening and learning from all views, especially those of critics. Vigorous
debate marked the earliest stages of brainstorming the Peace Corps.[13]

It continued through the six weeks of work of the task force, amicably called "Shriver's Socratic Seminar."[14] And it set the quality and character of the management style that would continue through the early years of the Peace Corps administration. Shriver never ceased to involve himself in every aspect of organizational decision-making. Yet he commanded the respect and admiration of his staff, mainly because of the personal relations he cultivated and their sense of participation in shaping an organization they believed accomplished things of value.[15]

A third feature was the organizational autonomy of the Peace Corps. In the early months of 1961, a debate arose whether it should be set up as a grant-issuing organization, leaving control of projects to other agencies, and installed within the existing US foreign aid establishment. The reaction to this was fierce, and considerable debate followed. In the end, the vision that prevailed was of an independent, non-political organization, disconnected from all other foreign aid or political organizational influences, with complete control over its own programs.[16] This stamped the Peace Corps with its distinctive character and ability to focus resolutely on its goals of welfare and dignity. To be sure, independence created problems in the launch and funding of the Peace Corps.[17] But Shriver was adamant. He insisted in striking a "Treaty" that would "establish an impenetrable firewall between the Peace Corps and the CIA."[18] And four years later, in September 1965, shortly after the outbreak of war between India and Pakistan, when President Johnson cited political reasons for a halt to sending Peace Corps volunteers to India, Shriver sent a "blistering memorandum" that would eventually persuade Johnson to back down.[19] In Shriver's words, "The fact that we are not an instrument of diplomacy has contributed immeasurably to the trust and confidence placed in us around the world."[20]

A fourth organizational feature that marked the operation of the Peace Corps was the focus on transformative learning. From the earliest months, Shriver built into the Peace Corps rigorous standards and procedures for organizational self-awareness and self-evaluation.[21] This was largely because of the enormous importance attached to the role of personal relations in the international reputation of the Peace Corps. The smallest misstep of a Peace Corps volunteer could easily be misinterpreted, escalating into an international incident that threatened the credibility the organization needed to do its work. But it also had to do with Shriver's insistence that Peace Corps volunteers not only assist people in developing countries, they also learn from them.[22] His commitment was to transformative learning on both individual and organizational levels, and this required procedures for self-reflection and self-evaluation. Early on, an impetus for this learning arose from an incident involving a postcard written by a volunteer, and accidentally dropped in the streets of Ibadan, Nigeria. A casual comment intended for an American friend back home was quickly taken as an insult to Nigerians, and considerable work had to be done to control the damage and repair relationships. Shriver took the event as an occasion for learning, and he quickly put in place a self-evaluation program whose rigor and commitment to "merciless objectivity" would bring enormous benefits as well as endless headaches in the years to come. For Shriver, the value of the transformative self-knowledge provided by the Evaluation Division was worth the difficulties it imposed.

Arguably, however, the most important organizational feature determining how the Peace Corps "works" would be the set of five "simple rules" that Shriver described in his speech to his California audience in 1983:

> The rules are few and simple. First, learn the language of the people with whom you work. Second, make up your mind that the work of developing nations is worth the price of personal sacrifice. Third, anchor yourself in the customs and traditions of the country where you are serving. Fourth, take your standard of living down near enough to the local level to make it possible to mix freely and easily with the people – get down to eye level with them. Fifth, believe in the power of personal integrity, humility and determination.[23]

These "simple rules" channel the skills and energy of volunteers, they put the core values of welfare and dignity of the program into action, and they concretely structure the way volunteers treat the people they meet in their host countries. This set of practical program guidelines – learn the language, commit personally to development work, embrace local customs, live at or near local standards of living, cultivate personal integrity, humility, and determination – patterns the personal relations of Peace Corps volunteers and host country nationals as relations of service and self-sacrifice. By putting themselves in service to human welfare and dignity, volunteers enter into patterns of cooperative relationships with their partners, they level the barriers and hierarchies created by economic, social and cultural difference, they open up possibilities for mutual understanding based on shared human experience, and in so doing, create conditions for the transformative personal experiences that dispel older impressions and usher in new ways of relating based on a lived reality of a shared humanity.

The formula that guided how the Peace Corps works involves three steps: first, peace involves personally transformative experiences;

second, the conditions for these experiences are authentic personal relationships; and third, the relevant relationships are those involving self-sacrifice and dedication to the service of welfare and dignity of others. At the celebration of the twenty-fifth Anniversary of the Peace Corps, September 20, 1986, Shriver recounts the events of the early years and contrasts the "world" of the Peace Corps with the typical "world" lived at home in the US.

> Unlike the Peace Corps world overseas, our USA world, is dominated by the lust for power: -economic, political, cultural, bodily, and scientific power! ... The Peace Corps world is different: – Much of it is poor, threatened, hopeless.
>
> Within this endangered and impoverished world, when even one PCV appears and begins to work humbly, compassionately, effectively for humanistic goals, every one spontaneously realizes that this is a person whose very presence and conduct bespeaks the existence of another America than the one I have just described.[24]

The result of this is an experience of personal change, a transformation in beliefs and attitudes of host country nationals. Shriver goes on to say more about what this change involves.

> The Peace Corps seeks peace through service, not through economic strength or military power. Service is the heart and soul and substance of the Peace Corps. Service is a discredited word these days. Who wants to be a servant? No one! Service implies servitude, failure to achieve even equality, let alone dominion. Yet the Peace Corps exists to serve, to help, to care, for our fellow human beings. It works its magic from below, not from above. It concentrates on basics - food, health, education, community development ...
>
> Serve, Serve, Serve! That's the challenge.
>
> For in the end it will be the servants who save us all.[25]

In 1965, in an address to The Experiment in International Living, the project that had planted the seeds for the idea of the Peace Corps by sending Shriver to Europe in the 1930s, he says more about how both the Peace Corps and The Experiment accomplish their goals.

> This is the third main lesson that The Experiment taught: that there is a way to bring about peaceful change and it works. This way is by focusing on people, by making people the target, by reaching the minds and hearts of people, and by doing all this through the direct participation

of the people ... On a significant but still pilot scale has The Experiment demonstrated that the vicious circle of alienation can be broken if people will cross cultural boundaries to meet each other, to listen and talk to each other, to live and work with each other. Above all, the communication must be two-way. The foreign volunteer, the outside social worker, the policeman from downtown, must lose their paternalism. They must above all learn – learn about the complexities of the culture in which they are working, learn what the people in that culture feel and think and suffer and hope for.

The Experiment has proved that this can be done. The Peace Corps, now with 12,000 volunteers in service, is proving that it can be done.[26]

The interesting feature of the Peace Corps is that it does its work, not simply through the personal transformative experiences of host country nationals, but also by transforming the volunteers themselves. In his June 9, 1963, commencement address to Springfield College, Shriver explores how Peace Corps volunteers return having been changed by their work with their host country partners.

But, more important, they come back with a new maturity and with the knowledge that they have participated in the world's great events. We know now that the career aspirations of returning Volunteers are different from the ones they had when they went, and they want jobs after the Peace Corps which offer full scope for service jobs which make a difference.[27]

This change is noticeable, and Shriver goes on to argue how it affects diverse aspects of American society.[28] While the change is intensely personal, it has widening circles of effects on society and on Americans' sense of participation in the world. Shriver speaks about the Peace Corps' influence:

on our society, on institutions and people, on the creation of a new sense of participation in world events, an influence on the national sense of purpose, self-reliance, and an expanded concept of volunteer service in time of peace.[29]

The locus of this change is personal interiority, in the free conscience of persons, and it does its work through the free and personal commitment to the principle of service to others.

In his January 1965 address to his poverty audience in Tucson, Shriver offers a recap of how the Peace Corps works:

First, Peace Corps Volunteers do not live apart. They live in a country, not off it! They live in a culture, not despite it! They drink the same drinking water, eat the same food, live in the same kinds of houses, use the same transportation, and speak the same language as the people!

Second, in order to survive, Peace Corps Volunteers must adapt! And this means they must learn from the only people who can teach them – the local people. They learn about the local culture, the local habits and local customs. The local people teach the Peace Corps Volunteers to recognize and avoid dangers, to know and use the local resources.

And because of this, every Bolivian, every Indonesian, every Nigerian can teach something important to our Volunteers. And for the first time, a situation exists where Americans must learn from others – where the local people know they have something to offer. And because the people know this they can also accept the Volunteer's advice, his help and his contribution – because that advice comes as part of a mutual giving and taking. It is not noblesse oblige; it is not a distribution of charity; it is not a way of asserting superiority! It is part of a "give and take" in which each person keeps his dignity because each has something to contribute and something to learn!

Third, and finally, Peace Corps Volunteers are not out to impose their way of thinking, their way of life, their political ideology and values on their hosts. Peace Corps Volunteers have only one purpose:

To help, to place their talents and energy at the disposal of others, to solve the problems others think are important in ways that make sense and are acceptable to others.[30]

Interiority and Spirituality

To understand how Shriver's spiritual values influenced the organizational structure of the Peace Corps, it would be helpful to step back and reflect again on the character of spiritual values and the role they play in building peace. Four years before the launch of the Peace Corps, in 1957, Bernard Lonergan's *Insight* was published in London, England, and in the years following, as Shriver was building the Peace Corps, Lonergan was delivering the lectures and courses at Regis College, Toronto (1962), Georgetown University (1964), and the Gregorian University, Rome (1959–64), where he would develop the ideas from *Insight* into a method for interdisciplinary collaboration he would later publish as *Method in Theology* (1972).[31] In chapter 20 of *Insight*, Lonergan takes core insights on natural law and charity from Catholic tradition and transposes them into a framework of interiority that recognizes achievements from modern science and historical consciousness, and he incorporates these insights into a broad-based analysis applicable to diverse traditions and contexts. In the first seventeen pages of the chapter, Lonergan lays the groundwork for understanding the role of spirituality in social and political life by offering an analysis of the obstacles encountered in the pursuit of the human good. He sketches the structure of the problem of personal and social evil, and offers an analysis of how spirituality effects a transformation in social life that works through freedom and personal relationships to create conditions for personal transformations that get to the core of evil.

Lonergan develops his analysis of the problem of evil through his turn to interiority – his analysis of the structure of human consciousness. Instead of appealing to the abstract theory of "human nature" that was the basis of the older natural law, he invites his readers to engage in a methodical exploration of the structure of their own consciousness to discover a normative or self-transcending orientation in the operations of meaning at work in everyday life. The result is a transposed version of the natural law, a framework based on interiority for understanding how we relate to each other socially when we are acting at our best. This framework provides diagnostic tools for explaining what goes wrong in social life when we fail to live up to the best of ourselves.

The basic problem in human living is rooted in the structure of consciousness itself. It is the fact that the demands of living forever outstrip our capacities to meet them.

> the present is ever a pattern of lags. No one can postpone his living until he has learnt, until he has become willing, until his sensitivity has been adapted. To learn, to be persuaded, to become adapted, occur within living and through living. The living is ever now, but the knowledge to guide living, the willingness to follow knowledge, the sensitive adaptation that vigorously and joyously executes the will's decisions, these belong to the future, and when the future is present, there will be beyond it a further future with steeper demands.[32]

The result of this structure is not simply a lack in human capacity, but also a bias or distortion in the way our conscious operations are engaged in solving the everyday problems of social life. We have to live before we can learn how to live fully and responsibly. This means that yesterday's learning has the effect of shaping our habits of living for today and tomorrow. Most important, yesterday's learning is not simply about facts, it is about values, notably values related to justice and social order that play a role in shaping persons and societies. The terrible problem in all this is that yesterday's experiences of suffering and harm stamp their imprint upon the ideas and feelings about justice and social order that prevail in our living today and tomorrow. The "real world" experiences that school our learning about justice are experiences of both success and failure. Yet we must live before developing the tools for differentiating between the two. Our resolute commitment to "realism" results in our replicating not only yesterday's successes but also yesterday's failures. And through it all, we remain incapable of sorting out the difference.

The problem gets magnified as yesterday's distortions get institutionalized in social systems that proliferate them. The result is that institutions become dysfunctional and empirical intelligence now has ample evidence to prove that social life is hostile and requires the mobilization of attack and defence for survival. The result is social conflict on a wide scale. The expectations of harm give rise to the proliferation of actions that reciprocate in kind in the name of defence. As textbooks get written and institutions built on the basis of these "realist" explanations of "the human condition," the stage is set for the formation of countless future generations in patterns of attack-defence that are prescribed as essential for survival.[33] Most important, the textbooks gain credence because they appeal to the ample historical evidence of distorted practice as basis for their "realism."

Lonergan's analysis of the solution to the problem has, at its core, an experience of personal transformation that breaks the link between past experience of harm and present deliberations and decisions. The effect is to de-link our feelings and deliberations from past harm so that present and future actions are freed up to pursue the welfare and dignity of others.[34] He examines this transformative experience using the older Catholic language of "charity," but by now he has transposed its meaning via the turn to interiority. In later texts, Lonergan will speak about charity using the language of "religious conversion," by which he means "being in love in an unrestricted fashion."[35] The core experience of charity is love. But because of its origin and scope, it is special kind of love. The transformative experience is not something we produce ourselves. Rather, like other "big" insights in our lives, it has its origins both within and beyond us, in this case in our encounter with transcendence. And because it is love writ large, its effect is to reorient our feelings, habits, horizons, and inclinations in new directions oriented to self-sacrifice and service to others.

Charity works as a habit of willingness to engage humbly in actions that promote the welfare of others, regardless of past experiences of harm, and regardless of the cost to ourselves. It is a willingness to commit to self-sacrifice and service whose origins lie in a subtle but profoundly transformative experience of transcendence arising in our own lives. Its first effect is to break the link between past harm and present action in ourselves. But its subsequent effect is that our actions now provide evidence and a catalyst for future transformative experiences in others.[36] This is because our actions now create conditions for others to experience something that marks a departure from past cycles of harm and recrimination in their own lives. The self-giving commitment to service, welfare, and dignity introduces conditions for further transformative experiences that open possibilities for trust and relationship-building.

The final ingredient in the analysis involves insights into ways we collaborate with charity to institutionalize patterns of relations so that such formative and transformative experiences occur more frequently. Traditionally, Catholic theology tended to assume that the Church would be the place where this institutional collaboration occurred. Lonergan, however, opens the analysis to recognize authentic religious experiences of charity in diverse religions and traditions.[37] He recognizes that diverse communities can be formed that take their stand on a religious principle, understood as "God's gift of his love."[38] And he recognizes that within the broader institutional life of political society, we need various forms of organizations that support the ongoing renewal of community and society through our cooperation with transformative experiences of love.

> There are needed, then, individuals and groups and, in the modern world, organizations that labor to persuade people to intellectual, moral, and religious conversion and that work systematically to undo the mischief brought about by alienation and ideology.[39]

Like Shriver, Lonergan counts the Christian churches as "among such bodies."[40] And in so doing, he recognizes that we can expect to find organizations other than churches dedicated to the self-sacrifice and service that are the hallmarks of charity.

Spiritual Values and the Peace Corps

The parallels between Lonergan's analysis of charity and Shriver's understanding of the Peace Corps are striking. We argue that Lonergan's work explains how Shriver's spirituality could become part of the policies and programs of the Peace Corps. We suggest that Shriver was able to build elements of this spirituality into the organizational fabric of the Peace Corps so it could become a service informed by "religious conversion" and committed to "undo[ing] the mischief brought about by alienation and ideology."

The first element in the spirituality at the heart of the Peace Corps is the role played by *transformative experience* in shifting personal attitudes from past expectations of harm and recrimination to new openings for trust and confidence. As Lonergan argued, the problem with basic evil is that it cannot be fixed by the common-sense pursuit of power or justice. Rather, it requires an opening to personal transformation that arises, not from our direct efforts, but from the gift of charity. Shriver's analysis of the Peace Corps reflects this recognition. He states that building peace in worlds that are "poor, threatened, hopeless"[41] can never be achieved "through economic strength or military power."[42] Instead, his focus is on the experience of personal change that emerges in contexts where Peace Corps volunteers engage actively in programs of service to the welfare and dignity of others.

> Within this endangered and impoverished world, when even one PCV appears and begins to work humbly, compassionately, effectively for human-istic goals, every one spontaneously realizes that this is a person whose very presence and conduct bespeaks the existence of another America.[43]

Shriver knew that the "realization" arising "spontaneously" in host country nationals was a personal transformation that could not be man-aged or manipulated by diplomacy or marketing. From the very begin-ning, he was adamant that the Peace Corps never be allowed to become "an instrument of diplomacy,"[44] and he built this into the core of its policies and programs. More important, however, is how Shriver under-stands this experience. His use of the term "compassion" is revealing. We know, from our analysis of Shriver's speeches in Chapter 3, that "com-passion" was his way of speaking about the role of spirituality in politics. It was the word he used to transpose the language of "charity" from the narrow framework of Catholic tradition into the broader framework of interiority required for application to public life.

Shriver speaks of the volunteer's goals as "humanistic," but it is the way these goals are pursued that signals the role of spirituality in Peace Corps programs. For Shriver, the normal instruments of human power do not succeed in achieving peace in contexts dominated by past histories of harm and recrimination. For Shriver, "economic, political, cultural, bod-ily, and scientific power"[45] are impotent in face of the real challenges posed by peace. Approaching peace appropriately requires understand-ing that we never achieve peace directly. We approach it only obliquely by committing ourselves to service. Service is our way of engaging spir-itually in laying the groundwork for receiving and welcoming the shifts in horizons and hearts that arrive in their own good time. Central to this spirituality is the peace-filled conviction that these experiences can indeed be trusted to occur and they remain the heart of peacebuilding. This is why Shriver calls "service" "the heart and soul and substance of the Peace Corps".[46] Engaging in service to others, we cooperate with the Spirit in establishing favourable conditions for the emergence of the personal transformations that "undo the mischief brought about by alienation and ideology." For Shriver, the volunteer's humble and compassionate dedication to the service of others is how the Peace Corps cooperates with the transformative power of charity to effect peace in contexts where no other strategy is "realistic."

The second element in the spirituality of the Peace Corps is the role played by *personal relations* in establishing conditions for the emergence of the transformative experiences involved in peacebuilding. The experiences of personal change required for peace cannot be manipulated or pursued directly, but they can and do emerge spontaneously in contexts defined by the volunteer's authentic dedication to service. For Shriver, cultivating the organizational climate for the personal relations essential for this work of service played a key role in the design of the Peace Corps from the earliest years.

From the earliest months of "Shriver's Socratic Seminar," and in his relations with colleagues and staff through the early years of the Peace Corps, Shriver never ceased to command respect and admiration, largely because of the sense of participation they felt in a project that was worthy of their commitment.[47] Cultivating and sustaining these personal relations of trust and good will was a central focus of Shriver, both at home and abroad. His policy of independence from outside political and financial control, his "Treaty" to "establish an impenetrable firewall between the Peace Corps and the CIA," and his 1965 "blistering memorandum" to President Johnson opposing a halt to sending volunteers to India, all of these measures were his way of ensuring that the Peace Corps remained dedicated to living up to "the trust and confidence placed in us around the world."[48]

It is the five "simple rules," however, that reveal the distinctively spiritual character of Shriver's commitment to personal relations. Peace Corps volunteers achieve their goals of service, not simply by performing tasks, but by performing them within patterns of relations of equality, mutual respect, and trust. They learn the language of host country nationals, they commit personally to development work, they embrace local customs, they live at or near local standards, and they cultivate personal integrity, humility, and determination.[49] In so doing, they make their own lives into instruments for the transformative work of charity. Following Lonergan's analysis, personal relations of service can be understood as the social and institutionalized form of the "habit of willingness" that disengages present action from the formative influence of past cycles of harm and recrimination. In social contexts dominated by the legacy of past cycles of evil, personal relations of service are incarnate gestures that speak the language of good will and mutual care. And they do their work by creating favourable conditions for the emergence of transformative experiences in host country nationals.

We suggest that this appreciation of the spiritual significance of personal relations is at the heart of Shriver's focus on "people" in his 1965 Experiment in International Living speech.

> there is a way to bring about peaceful change and it works. This way is by focusing on people, by making people the target, by reaching the minds and hearts of people, and by doing all this through the direct participation of the people.[50]

While Shriver has often been praised for his abilities as a salesman,[51] his marketing never instrumentalized people. Rather, he sought only to market the ideas and institutions that would promote the authentic personal relations at the heart of peacebuilding. Shriver understood that:

> the vicious circle of alienation can be broken if people will cross cultural boundaries to meet each other, to listen and talk to each other, to live and work with each other.[52]

There can be no doubt that Shriver understood the spiritual significance of these words. Grounded as he was in the theology of Thomas Aquinas, Shriver understood the theological virtue of charity, its form of operation in transforming human hearts, and our cooperation with the Spirit in living out the required habits of willingness in personal, social, and institutional life.[53] Shriver's commitment was to make the Peace Corps into an institution committed to enabling and supporting the work of volunteers in introducing novel personal relations that carry the healing influence of charity into contexts dominated by past histories of harm and recrimination.

There is a third element in the spirituality of the Peace Corps, and this is the role played by the *transformative experiences of Peace Corps volunteers*. When Shriver first set the Peace Corps in motion, his plan was to select volunteers that would be fit for the job. What he discovered, however, was that the job had a formative influence on volunteers themselves. And we argue this influence is central to the transformative spirituality at the heart of the Peace Corps policies and programs.

And, as a result, the Peace Corps Volunteers get more than they give ...
they come back with a new maturity and with the knowledge that they have
participated in the world's great events.[54]

One of the conditions for this change is the requirement that volunteers
dedicate themselves to transformative learning. Peace Corps programs
require them to learn deeply how to understand, appreciate, and live
alongside their host country colleagues and friends. Shriver is adamant
on insisting in this learning:

> They must above all learn – learn about the complexities of the culture in
> which they are working, learn what the people in that culture feel and think
> and suffer and hope for.[55]

There can be no doubt that this learning is transformative. But Shriver
also understood how this transformation of volunteers plays a role in the
sequence of events unfolding in the spiritual "logic" of charity. There is
an interesting pattern of reciprocity that Shriver envisions happening in
the spirituality of peacebuilding.

> [volunteers] learn about the local culture, the local habits and local cus-
> toms. The local people teach the Peace Corps Volunteers to recognize and
> avoid dangers, to know and use the local resources.
>
> And because of this, every Bolivian, every Indonesian, every Nigerian can
> teach something important to our Volunteers. And for the first time, a situ-
> ation exists where Americans must learn from others – where the local peo-
> ple know they have something to offer. And because the people know this
> they can also accept the Volunteer's advice, his help and his contribution –
> because that advice comes as part of a mutual giving and taking. It is not
> noblesse oblige; it is not a distribution of charity; it is not a way of assert-
> ing superiority! It is part of a "give and take" in which each person keeps
> his dignity because each has something to contribute and something to
> learn![56]

Peace Corps policies and programs are structured so that volunteers are
required to fit themselves into patterns of personal relations of equality,
respect, and service to host country nationals. But once these relations of
service are achieved, an interesting scheme of events is set in motion, a
scheme in which transformative experiences begin emerging spontaneously in both volunteers and hosts. The learning of volunteers changes
them, but their openness to learning has a reciprocal transformative
effect on their hosts, who begin observing, perhaps for the first time,

that volunteers do not fit the patterns established by past histories of harm and recrimination.

Shriver's critique of "charity" in this quote is not directed at the distinctively theological or spiritual meaning of charity understood here. Rather, his focus is the extrinsic and distorted meaning that became commonplace in popular culture. What Shriver rejects are the distorted relations that often accompany donations of money by the wealthy to the poor. His call, rather, is to overcome the harmful legacy of these distorted relations, and he lived out this calling by institutionalizing Peace Corps practices that give rise to the reciprocally transforming events of the spiritual scheme of authentic charity.

It would be difficult to imagine that the parallels between Lonergan's analysis of charity and Shriver's understanding of the Peace Corps could be mere coincidence. Steeped as he was in the daily practices of his Catholic faith, familiar as he was with the theology of Aquinas and his contemporary interpreters, committed as he was to living out his public life as an authentic religious vocation, passionate as he was in transposing the spiritual resources from his faith tradition, via the turn to interiority, into a language fit for the diverse publics of democratic politics, Shriver could not have avoided thinking about the Peace Corps in spiritual terms. We suggest that Lonergan's work provides the best framework for explaining why this line of thinking makes sense and how we can build on Shriver's example in developing creative ways of relating religion and politics in present and future years.

Resolving Conflicts and Building Peace: The Peace Corps and the Insight Approach

To this point, our focus has been on the healing role that spirituality plays in transforming situations marked by past histories of harm and recrimination. We have drawn on Lonergan to explain how Shriver institutionalized a spiritual dimension into the Peace Corps so that its policies and programs established conditions for this transformative work. What we have yet to explain, however, is why this work can be understood precisely as "peace." There is a distinctive character to the construction and resolution of conflicts that is key to the meaning of "peace."

In this final section, we draw on the work of scholars from the Insight approach to conflict to examine this key meaning. In "Interiority and Conflict: The Insight Approach" from Chapter 4, we introduced some of these scholars and outlined how conflict and resolution are understood and practised in the Insight approach.[57] We situated the Insight approach within the wider range of studies that apply Lonergan to diverse fields of scholarship and professional practice. We explained how scholars in the Insight approach move beyond Lonergan to new applications that Lonergan himself never developed. We show how these new developments remain rooted in the theory and method of Lonergan, notably the method of self-appropriation. And we point out texts of Lonergan, most notably *Insight*, chapter 20, that have informed our own study of spirituality and conflict. In the pages that follow, we apply this approach to the analysis of spirituality and the Peace Corps.

Central to the Insight approach, as presented in Melchin and Picard, *Transforming Conflict through Insight*, is an understanding of the curious character of insights, an understanding achieved by following Lonergan's methodical turn to interiority.[58] Insights are neither the passive reception of data, nor are they the active or deliberate construction of concepts. Rather, they involve both active pursuit and passive reception. Most important, when they arrive, they transform our consciousness from one state to another. Insights are not something we acquire, they are a change in state of "us." Prior to insights, we cannot imagine them. After gaining them, we cannot retrieve our prior state of confusion. With small insights, the drama of this transformation is not always easy to observe, but with large insights, it is unmistakable. Our big insights change our horizons.

In the Insight approach, we explain conflict as a deformation that unfolds progressively and cumulatively in relations of meaning among persons. The deformation involves a pattern in which past experiences of harm frame interpretations of another's meanings, and the back-and-forth sending and interpreting of meanings rooted in mutual expectations of harm results in mistrust and hostility building cumulatively. The past experiences of harm can involve past interactions with the same person, but usually they also include a re-feeling of older harm narratives from interactions with others. The re-feeling of the past harm generates expectations of the certainty of future threat, these expectations get attached or linked to the actions of others, and the interpretive complex arising from this linkage ends up framing responses that generally take the form of attack-defence. The cycle emerges when the same occurs in the other person, and both parties cumulatively provide more and more evidence that the attack-defence responses are justified.

The operations that link past harm narratives to present actions are reflective insights that capture and express feelings about how things parties care about are threatened by the meanings and actions of others. The insights may have elements of plausibility, but usually this plausibility is not at all recognized by the other person. The other party has her own "story," and both stories invariably involve feeling-saturated components from past narratives that are linked via threat-to-care insights to the components from the present conflict. What is interesting is that the reflective insights that sustain the conflict are not simply fact-insights, they are mainly value-insights. Parties in conflict invariably seek to promote and achieve cares or values. The expectations of threat to these values provide the links between past narratives and present experiences, and they yield explanatory frameworks for interpreting others and justifying responses.

Getting to the core of these threatened cares or values is one of the principal tasks of Insight mediators. Conflicts are difficult because values are often compacted in feelings whose meanings have not been probed by the parties themselves. The feelings carry an "if-then" logic to them that connects past harm narratives with present events to generate expectations of similar future harm that justify attack-defence responses. These future expectations are felt to be certain. The trouble is, the entire structure of this "if-then" narrative logic often is not understood explicitly by parties, it is only carried powerfully in feelings that apprehend the situation as an undifferentiated whole. The goal of Insight mediators is to probe these feelings, to help parties gain insights into the cares at the heart of their own meanings and those of others, and to help them understand how feelings of threats-to-cares project future scenarios they feel are certain.

When insight mediators are successful in this work of probing or deepening, some interesting things begin happening to parties. The first is they begin gaining insights into their own values, most notably the cares they feel are threatened in the conflict. When these cares and threats-to-cares are articulated in plausible ways by mediators, parties begin to feel "understood," and these feeling-saturated-insights, both direct and reflective, begin changing their stance in the conflict. The second thing arises when they listen to the mediator doing the same with the other person. What they often discover is that the threats-to-cares that lie at the heart of the other's meanings and actions are meanings they had not previously understood. They are usually surprised, sometimes astonished. Something new emerges in their understanding. And like other big insights that change horizons, this begins to change them.

We explain this change as a "de-linking of threats-to-cares." Central to conflicts are feelings of certainty about threats. When new meanings begin emerging, however, parties begin discovering that another's actions might be grounded in values quite different from those expected previously. The other's cares and feelings of threat may not center on them at all. The newly discovered cares express trajectories that could plausibly unfold in directions quite unrelated to them or de-linked from them. Also, understanding the deeper roots of one's own cares reveals that entrenched expectations of harm might not be warranted. Other avenues become imaginable. Expected threats-to-cares start to de-link from the events of the conflict as parties become curious about the implications of newly gained insights for possibly new trajectories that are opened up and now available to themselves and others.

The result is that parties' certainty begins to give way. Because they feel some security that their own cares are indeed plausible, there is a willingness to let the certainty slide. The effect of this is a de-linking or unravelling in the threats-to-cares at the heart of their own meanings and actions and those of the other. In its place what emerges is a curiosity about the other and an envisioning of possibilities for action presented by the new scenario.

Following the Insight approach, we understand peace as the state of personal relations in which parties move out of expectations defined by threat-to-care and into expectations defined by genuine curiosity and openness-to-care. We offer this approach as an explanation of what Sargent Shriver designed the Peace Corps to achieve. The state of peace that Shriver understood as central to the work of the Peace Corps was "a 'give and take' in which each person keeps his dignity because each has something to contribute and something to learn!"[59] What marks the mutuality of this "contributing" and "learning" and what guards each person's dignity is the volunteer's openness to care/value in the local person's knowledge about dangers to avoid and resources to use and the host's openness to care/value in the volunteer's advice, help, and contribution. The break in the "vicious cycle of alienation" that occurs when people "cross cultural boundaries to meet each other, to listen and talk to each other, to live and work with each other"[60] arises because new patterns of meeting, listening, talking, living, and working are established – patterns in which threats-to-cares are de-linked, opening spaces for a new openness-to-care.

The question we ask, then, is how Peace Corps programs bring about the transformation in patterns of personal relations from expectations defined by threat-to-care to expectations defined by openness-to-care. Does the Insight approach explain this transformation in ways that correlate with Shriver's understanding? Our answer is "yes," and to support this, we offer Shriver's account of Peace Corps cases from Peru and Venezuela.

Volunteers went to Arequipa, Peru, for example, to share the conditions of people who lived in abject misery – no running water or plumbing, no electricity or heat, crumbling hovels which scarcely afforded shelter from wind or rain and no tools to rebuild them. They found themselves under violent attack from the communists who harassed them with slogans scrawled on walls and walks, threatened to brand and burn them, accused them of poisoning children with tainted food.

But the volunteers moved in and went right to work. They helped build schools and houses taught hygiene and child care to mothers – provided medical clinics established sewing classes and offered all their capacities to elevate the lives of the people.

Soon their enthusiasm affected the middle class of Arequipa. Hitherto indifferent to their own slums, they became disturbed, began to come to the barriadas to work with the Volunteers. According to the American consul, the Volunteers are now so well accepted "that the demands for their assistance cannot be met. They have become so revered by the townspeople," he reported, "that the communists have ceased intimidating them out of fear of public reaction," And now they have received a silver medal from the President of the country and the people of Arequipa for their work in the slums.[61]

Clearly, Peace Corps volunteers are not conflict mediators. Their contexts are different and their roles are different. Yet Shriver's account reflects an interesting pattern, parallel to that arising from the work of Insight mediators, in the transformation of the conflict relation defined by threats-to-cares. The conflict situation is understood by Shriver to be not only the poverty and desolation in the living conditions of the Peruvians, but the anti-American sentiment revealed in their support for the communists and their initial hostility to volunteers.

They found themselves under violent attack from the communists who harassed them with slogans scrawled on walls and walks, threatened to brand and burn them, accused them of poisoning children with tainted food.[62]

The volunteers' response, however, was not defined by the reciprocal interpretive response of threat-to-care that is characteristic of escalating conflicts. Rather, their efforts focused entirely on understanding and responding to the needs and cares of their host country nationals.

They helped build schools and houses taught hygiene and child care to mothers – provided medical clinics established sewing classes and offered all their capacities to elevate the lives of the people.[63]

The effect of this response was to elicit an openness to the value of the work of volunteers in their hosts. In fact, this openness received such widespread acclaim that it drew other middle-class Peruvians into appreciating the cares of the poor, becoming "disturbed" by their plight, and joining in addressing their needs. The effect of all this was a transformative experience in the Peruvian hosts, an experience de-linking attitudes grounded in expectations of threat and opening spaces for attention to value in the work of Peace Corps volunteers. The signal markers of this openness-to-value, in Shriver's judgement, are the cessation of communist intimidation, the public reaction that keeps this intimidation at bay, an increased demand for their talents and services, and the President's silver medal recognizing their work.

The interesting feature of the situation's transformation, we suggest, lies in the correlation between the transformation as understood by the Insight approach to conflict and the transformation as explained by Shriver's spirituality of charity/compassion. The direct focus of the Peace Corps volunteers was not peacebuilding or conflict resolution, it was living out the "habit of willingness" to commit to self-sacrifice and service that Shriver inscribed as the attitude of mind and heart that would be central to the institutional structure of Peace Corps programs. But the transformative effect of this dedication, achieved obliquely or indirectly, was to de-link the threats-to-cares in the host country nationals and to open them, we can imagine, first, to curiosity about them, and then to the cares or values at the core of their work. The pattern of transformation in the spirituality inscribed in the Peace Corps is parallel to the pattern operative in the Insight approach to conflict – a pattern whose central ingredient is a dedication to service that de-links present action from past legacies of harm and recrimination.

Shriver's account of the Venezuela case offers further support for this explanation of the structure at play in the transformative work of spirituality, the resolution of conflicts, and the building of peace, as these are applied to conflict by scholars in the Insight approach.

In Venezuela the Peace Corps works side-by-side with the YMCA. We have found what you had already discovered – conditions in the poor, crowded urban sections of Caracas where young people grow up in substandard housing, with insufficient food, limited formal education, little sanitation, few jobs and daily companionship with crime and delinquency. More than sixty percent of the slum dwellers in Venezuela are between the ages of 14 and 19.

To help these young people, the "Y" has established neighborhood centers. Volunteers are working at these centers in seven cities. Try to tell them that "enthusiasm" and a "crusading spirit" are out of date. Daily they must deal with unemployment, delinquency, and anti-American passions. The walls of one slum where Volunteers are working are smeared with slogans like "CUBA SI YANKIS NO" and it was in this section that Vice President Nixon was stoned in 1958.

But the real challenge is the youth. Children come to the centers not only to play baseball, volleyball, basketball and other-games, but also to seek affection, guidance and friendship. Volunteers become more than recreation leaders – in the spirit of the "Y" they must become counselors, confidants, teachers and friends.

Their tools are patience, resourcefulness, initiative – and enthusiasm. A lack of facilities does not discourage them. Peace Corps Volunteers have established three new YMCA neighborhood centers. They did this by getting donations of land and building material. The work was done by the people who caught the Peace Corps germ of enthusiasm. Two Volunteers, Will Pryor and Jim Oliver, have completed one of the new centers in Valencia. It's located on several acres of land which are beautifully landscaped. The people of Valencia are thrilled. They see their young people engaged in wholesome activities with a new kind of Yankee – the Peace Corps Volunteers who rolled up their sleeves and dug in right beside them. They also have an outstanding field for their national game, bolas criollas, which the Volunteers have learned to play.

The effect of the Peace Corps Volunteers has been far reaching.

Recently two Volunteers were walking through a barrio and came upon a street fight. They recognized the boys beating up another boy as a gang which had been disrupting their "Y" activities. The Volunteers stepped in to break up the fight and found themselves attacked by the gang. Then something very interesting happened. Observers on Latin America, and slum areas everywhere, for that matter, were amazed at the outcome.

The older men looking on the fight came to the defense of the Peace Corps Volunteers.

Not to the defense of the gang. Not to chase off the Volunteers. But to help them.[64]

Once again, while Peace Corps volunteers do not act as conflict mediators, their contributions in the conflict situation do have the effect of shifting patterns of personal relations. The situation clearly is one marked by past cycles of harm and recrimination. The "anti- American passions," the slogans smeared on the walls, "CUBA SI YANKIS NO," the stoning of Vice-President Nixon in 1958, and the street fight attack on the volunteers, all of these signal a legacy of hardened conflict between Venezuelans and Americans. The volunteers, however, enter this situation with new patterns of personal relations. They help the youth by establishing and working in neighborhood centers in seven cities. They become "counselors, confidants, teachers and friends."

The effect of these actions and relations is to de-link threats-to-cares and establish an openness-to-cares that grounds new directions for curiosity and action. The youth begin turning to volunteers, not only for "baseball, volleyball, basketball and other games," but also for "affection, guidance and friendship." Donations of land and building materials acquired and accumulated by volunteers results in work on three new youth centers that is performed by "people who caught the Peace Corps germ of enthusiasm." According to Shriver's account, "The effect of the Peace Corps volunteers has been far reaching."

The de-linking has the effect of disengaging present deliberations and decisions from past formative legacies of harm and recrimination. Volunteers, finding themselves attacked after intervening on behalf of a boy being beaten up by a gang, encounter a radically novel departure from past patterns. "The older men looking on the fight came to the defence of the Peace Corps volunteers." The departure from the patterns of the past is so novel it is noticed by "Observers on Latin American, and slum areas everywhere."

The transformation involves a novel habit of willingness of self-sacrifice and service inscribed in the structure of Peace Corps programs and lived out in the personal relations of volunteers. Ever up-beat, Shriver uses the word "enthusiasm" to describe this habit of willingness. Yet, while "enthusiasm" may have been the word Shriver chose to communicate best to his audience, it fails to capture the depth of commitment elicited by Peace Corps programs and displayed by volunteers. Their willingness was to enter into and live alongside their hosts "in the poor, crowded urban sections of Caracas where young people grow up in substandard housing, with insufficient food, limited formal education, little sanitation, few jobs and daily companionship with crime and delinquency." Their willingness was to enter situations of personal danger, walking through barrios and coming to the aid of victims of gang violence. Their willingness was to move in and help residents of a slum where anti-American sentiment was so rampant that Vice-President Nixon was stoned five years earlier. Shriver speaks of "patience, resourcefulness, initiative" to describe volunteers. But the term that best captures the truth of their willingness is "compassion," the term he used to signal the presence of the theological virtue of charity.

Finally, the effect of this habit of willingness, as it is expressed and lived out in the personal relations established by the actions of volunteers, is a transformation in Venezuelans. The youth and then the adults find themselves engaged with "a new kind of Yankee." As Shriver states clearly: "The people of Valencia are thrilled." "The effect of the Peace Corps volunteers has been far reaching."

Concluding Remarks

On the face of it, the process seems simple. If you want to build peace, all you have to do is dedicate your life to self-sacrifice and service to others, move in among people who consider you an enemy, live in conditions shared by them, on terms specified by them, performing community, technical, educational, medical, family, and other services needed and requested by them, all free of charge, asking nothing in return, selling nothing, imposing no political, economic, or religious doctrines, working with them not employing them, listening to them not preaching to them, learning from them, performing services as they request, eating their food, obeying their laws, and sharing their lives.

It seems this is how Shriver understood things. Of course, the apparent simplicity in all this may not be obvious to all. Appearances can be deceiving. We suggest this is because peacebuilding has the same structure as all insights: before you get it, you cannot imagine it, after you get it, you cannot retrieve your prior state of un-knowing. Like all insights, the simplicity only seems so afterwards, and the apparent simplicity conceals a deeper complexity whose perplexing challenges are resolved by the change in ourselves as persons. The simplicity involves an integrity that unifies a rather large set of complex relations. Beforehand, we cannot imagine anything other than the threats-to-cares that define our horizons, channel our questions, and block our curiosity about the cares of adversaries. After the transformative experiences that de-link threats-to-cares, a new curiosity emerges that opens novel forms of engagement with the cares at the center of their meanings and actions.

Clearly, in the examples of Panama, Peru, and Venezuela, in the accounts of Shriver's biographer, in Shriver's 1960s speeches in Tucson, Bangkok, California, New York, and Washington, and in his own reflections 25 years later in Washington, DC, Shriver's understanding reveals this pattern of transformative action at work in the programs of the Peace Corps. The central ingredient in this pattern is a dedication to personal relations of service that gives rise to transformative experiences that de-link present action from past legacies of harm and recrimination. This pattern can be understood as a spirituality whose origins were in Shriver's own religious vocation to public life. It was expressed originally in the language of his traditional Catholic faith. But eventually this spirituality gained expression in a new language, now open to diverse audiences, reflecting a transposition to interiority that is best articulated by Lonergan. This pattern of transformative action is the work of a spirituality that stops cycles of harm and recrimination and begins anew the work of cooperating with transcendence to build the human good. And the Insight analysis of conflict reveals this structure at work in building peace in situations of conflict. We suggest this offers a compelling model to follow in relating religion and politics in present and future generations.

Chapter Six

The Way Forward

This book ends where another needs to begin. The careful analysis of permissible forms of religion-politics relations cannot go forward under the banner of "a wall of separation." It remains true that politics must be differentiated from religion and must never be permitted to operate as religion in making ultimate or comprehensive claims. This requires some forms of institutional differentiation. Still, differentiation is not separation. Real positive influences do flow and must continue to flow to politics from both philosophical and religious belief traditions. These positive influences must now be permitted to flow amply and diversely. The principal conduit remains the conscience of citizens, and this remains so even when the constitutions and institutions of politics are constructed wisely to facilitate these flows for the common good.

Simplistic images do violence to the complex relations that must be understood and affirmed for politics to receive the supports required from religious and philosophical belief traditions. Both types of traditions function as religions in supplying comprehensive or ultimate values that, for better and for worse, shape the directions of politics. Politics needs religion to do its work. Still, not all influences from such traditions are healthy. This means that sorting out the "how" requires the ongoing work of careful analysis that differentiates the positive from the negative in both types of traditions.

To be sure, we must guard against coercion. In technological societies, however, when complex public-private partnerships establish the conditions for the delivery of public goods to citizens, institutional names and flows of payments are not always adequate markers of coercion. In fact, when citizens fail to recognize the negative influences flowing from philosophical belief traditions not regarded as religious, the focus on overt religion blinds us to coercive forces operating quietly in our midst. Both religious and secular belief traditions need the vigorous work of critical philosophies and theologies operating from within to ensure that such negative influences do not find their way into the programs and policies of politics.

The way forward, then, requires assembling tools for this task of careful scrutiny. We argue that navigating this work of careful analysis requires a philosophy that can mediate between belief traditions and political deliberation. A first ingredient of this philosophy, we suggest, is provided by political philosopher, John Rawls. His insight into the role of *comprehensive doctrines* in politics helps set the task on a proper footing. Next, we suggest, is the call for a *philosophical method*. We believe that while Rawls's analysis of the problem is wise, the solution he provides falls short. We suggest that a philosophy adequate to the task must be fully methodical. It must be accessible as a methodical practice that women and men from all comprehensive doctrines can engage in performing. This, we argue, is provided by Lonergan. Finally, to point the way, we need *exemplary figures*. Our purpose in writing this book, then, has been to examine one such exemplary figure, Sargent Shriver, as a model for both diagnosing problems and signaling paths forward.

Comprehensive Doctrines

Readers familiar with John Rawls's *Political Liberalism* know that his book summarizes a shift in his work from a comprehensive ethical-political philosophy of liberalism, as outlined in *A Theory of Justice*, to a more modest political theory. He proposes that the more modest work could reasonably claim the allegiance of wide ranges of citizens in a democracy because it does not require holding to the more comprehensive system of liberalism. A central ingredient in this shift is his formulation of the idea of comprehensive doctrines.

For Rawls, a democracy is the sort of political system in which citizens participate fully in determining what sort of society they will make for themselves. If members of a society were of one mind in their thinking and valuing, then the direction of this participatory work would follow the line of values championed by the group. But in modern, cosmopolitan societies, this is not the case. Rather, for Rawls, democracy has a very specific problem it must solve, the problem posed by the fact of major differences about the ultimate or comprehensive values governing human living. "The political culture of a democratic society is always marked by a diversity of opposing and irreconcilable religious, philosophical, and moral doctrines."[1] The term Rawls coins for these diverse comprehensive values sets is *comprehensive doctrines.*

This means that of all the values citizens champion in life, there needs to be a clear delineation between two types of values. The first will be those that govern their respective religious, philosophical, or moral belief traditions. These are comprehensive because they govern the whole of life. The second, however, cannot govern the whole of life. Rather, in a democracy, there must be a smaller set of values, distinctly relevant to the sphere of politics that we must agree to hold in common with others from diverse and conflicting comprehensive doctrines. These are required so we can work through the challenges arising from our differences.

The important step Rawls takes is recognizing that citizens who are not religious do not escape to a place of neutrality with respect to religion. Rather, they simply shift to other comprehensive doctrines that function exactly like religions. These doctrines continue to pose the same challenges for democracy as overt religions. Thinking adequately about religion and politics today, we argue, requires taking this first step proposed by Rawls.

Rawls recognizes that citizens from diverse comprehensive doctrines will engage in debates about how their respective belief traditions will influence the course of political life. Notice he presumes such influences will flow. What is interesting is his response to the question: How? In order to secure democratic pluralism, politics must be identified exclusively with no particular comprehensive doctrine. But this does not mean that politics cannot accept the influences from particular comprehensive doctrines. Rather, it means these influences must flow diversely through ongoing public debates in which citizens offer arguments in terms that are accessible to all. It remains that a citizen's basic justifications will appeal to personal reasons that are non-public, meaning they are distinct to her own comprehensive doctrine. But for her arguments to influence an overlapping consensus among representatives from diverse traditions, their substance must be framed in terms accessible to all. They must be fully public reasons. The lion's share of Rawls's work in *Political Liberalism*, then, is devoted to working out how these fully public reasons might be worked out.

The starting point for moving forward on religion and politics, we argue, requires Rawls's recognition that the central category for analysis is not explicit religion as institution, rather it is the comprehensive doctrine operative as ultimate or comprehensive horizon of value. What distinguishes this higher doctrine is the way it operates in consciousness to govern or influence the whole of life. What distinguishes politics, on the other hand, is its narrower, more restricted range. This distinction remains central even when influences flow to politics from comprehensive doctrines. The guard against a belief tradition operating coercively lies not in the mere fact of an institutional relation. Politics must not identify exclusively with any particular comprehensive doctrine, but this does not rule out particular forms of relations when these proliferate diversely. Rather, the guard against coercion lies in the critical analysis of benefit and harm to society that can be reasoned in terms accessible to all.

In *Political Liberalism*, Rawls devotes considerable attention to working out how this universal accessibility is to be achieved. His solution is based on an interesting philosophical device he calls "the original position under the veil of ignorance." An alternative solution offered by his colleague Jürgen Habermas is based on a discourse ethic that arises from an analysis of the social structure of discourse. Both proposals, we suggest, are worth examining. As we've made clear through these chapters, we propose the philosophical method of Bernard Lonergan.[2] What is important, however, is the starting point. We believe conversations on religion and politics get launched on a proper footing when the central category for analysis is not explicit religion as institution but comprehensive doctrine as horizon of consciousness and belief tradition. Distinctions and relations between comprehensive doctrines and politics as narrower, delimited spheres of value, then, must be worked out using methods that can secure the reasoned agreement of all.

Philosophical Method

When Lonergan wrote his book, *Method in Theology*, he chose the title to reach a particular audience at the time. What is interesting, however, is the book provides resources for a method that can be implemented equally in disciplines that would not be called "theology" today. His proposal is for a method that can be performed by women and men from diverse comprehensive doctrines engaged in working through religion-politics questions of our time. At the core of the method lies a way of understanding religion, not first as institution, but as ultimate or comprehensive horizon of consciousness.[3] His approach begins by examining religion as a pattern of ultimate questioning, rather than as an institution providing answers to such questions. This, we suggest, lends itself to the way forward in examining religion and politics today.

The philosophical method he proposes is a self-reflective empirical method that is cultivated through a regular practice of skill development.[4] The skills aim at honing and focusing attention on the operations of consciousness we employ in our daily involvements in social and political life. Our daily living brings us into meaningful involvements with others. These involvements arise, in part, from our encounter with externalities that present themselves to us. More significantly, however, they arise from our performance of operations that respond to these externalities as they are mediated to consciousness. These operations change us and they change our engagements with others. We need to understand what is involved in the performance that brings about these changes. We have been performing these operations since our earliest days of childhood. Our operations of consciousness are so familiar, they remain as obscure and as difficult to discern as the lenses of our eyes. They reside and do their work in the background, not the foreground of our consciousness. Because of the spontaneously extroverted structure of our consciousness, they seldom "appear" to us as present and operative. Yet, their performance determines our forms of involvement in social and political living. Understanding political living requires understanding this performance.

The philosophical method is difficult, but with practice it can be learned. Most important is the task of gaining entry. The initial hurdles are the most daunting because standard modes of communication in philosophy involve reading books and the method of self-appropriation cannot be learned simply by reading books. Rather, it requires practice in mobilizing a self-reflective attention to operations of consciousness while engaged in performing these same operations. This is not taught easily using standard teaching methods of philosophy. It requires a method closer to that used in learning to play musical instruments. The first step requires developing the habits of calm engagement in some sort of task of inquiry and discovery, then coupling this engagement with a second-order pattern of self-questioning that examines the operations we use in the inquiring and discovering.

What emerges from practice is a cultivated ability to identify and examine characteristics of the operations of consciousness we use in our engagements in social and political living. Most important for our purposes is the universal accessibility of the method. The method can be performed by women and men from all comprehensive doctrines because it both employs and focuses on the operations of consciousness used by all of us in our daily living. Like the methods of the natural sciences, the method may have arisen historically in a particular culture, but it can be implemented by women and men from all cultures because it involves a particular differentiation of operations that all of us employ daily.

What the method reveals is a distinction between the ultimate or comprehensive horizon of consciousness, and narrower, more particular patterns of cooperation that are operative in the spheres of family, economy, society, and politics. The method provides tools for examining these narrower spheres both descriptively and normatively. And it provides resources for exploring how higher order comprehensive doctrines can operate both positively and negatively in influencing these narrower patterns of cooperation. Because the method focuses on operations of meaning, the spheres of family, economy, society, and politics can be studied not simply as outward institutional forms but as inner-structured patterns of linkages among operations of meaning of participants. This, we argue, lends itself to the questions arising in the religion-politics conversations.

At the center of the method lies a particular operation that is most elusive – the operation of insight. Insights come very quickly, they often catch us by surprise, and they transform us from one state to another. They are difficult to observe, yet we can learn to pay attention to the "before" and "after" of insights, and we can examine the transformations they effect in our states of consciousness. Implementing the method, we observe different types of insights. Some result in new intelligibilities becoming present to us, intelligibilities that emerge as answers to questions. Others result in judgements about these answers, judgements that they do or do not respond adequately to our questions.

We discover that within and among our operations of consciousness there is an intrinsic normativity that guides us through the learning of everyday life. We can observe this normativity, we can make it explicit. We can learn to follow it more deliberately as we move our public reasoning towards objectively valid judgements of fact and value. We can apply the method to the discernment of discourse norms that govern the processes of public conversations. But we can also apply the method to the content of the issues themselves, seeking more and more adequate ways of understanding the patterns of social cooperation at work in public living. We can reflect both descriptively and normatively on these patterns, discerning the intrinsic norms operative in the demands they make upon citizens who rely on them for their living. And we can draw on the method in offering publicly accessible reasons for evaluating strategies proposed for re-shaping their future operation.

Implementing the method, we can discover a spontaneous dynamism that is operative in our consciousness that carries us from one operation to another: from questions, to insights, to questions for verification, to judgements that assemble evidence, to questions about values and actions, to judgements of value, and finally to decisions that implement values in actions. All of this can be observed by anyone choosing to learn and practice the method. We suggest that performing the method reveals a set of insights about our operations of consciousness that enables us to transpose resources from particular comprehensive doctrines into an open philosophy that can ground a way of thinking about religion and politics in democratic societies.

Exemplary Figures

Most important in pointing the way forward are exemplary figures whose actions yield results we have found reliable. We offer the example of Sargent Shriver as one such figure. Shriver's speeches reveal his attention to the spiritual experiences that renew and liberate personal relations in political life. He drew on his tradition to understand and appreciate the role of the religious gift of charity as the transformative experience of compassion in politics. Yet his appeal to tradition was not a slavish or mechanical replication of exterior forms. He turned to interiority to transpose the traditional religious categories of natural law and charity into a broader, more open method for "spiritualizing" politics. Most important, he understood how transformative spiritual experiences play a vital role in institutions that help build peace at home and abroad.

Our analysis shows how Shriver's transposition of religious resources from his Catholic tradition left its mark on the structure of the Peace Corps. Peace is not only a work accomplished in the life of an individual person motivated by religious faith. It can also be a public incarnation of the spiritual resources of this vocation. Shriver saw the Peace Corps as establishing the institutional conditions for facilitating the transformative experiences that he understood in the language of his tradition as the Divine gift of charity. Shriver knew we are open to spiritually transformative experiences that can shift us from indifference or hate to engagement and love. This, he believed, is the way the gift of charity works. And in true fidelity to the Catholic doctrine of cooperative grace, he structured the Peace Corps to do just that.

Shriver knew that building peace in worlds that are "poor, threatened, hopeless"[5] can never be achieved through military or economic force. Instead, his focus was on the experience of personal change that emerges in contexts where Peace Corps volunteers engage actively in programs of service to the welfare and dignity of others. He knew that a change of heart in host country nationals could only arise from volunteers dedicating themselves to service. He knew that personal transformation does not arise from manipulation, diplomacy, or marketing. From the very beginning, he was adamant that the Peace Corps never be allowed to become an instrument of diplomacy[6] and he built this into the core of its policies and programs.

The key element in the spirituality at the heart of the Peace Corps is the role played by transformative experience in shifting personal attitudes from past expectations of harm and recrimination to new openings for trust and confidence. As Lonergan explained, the problem with basic evil is that it cannot be fixed by the common-sense pursuit of power or justice. Rather, it requires an opening to personal transformation that arises, not from our direct efforts, but from a Divine gift of charity. Shriver's analysis of the Peace Corps reflects this recognition. But his analysis does not remain within the language of his tradition. He transposes the core insights into terms that are widely accessible. And he incorporates these insights into the structure of a public institution, the Peace Corps, that would be open to participants from all comprehensive doctrines.

Shriver and the Peace Corps provide examples of the way forward. We know from our analysis of Shriver's speeches that his work in politics and the Peace Corps was dynamized by the religious values at the heart of his Catholic tradition. Yet he was able to transpose his insights into terms more widely accessible. This, we argue, is the method in action.

This book may appear as an argument. Yet perhaps it would be better called an illustration. Shriver illustrates our proposal in action. Shriver's speeches illustrate a pattern of spiritually transformative action at work in his understanding of the Peace Corps. The central ingredient in this pattern is a dedication to the service of others that gives rise to transformative experiences that disengage present actions from past legacies of harm and recrimination. This pattern can be understood as a spirituality whose origins were in Shriver own religious vocation to public life. It was expressed originally in the language of his traditional Catholic faith – his comprehensive doctrine. But eventually this spirituality gained expression in a new language, now open to diverse audiences, reflecting a transposition to interiority that is best articulated by Lonergan's philosophical method. This pattern of transformative action is the work of a spirituality that stops cycles of harm and recrimination and begins anew the work of cooperating with transcendence to build the human good. We suggest this offers a compelling model to follow in relating religion and politics in present and future generations.

Notes

1. Religion and Politics: Doing Things Differently

1 Stossel, "The Good Works of Sargent Shriver," 3.
2 See our discussion of this issue of objectivity in Chapter 4.
3 SSPI 1963.12.11 Foreign Policy, 2.
4 SSPI 1963.12.11 Foreign Policy, 3.
5 See our discussion of these issues in Chapter 2.
6 See Komonchak, "Vatican II and the Encounter between Catholicism and Liberalism," 85–6; Gleason, "American Catholics and Liberalism, 1789–1960," 45–7.
7 Taylor, *A Secular Age.*
8 For resources on the method of interiority, see Lonergan *Method in Theology*, 3–25, 101–7, "Cognitional Structure," "Merging Horizons," and "Sacralization and Secularization." See also Byrne, *The Ethics of Discernment.*
9 SSPI 1963.01.15 Religion and Race, 2; see also SSPI 1963.06.12 Fordham, 1–2.
10 SSPI 1963.01.15 Religion and Race, 2.
11 See McCarthy, "Shriver: The Lightweight Label," 9–10; see also our discussions of Maritain's influence on Shriver in Chapters 3 and 5.
12 See, e.g., Lonergan, "The Transition from a Classicist World-View to Historical-Mindedness," "Theology in its New Context," and "Revolution in Catholic Theology."
13 See, e.g., SSPI 1955.02.09 Kenwood, 1; SSPI 1956.06.16 Veterans, 2; SSPI 1957.04.17 Leadership, 4; SSPI 1958.04.27 Men Money, 6–7; SSPI 1963.01.15 Religion and Race, 2.
14 Cited in Stossel, *Sarge*, 193–4.
15 SSPI 1963.06.12 Fordham, 3.
16 SSPI 1963.06.12 Fordham, 1 (emphasis added).
17 SSPI 1963.06.12 Fordham, 3.

18 SSPI 1964.01.28 Secret, 3.

19 SSPI 1963.10.11 Commonwealth Club, 4.

20 SSPI 1963.12.11 Foreign Policy, 3.

21 SSPI 1963.05.28 Salem, 3.

22 See, e.g., Price and Bartoli, "Spiritual Values, Sustainable Security, and Conflict Resolution"; Price, "Method in Peacemaking"; Melchin and Picard, *Transforming Conflict through Insight.*

23 Stossel, "The Good Works of Sargent Shriver," 5, and *Sarge*, 673–82.

24 Rawls, *Political Liberalism.*

25 We are not aware of another study that explores the influence of Shriver's spirituality on the design and launch of the Peace Corps. For other studies of the Peace Corps, see, e.g., Fischer, *Making Them Like Us*; Fuchs, *"Those Peculiar Americans"*; Hoffman, *All You Need is Love*; Kittler, *The Peace Corps*; Redmon, *Come As You Are*; Reeves, *The Politics of the Peace Corps and VISTA*; and Rice, *The Bold Experiment.* As noted in the "Preface," this study presents a positive assessment of Shriver's achievements. We believe that, given the importance of the issues related to religion and politics and the novel approach offered here, our focus on the positive is warranted. A variety of critical appraisals related to the Peace Corps can be found in the works cited above.

26 In "Interiority and Conflict: The Insight Approach" from Chapter 4 and "Resolving Conflicts and Building Peace: The Peace Corps and the Insight Approach" from Chapter 5, we provide an overview of core ideas of the Insight approach to conflict. The Insight approach was launched with the publication of Melchin and Picard, *Transforming Conflict through Insight* in 2008. See also, Price and Bartoli, "Spiritual Values, Sustainable Security, and Conflict Resolution."

2. The Public Faith of Sargent Shriver, 1955–1959

1 The letters to the Shriver family that arrived from all over the world following death of Shriver provide evidence of this recognition. See Sargent Shriver Peace Institute, "Letters Page."

2 Stossel, "The Good Works of Sargent Shriver," 3.

3 SSPI 1957.03.09 Public Relations, 4; see also SSPI 1956.11.19 School Boards, 5; SSPI 1957.04.17 Leadership, 4; SSPI 1957.10.13 Rutledge, 3.

4 We are grateful to Charles Hefling for help in understanding charity as a properly theological virtue, distinct from the natural virtue of justice. See Hefling, "Creation."

5 See, e.g., SSPI 1955.02.09 Kenwood, 1; SSPI 1956.06.16 Veterans, 2–3; SSPI 1957.04.17 Leadership, 4; SSPI 1958.04.27 Men Money, 6–7; SSPI 1963.01.15 Religion and Race, 2.

6 SSPI 1956.04.25 Racial Harmony, 1 (emphasis in the original).
7 See, e.g., SSPI 1957.11.18 Saints Church, 2, 3, 9; SSPI 1957.09.03 Champaign, 7; SSPI 1957.07.09 Education Future, 6; SSPI 1957.03.21 Ancient Mystery, 2; SSPI 1957.03.30 Career Conference, 6; SSPI 1958.02.11 Christians and Jews, 7; SSPI 1958.10.07 Everyone, 7; SSPI 1959.02.03 Your Brother, 8.
8 SSPI 1957.03.04 Livingston, 7.
9 SSPI 1957.03.14 Citizenship, 5.
10 See, e.g., Stossel, Sarge, 80, 231, 673–6.
11 SSPI 1956.01.16 Finance Committee, 5; SSPI 1956.02.28 Junior Association, 5; SSPI 1956.03.06 Women's Aid, 4.
12 SSPI 1957.06.09 Education America, 4; SSPI 1957.10.13 Rutledge, 4.
13 SSPI 1957.03.09 Public Relations, 4; see also SSPI 1956.11.19 School Boards, 5; SSPI 1957.04.17 Leadership, 4; SSPI 1957.10.13 Rutledge, 3.
14 SSPI 1959.06.04 Procopius, 2–4.
15 Stossel, Sarge, 675. See also Shriver's discussion of Opus Dei in SSPI 1959.06.04 Procopius, 4–5, and his reference, "to work is to pray," in SSPI 1956.10.26 Vocational Education, 3. See also Stossel's reference to Shriver's commitment to sexual fidelity, Stossel, Sarge, 41.
16 Douthat, "Sargent Shriver's Christian Politics," 2.
17 Stossel, Sarge, 9–13.
18 Stossel, Sarge, 18, 22–3.
19 Stossel, Sarge, 32, 36–7.
20 Stossel, Sarge, 40–1, 43–4, 80.
21 See, e.g., SSPI 1955.02.09 Kenwood, 1; SSPI 1956.06.16 Veterans, 2–3; SSPI 1957.04.17 Leadership, 4; SSPI 1958.04.27 Men Money, 6–7; SSPI 1963.01.15 Religion and Race, 2.
22 SSPI 1958.01.21 Big Sisters, 1–2.
23 SSPI 1958.02.07 Schoolmasters, 7.
24 SSPI 1959.06.04 Procopius, 7; see also SSPI 1958.04.27 Men Money, 7.
25 See, e.g., SSPI 1956.04.25 Racial Harmony, 4–5; SSPI 1957.03.04 Livingston, 7; SSPI 1957.03.14 Citizenship, 5; SSPI 1957.07.09 Education Future, 5–6; SSPI 1958.02.11 Christians and Jews, 6–7; SSPI 1958.10.26 Hoey Award, 4–5; SSPI 1959.02.03 Your Brother, 7–8.
26 See Komonchak, "Vatican II and the Encounter between Catholicism and Liberalism."
27 Komonchak, "Vatican II and the Encounter between Catholicism and Liberalism," 77.
28 See the excellent presentation provided by Charles Curran in American Catholic Social Ethics.
29 Stossel, Sarge, 20, 27. Stossel's account may leave readers with the impression that Commonweal was founded by Shriver and Skinner in 1929. The magazine's inaugural issue was dated November 12, 1924, and the person

regarded as behind its founding was its first editor, Michael Williams. See Bredeck, *Imperfect Apostles*, 27–33. Williams is credited with gathering a group of supporters around him to promote the magazine and to assure its survival. We can gather from Stossel's account that Hilda and Robert Shriver were active members of this group. There are indications that the magazine played a significant role in Shriver's life. Stossel speaks about the influence of Dorothy Day on Shriver during his years at Yale, Stossel, *Sarge*, 44. And he points to the influence of Jacques Maritain on Shriver, Stossel, *Sarge*, 628. See also McCarthy, "Shriver: The Lightweight Label," 9–10. Both Day and Maritain are regarded as significant contributors to *Commonweal*. See Johnson, "The Commonweal Catholic."

30 See Gleason, "American Catholics and Liberalism, 1789–1960," 45, 58, 65. Gleason points to a volume of essays collected from *Commonweal* that provides a good indication of these perspectives on religion and politics, Commonweal, *Catholicism in America*. See also the analyses throughout Bredeck, *Imperfect Apostles*.

31 Gleason, "American Catholics and Liberalism, 1789–1960," 49–50. See also the excellent discussion of these issues in Hughson, *The Believer as Citizen*.

32 This discussion is developed throughout Bredeck, *Imperfect Apostles*, and can be observed in the essays collected in Commonweal, *Catholicism in America*.

33 Gleason, "American Catholics and Liberalism, 1789–1960," 65.

34 Gleason, "American Catholics and Liberalism, 1789–1960," 64.

35 See, e.g., Bredeck, *Imperfect Apostles*, 139–60.

36 Shriver seems to have been influenced significantly by Maritain. See McCarthy, "Shriver: The Lightweight Label," 9–10; and Stossel, *Sarge*, 628. See Shriver's references to Maritain in his speeches: SSPI 1957.10.28 Teachers Union, 8; SSPI 1963.01.15 Religion and Race, 6; SSPI 1967.04.17 Yale, 1; SSPI 1972.10.11 Brave Ones, 3; SSPI 1981.09.22 Job Corps, 3; SSPI 2002.09.17 Washington and Lee, 3; SSPI 2002.11.16 Knights, 3; Shriver, *Point of the Lance*, 201. See also in SSPI 1958.02.11 Christians and Jews, 7, his reference to "a great man" in this text is to Maritain, *Ransoming the Time*, 136, reprinted in *Christianity, Democracy, and the American Ideal*, 98.

37 On Maritain and *Commonweal*, see Johnson, "The Commonweal Catholic." Reading through Shriver's speeches of the 1950s, it is not difficult to discern a resonance with core ideas of Maritain's approach to natural law and his Christian humanism as it is expressed in the volume of selected readings, *The Social and Political Philosophy of Jacques Maritain*, 155–70, particularly 166–70. Colman McCarthy recounts a meeting in which Shriver took out this book and began reading pages aloud to him. See McCarthy, "Shriver: The Lightweight Label," 10. On page 166, Maritain refers to the natural law basis for Christian humanism, and he develops his analysis of natural law on pages 28–36. The chapter on Christian humanism was published initially in

The Range of Reason, 185–99, and the chapter on natural law was published initially in *Man and the State*, 84–94.

38 Maritain presents core elements of these three sets of ideas and begins applying them to religion-politics distinctions and relations in three essays of *The Social and Political Philosophy of Jacques Maritain*, 3–9, 28–36, and 163–70. The first essay dealing with the natural-supernatural relation was published earlier in *The Person and the Common Good*, 31–44, the second on natural law appeared initially in *Man and the State*, 84–94, and the third on the theological virtue of charity is from his chapter, "Christian humanism," in *The Range of Reason*, 185–99. His positive analysis of American democracy is evident in, e.g., *Man and the State*, 182–4.

39 Shriver never ceased to believe in the reality of the supernatural and its import for the natural world of social-political life. Two dramatic examples are provided in two speeches from his years of public life after the Peace Corps, SSPI 1964.04.19 Dedication, and SSPI 1982.07.01 Dedication. For an excellent analysis of the significance of the natural-supernatural distinction for issues related to religion and politics, see the essay by Hefling, "Creation."

40 Shriver's commitment to natural law is revealed in his explicit endorsement of natural law as a basis for a Catholic ethical response to political challenges related to economic life. See SSPI 1982.11.14 Bishops Economy, 4–5. For Maritain's understanding of natural law, see Maritian, *The Social and Political Philosophy of Jacques Maritain*, 29–36. What is interesting is that as late as 1982, Shriver remained committed to the importance of a natural law approach. During the 1980s a consensus was emerging that the natural law tradition no longer provided adequate resources for this work. See, e.g., West, "The Common Good and the Participation of the Poor," 21–2, 26–9; Collins, "The Biblical Vision of the Common Good," 50; Curran, "The Common Good and Official Catholic Social Teaching," 113–17. These essays were written for a 1986 conference on the very project Shriver addressed in his November 14, 1982, speech, the American Catholic bishops' consultations on Catholic teaching and the American economy. Our argument through this book is that, while other Catholic theologians were distancing themselves from the natural law, Shriver was able to develop his own novel approach to religion and politics because he did not follow their path. Instead of giving up on a natural law framework, Shriver transposed it, in practice, in a way that is best explained in theory by Lonergan. See our discussions in Chapter 4, "Explaining What Shriver Did."

41 For evidence of Shriver's belief in the significance of the theological virtue charity, see SSPI 1957.11.18 Saints Church, 2, 3, 9; SSPI 1957.09.03 Champaign, 7; SSPI 1957.07.09 Education Future, 6; SSPI 1957.03.21 Ancient Mystery, 2; SSPI 1957.03.30 Career Conference, 6; SSPI 1958.02.11 Christians and Jews, 7; SSPI 1958.10.07 Everyone, 7; SSPI 1959.02.03 Your Brother, 8.

For texts by Maritain on charity, see Maritian, *The Social and Political Philosophy of Jacques Maritain*, 3–9, 163–70.

42 For Maritain, natural law is the basis for possible agreement on human rights among women and men from diverse traditions. See *Man and the State*, 76–107. For his discussions of the significance of his natural law approach to reason in pluralist democracies, see *The Range of Reason*, 165–84.

43 For discussions of the role of spiritual practice in enabling and liberating moral life, see Maritain, *The Range of Reason*, 108–17, 192–9.

44 In notes 29, 36, and 37 of this chapter, we provide evidence that Maritain and Dorothy Day were important influences on Shriver. The personalism of Maritian is well known. See, e.g., *The Person and the Common Good*. Curran, in *American Catholic Social Ethics*, 30–2, traces the influence of personalism on Dorothy Day and her involvement with The Catholic Worker. Hughson, in *The Believer as Citizen*, 25–7, argues for the influence of personalism on Vatican II and John Courtney Murray, and Shriver refers positively to Vatican II's endorsement of Murray in SSPI 1982.11.14 Bishops Economy, 3.

45 See Maritain, *Man and the State*, 157–65.

46 This is the title of Hughson's book on John Courtney Murray, *The Believer as Citizen*.

47 For a discussion of similarities and differences between Maritain and John Courtney Murray on various ways that religious institutions may and may not work to shape the "hearts" of citizens in American democracy, see Hughson, *The Believer as Citizen*, 59–61. Hughson's discussion includes an analysis of the personalist approach to the religion-politics relation in the work of Murray, 25–7.

48 Stossel, *Sarge*, 36–7.

49 Stossel, *Sarge*, 35.

50 It would be interesting to explore to what extent Shriver's interpretation of Maritain was influenced by his own reading of Aquinas, and how this interpretation may have pushed him beyond Maritain. See Stossel, *Sarge*, 32. In Chapter 4 we show how Shriver's work moves beyond limitations in Maritain, and we argue that Lonergan's work, while it may not have influenced Shriver directly, offers a better framework for explaining Shriver's achievements.

51 See *Everson v. Board of Education; Engel v. Vitale*, and *Wallace v. Jaffree*.

52 For an account of these decisions, see Cord, "The Nationalization of the Bill of Rights," 58–63.

53 *Cantwell v. Connecticut*, 310 US 296 (1940).

54 For a history of the Supreme Court jurisprudence before and after 1940, see Hitchcock, *The Supreme Court and Religion in American Life*.

55 For background on Justice Black, see Suitts, *Hugo Black of Alabama*.

56 *Everson v. Board of Education*, 1, 10–11.

57 *Everson v. Board of Education*, 1, 18.

58 *Everson v. Board of Education*, 1, 16.

59 *Everson v. Board of Education*, 1, 18.

60 The metaphor of the First Amendment as a "wall of separation between Church and State" is not original to Justice Black. Thomas Jefferson created the metaphor in a letter to the Danbury Baptist Association, January 1, 1802, and Chief Justice Waite later cited Jefferson and the metaphor in *Reynolds v. United States*, 98 U.S. 145, 164 (1878). Black, however, does not cite these references. The way he uses and interprets the metaphor appears to be his own.

61 As Justice Black expressed his dissent: "Here the sole question is whether New York can use its compulsory education laws to help religious sects get attendants presumably too unenthusiastic to go unless moved to do so by the pressure of this state machinery. [...] New York is manipulating its compulsory education laws to help religious sects get pupils. This is not separation but combination of Church and State." *Zorach v. Clauson*, 343 U.S. 306, 318 (1952).

62 SSPI 1957.07.09 Education Future, 5.

63 SSPI 1957.07.09 Education Future, 5.

64 SSPI 1957.07.09 Education Future, 5; see also SSPI 1957.09.03 Champaign, 5–8.

65 SSPI 1958.02.07 Schoolmasters, 6.

66 SSPI 1958.02.11 Christians and Jews, 6.

67 Stossel, *Sarge*, 29–30.

68 Stossel, *Sarge*, 47–51.

69 SSPI 1957.07.09 Education Future, 4; SSPI 1957.09.03 Champaign, 5; SSPI 1958.02.07 Schoolmasters, 5.

70 SSPI 1957.07.09 Education Future, 4–6; SSPI 1957.09.03 Champaign, 5–7; SSPI 1958.02.07 Schoolmasters, 5–7.

71 SSPI 1957.07.09 Education Future, 5–6; SSPI 1957.09.03 Champaign, 7; SSPI 1958.02.07 Schoolmasters, 7–8.

72 SSPI 1958.10.07 Everyone, 4–5.

73 SSPI 1957.07.09 Education Future, 6; SSPI 1957.09.03 Champaign, 7; SSPI 1958.02.07 Schoolmasters, 8. In three other texts, Shriver identifies this as a quote from Maritain: SSPI 2002.09.17 Washington and Lee, 3; SSPI 2002.11.16 Knights, 3; Shriver, *Point of the Lance*, 201. We have not been able to find this text in Maritain. Perhaps other scholars will. To be sure, the ideas are in line with Maritain's overall framework and perspective and another formulation could have been written by him.

74 Pius XII, *Summi pontificatus*, pars. 81, 83.

75 See the comments and resources referenced in notes 29, 36–45, 47, and 50 of this chapter, tracing Maritain's influence on Shriver.

76 SSPI 1956.04.25 Racial Harmony; SSPI 1957.11.18 Saints Church; SSPI 1958.10.26 Hoey Award; SSPI 1959.02.03 Your Brother.
77 SSPI 1957.03.14 Dunbar, 1–2; SSPI 1957.03.30 Career Conference, 6; SSPI 1958.02.06 Problems, 1; SSPI 1958.02.11 Christians and Jews, 5–7; SSPI 1958.10.07 Everyone, 7–8.
78 SSPI 1957.07.09 Education Future, 6; SSPI 1957.09.03 Champaign, 7; SSPI 1958.02.07 Schoolmasters, 7–8; SSPI 1958.10.07 Everyone, 4–5.
79 Stossel, *Sarge*, 13, 19.
80 This account of Shriver's involvement in religion and civil rights in the Chicago years is taken from Stossel, *Sarge*, 119–29.
81 Stossel, *Sarge*, 128–9.
82 See also the long lists of anti-racism projects that are itemized in Shriver's speeches: SSPI 1956.04.25 Racial Harmony, 3–4; SSPI 1957.11.18 Saints Church, 6–7; SSPI 1958.10.26 Hoey Award, 3–4; SSPI 1959.02.03 Your Brother, 4–7.
83 See SSPI 1958.10.26 Hoey Award.
84 National Catholic Welfare Conference, "Racial Discrimination and the Christian Conscience."
85 Stossel, *Sarge*, 148, 144–7.
86 Stossel, *Sarge*, 159.
87 Stossel, *Sarge*, 149.
88 Stossel, *Sarge*, 158–62.
89 Stossel, *Sarge*, 168–9.
90 Stossel, *Sarge*, 143–4.
91 Stossel, *Sarge*, 162–9.
92 Stossel, *Sarge*, 128.
93 SSPI 1956.04.25 Racial Harmony, 4; SSPI 1957.11.18 Saints Church, 9.
94 SSPI 1958.10.07 Everyone, 7–8; SSPI 1958.02.11 Christians and Jews, 5–7.
95 SSPI 1957.04.17 Leadership, 4; SSPI 1958.04.27 Men Money, 7.
96 SSPI 1955.02.09 Kenwood, 1; SSPI 1956.06.16 Veterans, 2.
97 SSPI 1958.04.27 Men Money, 6; see also 6–7.
98 SSPI 1958.10.07 Everyone, 4.
99 SSPI 1956.11.30 Mary McDowell, 4–5.

3. Shriver on Spirituality and Politics, 1961–1964

1 SSPI 1961.03.24 Youth Forum; see also, e.g., SSPI 1961.06.29 Student Education; SSPI 1961.07.24 Higher Education; SSPI 1961.09.12 Agricultural; SSPI 1961.10.13 Corn Picking; SSPI 1961.10.13 Wisconsin; SSPI 1962.02.09 Student Editors; SSPI 1963.06.09 Springfield.
2 SSPI 1961.06.04 Notre Dame, 2, 4.
3 SSPI 1961.06.07 DePaul, 4.

4 SSPI 1962.06.02 St. Louis, 1.

5 SSPI 1963.01.15 Religion and Race, 2.

6 SSPI 1963.01.15 Religion and Race, 4.

7 SSPI 1963.01.15 Religion and Race, 5.

8 SSPI 1963.01.15 Religion and Race, 2–3.

9 SSPI 1963.01.15 Religion and Race, 3.

10 SSPI 1963.02.24 Knights of Columbus, 14–15.

11 SSPI 1963.06.12 Fordham, 3.

12 SSPI 1986.09.20 Volunteers, 3; see also SSPI 1967.10.04 University of California, 3.

13 SSPI 1982.07.01 Dedication.

14 The other states were: Alabama, Arizona, Arkansas, Florida, Georgia, Idaho, Kansas, Louisiana, Maine, Mississippi, New Hampshire, New Jersey, New Mexico, North Carolina, Rhode Island, South Carolina, South Dakota, and Tennessee. See, *Abington v. Schempp*, 203.

15 *Abington v. Schempp*, 203, 208.

16 *Abington v. Schempp*, 203, 212.

17 *Abington v. Schempp*, 203, 208.

18 *Abington v. Schempp*, 203, 212.

19 *Abington v. Schempp*, 203, 222.

20 *Abington v. Schempp*, 203, 226.

21 *Abington v. Schempp*, 203, 222.

22 *Abington v. Schempp*, 203, 223–4.

23 See Wald, *Religion and Politics in the United States*, 128–9. See also two articles cited by Wald: Ellis Katz, "Patterns of Compliance with the Schempp Decision," *Journal of Public Law* 14 (1965): 396–408; and Robert Birkby, "The Supreme Court and the Bible Belt: Tennessee Reactions to the 'Schempp' Decision," *Midwest Journal of Political Science* 10 (1966): 304–19.

24 Hair, *Freedom Under Siege*, 55.

25 See discussions in Hair, *Freedom Under Siege*, and Wald, *Religion and Politics in the United States*.

26 Wald, *Religion and Politics in the United States*, 195–7. See also two articles cited by Wald: "Lobbying for Christ," *Congressional Quarterly Weekly Report* (September 6, 1980): 2627–34; and Paul Simon, *The Glass House: Politics and Morality in the Nation's Capital* (New York: Continuum, 1984), 89–90.

27 See Rawls, *Political Liberalism*, for an analysis that recognizes how religious, political, ethical, and philosophical "Comprehensive Doctrines" all function in ways that are similar to religions to provide comprehensive frameworks that inform social and political life. See also Taylor, *Sources of the Self*.

28 SSPI 1963.06.12 Fordham, 1.

29 SSPI 1963.06.12 Fordham, 1–2.

30 SSPI 1963.06.12 Fordham, 2.

31 SSPI 1963.06.12 Fordham, 2.
32 SSPI 1963.01.15 Religion and Race, 2.
33 SSPI 1963.01.15 Religion and Race, 2.
34 SSPI 1963.01.15 Religion and Race, 2–3.
35 SSPI 1963.01.15 Religion and Race, 2.
36 SSPI 1963.01.15 Religion and Race, 1.
37 SSPI 1963.01.15 Religion and Race, 1.
38 SSPI 1961.03.24 Youth Forum, 1.
39 SSPI 1961.03.24 Youth Forum, 4, 5.
40 SSPI 1961.03.24 Youth Forum, 6, 5–6.
41 SSPI 1961.03.24 Youth Forum, 5.
42 SSPI 1961.06.29 Student Education, 1, 3. See also his references to "the whole man," the "idea of human dignity," and the "creative forces" that can transform society in SSPI 1964.11.15 Einstein, 2, 4.
43 SSPI 1961.07.24 Higher Education, 3.
44 SSPI 1961.07.24 Higher Education, 5.
45 SSPI 1963.05.28 Salem, 1.
46 SSPI 1963.05.28 Salem, 3; see also SSPI 1962.03.06 Higher Education, 3–4.
47 SSPI 1963.06.09 Springfield, 4.
48 SSPI 1961.07.24 Higher Education, 3.
49 SSPI 1961.10.18 Women, 4; SSPI 1962.06.03 Kansas State, 4; SSPI 1962.06.26 Women's Clubs, 6; SSPI 1963.05.28 Salem, 1, 3; SSPI 1963.06.09 Springfield, 3.
50 SSPI 1961.07.24 Higher Education, 2.
51 SSPI 1961.07.24 Higher Education, 2–3.
52 SSPI 1961.10.18 Women, 4; SSPI 1963.05.28 Salem, 1; SSPI 1963.06.09 Springfield, 1–2.
53 SSPI 1961.10.18 Women, 4.
54 SSPI 1962.06.03 Kansas State, 2.
55 SSPI 1963.05.28 Salem, 1.
56 SSPI 1963.06.09 Springfield, 2.
57 SSPI 1963.02.24 Knights of Columbus, 3, 5, 6.
58 SSPI 1963.02.24 Knights of Columbus, 5.
59 SSPI 1963.02.24 Knights of Columbus, 5.
60 SSPI 1963.02.24 Knights of Columbus, 6.
61 SSPI 1963.01.15 Religion and Race, 1.
62 SSPI 1963.01.15 Religion and Race, 2.
63 SSPI 1963.06.12 Fordham, 3.
64 SSPI 1964.04.19 Dedication, 1–2.
65 Stossel, *Sarge*, 170.
66 Stossel, *Sarge*, 169–72, 195–6.
67 SSPI 1964.01.28 Secret, 3.

68 Cited in Stossel, *Sarge*, 193–4.
69 Shriver, *Point of the Lance*, 69.
70 SSPI 1963.10.11 Commonwealth Club, 4.
71 SSPI 1964.01.28 Secret, 3.
72 SSPI 1963.06.12 Fordham, 3.
73 SSPI 1963.06.12 Fordham, 3.

4. Explaining What Shriver Did

1 The analysis here draws on Voegelin, *The New Science of Politics*; and Hughes, *Transcendence and History*. See also Keulman, *The Balance of Consciousness*.
2 See Voegelin, *Anamnesis*, and *The New Science of Politics*; as well as Hughes, *Transcendence and History*; and Keulman, *The Balance of Consciousness*.
3 See Voegelin, *The New Science of Politics*, chaps. IV, V, and VI; and Hughes, *Transcendence and History*, chaps. 2, 4, and 7.
4 SSPI 1956.05.07 Youth Citizenship.
5 See Charles Curran's discussions of Maritain's personalism and its influence on Catholic Social Thought in *Catholic Social Teaching 1891-Present*, 35, 73, 153–4, 157.
6 Shriver seems to have been influenced significantly by Maritain. See McCarthy, "Shriver: The Lightweight Label," 9–10; and Stossel, *Sarge*, 628. See Shriver's references to Maritain in his speeches: SSPI 1957.10.28 Teachers Union, 8; SSPI 1963.01.15 Religion and Race, 6; SSPI 1967.04.17 Yale, 1; SSPI 1972.10.11 Brave Ones, 3; SSPI 1981.09.22 Job Corps, 3; SSPI 2002.09.17 Washington and Lee, 3; SSPI 2002.11.16 Knights, 3; Shriver, *Point of the Lance*, 201. See also in SSPI 1958.02.11 Christians and Jews, 7, his reference to "a great man" in this text is to Maritain, *Ransoming the Time*, 136, reprinted in *Christianity, Democracy, and the American Ideal*, 98.
7 Shriver never ceased to believe in the reality of the supernatural and its import for the natural world of social-political life. Two dramatic examples are provided in SSPI 1964.04.19 Dedication, and SSPI 1983.00.00 Dedication.
8 See Maritain, *The Social and Political Philosophy of Jacques Maritain*, 1–9, 22–7, 163–70. See also the excellent discussion in Hefling, "Creation."
9 See, e.g., Murray, *We Hold These Truths*, 175–96.
10 For another example of an analysis of politics that stresses this fact that ultimate fulfilment lies beyond history, see Metz, *Faith in History and Society*. See also the discussion in Melchin, "Reaching Toward Democracy."
11 Shriver's convictions about the relevance of natural law are evident as late as 1982. See SSPI 1982.11.14 Bishops Economy, 4. On the historical influence of natural law on international law, see Craig Reeves, "Natural Law."
12 See Maritain, *Man and the State*, 76–107. See also Ralph McInerny, "Maritain, Jacques," 563–5.

13 The influence of natural law was not limited to the Roman Catholic tradi-
    tion, it has also been influential in the Anglican Church tradition. See, e.g.,
    William Temple, *Christianity and Social Order*, 80–4.
14 Maritain, *The Social and Political Philosophy of Jacques Maritain*, 3–9, 28–36.
15 Maritain, *The Social and Political Philosophy of Jacques Maritain*, 82–4.
16 Maritain, *Man and the State*, 2–4.
17 Maritain, *The Person and the Common Good*, 38–42.
18 Maritain, *Man and the State*, 48.
19 MacInerny, "Maritain, Jacques," 563–4.
20 Maritain, *The Social and Political Philosophy of Jacques Maritain*, 45–59.
21 See Hefling, "Creation."
22 Maritain, *The Person and the Common Good*. See also the discussion by McIn-
    erny in "The Primacy of the Common Good."
23 See Maritain's November 6, 1947, UNESCO address, in *The Social and Politi-
    cal Philosophy of Jacques Maritain*, 123–36, published earlier in *The Range of
    Reason*, 172–84.
24 See Maritain, "The Pluralist Principle in Democracy," in *The Range of Reason*,
    171. See also the discussions of natural law and pluralism as related to the
    work of John Courtney Murray by Hollenbach et al., "Theology and Philoso-
    phy in Public."
25 One author whose name shows up in the speeches of the 1950s and 1960s,
    when Shriver speaks in similar ways about charity and public life, is Léon
    Bloy. See, e.g., SSPI 1958.02.11 Christians and Jews, 6; SSPI 1966.06.05 Il-
    linois Wesleyan, 4; SSPI 1966.10.12 Catholic Charities, 3; SSPI 1966.02.12
    Xavier Alumni, 6.
26 Shriver refers frequently to charity in his early speeches. See, e.g., SSPI
    1957.11.18 Saints Church, 2, 3, 9; SSPI 1957.09.03 Champaign, 7; SSPI
    1957.07.09 Education Future, 6; SSPI 1957.03.21 Ancient Mystery, 2; SSPI
    1957.03.30 Career Conference, 6; SSPI 1958.02.11 Christians and Jews, 7;
    SSPI 1958.10.07 Everyone, 7; SSPI 1959.02.03 Your Brother, 8. Shriver's
    biographer, Scott Stossel, tells us that Shriver read the work of Thomas
    Aquinas carefully during his years at Yale, and it is not difficult to discern
    the influence of ideas from Aquinas in his speeches of the 1950s and 60s.
    Maritain's work, based as it is in Aquinas, explains much of this influence.
    Yet Shriver's own reading of Aquinas would likely have played a role in
    shaping his thought and action. For a brief discussion of the primacy of the
    theological virtue of charity in Aquinas, see, e.g., Jean Porter, *The Recovery of
    Virtue*, 168–71. Another avenue of influence on Shriver regarding the theo-
    logical virtue of charity would likely have been the idea of "social charity"
    from the Encyclical of Pius XI, *Quadragesimo anno*, of May 15, 1931, particu-
    larly pars. 88–90. For a discussion of social charity in a textbook that was
    influential in American Catholic circles during the years of Shriver's early

public life, see Cronin, *Social Principles and Economic Life*, 76–80. Charles Curran refers to the influence of Cronin's text in *American Catholic Social Ethics*, 1–2.

27 The influence of the work of Bloy on Shriver seems linked to Dorothy Day and her dedication to working with the poor in the Catholic Worker. Charles Curran makes the link between Bloy and Dorothy Day in *American Catholic Social Ethics*, 130. For a portrait of Léon Bloy that explores the links between the supernatural gift of charity and his personal dedication to the poor, see Dubois, *Portrait of Léon Bloy*, 69–79, 96, 100–2.

28 See Maritain's discussions related to charity and justice in his essay, "The Conquest of Freedom," in *The Social and Political Philosophy of Jacques Maritain*, 10–27. See also discussions of insights from Lonergan related to charity and justice, in Hefling, "Creation"; and Melchin, "Charity and Justice in Economic Life."

29 See Stossel, *Sarge*, 673–84; and our discussions in Chapter 3.

30 See Noonan, "Contraception," 124–6.

31 See the critical discussions of natural law methodology in *Humanae vitae* by 20 professors of theology and philosophy at the Catholic University of America in Washington, DC, in Curran et al., *Dissent In and For the Church*, 155–95.

32 See Curran, "Natural Law," 35–45.

33 For a defence of the application of the traditional Catholic natural law ethical methodology to the issue of contraception, see Smith, *Humane Vitae*. Her analysis contains a critical appraisal of an alternative approach to natural law developed by Grisez, Finnis, Boyle, and May, 340–70.

34 See Curran, "Utilitarianism, Consequentialism, and Moral Theology," 136–9.

35 Charles Curran offers an overview of the historical process in which natural law came to reveal its limitations. See Curran, "Natural Law." Thomist theories of natural law appeal to interpretations of Aquinas's understanding of human reason. For a critical discussion of limitations in Maritain's philosophy of reason in light of Lonergan, see Murnion, "Aquinas and Maritain on the Act of Understanding."

36 See Curran, "Natural Law," 45–9, "Modern Roman Catholic Moral Theology," 390, and *The Catholic Moral Tradition Today*, 21. We argue that Lonergan's understanding of what is involved in the transposition to historical consciousness is more complex than what seems to be suggested by Curran. See our discussion in the section, "Transposing the Tradition: Diversity and Interiority," of this chapter.

37 By 1976, Charles Curran, a Catholic moral theologian who consistently remained thoughtful and respectful in his accounts of the natural law tradition, had distanced himself from the natural law and opted for an ethical

model that he called "relationality and responsibility." See "Utilitarianism, Consequentialism, and Moral Theology," 136–9.

38 Mahoney, *The Making of Moral Theology*, 103–9.

39 See, e.g., the essays in Curran and McCormick, eds., *Readings in Moral Theology No. 2: The Distinctiveness of Christian Ethics*.

40 Mahoney, *The Making of Moral Theology*, 109–12.

41 See Curran, "Modern Roman Catholic Moral Theology," 390. See also the longer analysis of the effects of Jansenism on Catholic moral theology in Mahoney, 83–96. We can observe a reaction against this tendency to devalue "the world" in liberation theology. See, e.g., Gutiérrez, *We Drink From Our Own Wells*, 1–18.

42 Taylor, *Sources of the Self*, 211–302.

43 Mahoney, *The Making of Moral Theology*, 96–102.

44 Mahoney, *The Making of Moral Theology*, 253–4.

45 Curran, *The Catholic Moral Tradition Today*, 4–10.

46 Finnis, *Fundamentals of Ethics*, 18.

47 See the discussion by Melchin, "Revisionists, Deontologists, and the Structure of Moral Understanding." See also the analysis of Finnis in *Fundamentals of Ethics*, 80–105, 126–33.

48 For an excellent critical analysis of this self-reflective method in Finnis, see Snell, "Performing Differently: Lonergan and the New Natural Law," 365–87, particularly 377–85. See also Lawrence, "Finnis on Lonergan: A Reflection."

49 Finnis, *Fundamentals of Ethics*, 50–3, 120–4.

50 Smith, *Humanae Vitae*, 355; for her arguments in support of this claim see 340–70, particularly 352–61.

51 See the arguments of Curran et al., *Dissent In and For the Church*, 155–95.

52 For an overview of some the issues in these conversations, see Hollenbach, "A Communitarian Reconstruction of Human Rights." See also Melchin, "Reaching Toward Democracy."

53 Hollenbach, "Public Theology in America." See also *Claims in Conflict*; and Hollenbach et al., "Theology and Philosophy in Public."

54 See, e.g., Hollenbach, *Nuclear Ethics*, and *Justice, Peace, & Human Rights*.

55 See, e.g., Hollenbach's conversation with Alasdair MacIntyre in "A Communitarian Reconstruction of Human Rights."

56 Rawls presents the main lines of his argument in *Political Liberalism*, xv–xlvii, 3–46, 51–4, 217–18, 225–6.

57 The argument and some key ideas of the framework of Habermas are presented in Habermas, "Three Normative Models of Democracy," 21–30, "Popular Sovereignty as Procedure," 55–60, *Moral Consciousness and Communicative Action*, 43–115, and *Between Facts and Norms*, chaps. 7–8. See also Rehg, *Insight and Solidarity*, 56–83.

58 Charles Taylor, "The Politics of Recognition," 70. Notice the similarities here with the issues arising in Hollenbach's engagement with MacIntyre in "A Communitarian Reconstruction of Human Rights."

59 Taylor, "The Politics of Recognition," 67, 70–1, 72–3. See also the discussions in *The Ethics of Authenticity*, chaps. 7–8, and *Sources of the Self*, chap. 25. For an excellent analysis of Taylor and Lonergan see Braman, *Meaning and Authenticity*.

60 Hollenbach, "Public Theology in America." See also, *The Common Good and Christian Ethics*. Taylor's argument also recalls the decades-long debate between Habermas and Gadamer. For an excellent analysis of this debate see Lawrence, "'The Modern Philosophic Differentiation of Consciousness' or What is the Enlightenment?'"

61 Hollenbach, *The Common Good and Christian Ethics*, 138.

62 Hollenbach, "A Communitarian Reconstruction of Human Rights," 129–31, 142–4.

63 Lawrence, "'The Modern Philosophic Differentiation of Consciousness' or What is the Enlightenment?'"

64 Lawrence, "'The Modern Philosophic Differentiation of Consciousness' or What is the Enlightenment?'" 240–3.

65 Lawrence, "'The Modern Philosophic Differentiation of Consciousness' or What is the Enlightenment?'" 251–64.

66 Snell, "Performing Differently: Lonergan and the New Natural Law."

67 Lawrence, "'The Modern Philosophic Differentiation of Consciousness' or What is the Enlightenment?'" 266–76; Snell, "Performing Differently: Lonergan and the New Natural Law," 369–73, 383–7.

68 Lonergan's principal study of the structure of understanding is *Insight*. Other significant philosophical works include: *Understanding and Being, Phenomenology and Logic, Philosophical and Theological Papers 1958–1964*, and *Philosophical and Theological Papers 1965–1980*. Secondary works that provide helpful introductions to Lonergan include: Byrne, *The Ethics of Discernment*; Flanagan, *Quest for Self-Knowledge*; Morelli, *Self-Possession*; Mathews, *Lonergan's Quest*; Meynell, *Introduction to the Philosophy of Bernard Lonergan*; and Melchin, *Living with Other People*. For secondary works that situate Lonergan within wider conversations in philosophy, see McCarthy, *The Crisis of Philosophy*; Fitzpatrick, *Philosophical Encounters*; Crysdale, ed., *Lonergan and Feminism*; Meynell, *Redirecting Philosophy*; and Braman, *Meaning and Authenticity*. Lonergan's principal contribution to theology is *Method in Theology*. His most explicit discussion of the relevance of his cognitional theory to the field of education and learning is *Topics in Education*. For an excellent analysis of how Lonergan provides a framework for a theory of human rights that is rooted in the transposition to interiority, see Haughey, "Responsibility for Human Rights: Contributions from Bernard Lonergan."

69 See Lonergan, "Doctrinal Pluralism," 75–6.
70 Taylor, *The Ethics of Authenticity.*
71 See, e.g., the study of personal development by Conn, *Conscience: Development and Self-Transcendence;* and the study of historical development by Hughes, *Transcendence and History.*
72 See, e.g., Haughey, "Responsibility for Human Rights: Contributions from Bernard Lonergan." See also Lonergan, "Doctrinal Pluralism," 75–6.
73 For an excellent discussion of the scale of values see Byrne, *The Ethics of Discernment,* chaps. 13 and 14.
74 See, Lonergan, *Insight,* chap. 19, *Method in Theology,* chap. 4, and *Philosophy of God and Theology.*
75 See, Lonergan, *Insight,* chap. 19, *Method in Theology,* chap. 4, and *Philosophy of God and Theology.*
76 Derek Melchin, "Insight, Learning, and Dialogue in the Transformation of Religious Conflict"; Kenneth Melchin, "Charity and Justice in Economic Life"; Melchin and Picard, *Transforming Conflict through Insight;* Picard, *Practicing Insight Mediation,* "Learning about Learning"; Picard and Jull, "Learning through Deepening Conversations"; Price, "Method in Analyzing Conflict Behavior," "Method in Peacemaking," "Explaining Human Conflict," "Practical Idealism," "Sargent Shriver, Insight Skills, and Retaliatory Violence"; Price and Bartoli, "Spiritual Values, Sustainable Security, and Conflict Resolution"; Price and Melchin, "Recovering Sargent Shriver's Vision for Poverty Law"; Price and Price, "Insight Policing and the Role of the Civilian in Police Accountability"; Megan Price, "Intentional Peace," "The Process and Partnerships behind Insight Policing,"
77 See, e.g., Alfani, Bartoli and Garofalo, "Seeking Peace through Insights"; Jull, "Aspiring to Change"; McAuley, "A Note on Mindfulness"; Melchin and Price, "Religion and Politics in the Early Public Life of Sargent Shriver"; Peddle, "Spirituality, Insight and The Sermon on the Mount"; Picard, "Lonergan's Philosophy of Insight and its Significance for Conflict"; Megan Price, "The Practical Value of Linking the Personal and the Social"; Price and Obasi, "An Insight Approach to Theatre and Artistry."
78 See, e.g., *The Lonergan Review* volumes I (2009), II (2010), III (2011), and VII (2016); and *Theoforum* volumes 43 (nos. 1–2, 2012), 45 (no. 1, 2014), and 50 (no. 2, 2020).
79 See, e.g., Lonergan, *Insight,* chapter 20.
80 Price and Bartoli, "Spiritual Values, Sustainable Security, and Conflict Resolution."
81 Derek Melchin, "Insight, Learning, and Dialogue in the Transformation of Religious Conflict."
82 Bartoli, "The Insight Approach."
83 Melchin and Picard, *Transforming Conflict,* 76–101.

84 Picard, *Practicing Insight Mediation*; Picard and Jull, "Learning through Deepening Conversations."
85 Price and Bartoli, "Spiritual Values, Sustainable Security, and Conflict Resolution," 164–9; Melchin, "Charity and Justice in Economic Life," "Insight, Conflict, and Spirituality."

5. Religion, Politics, and the Peace Corps

1 Stossel, *Sarge*, 169–72, 195–6.
2 SSPI 1964.01.28 Secret, 3.
3 SSPI 1964.01.28 Secret, 3.
4 Shriver, *Point of the Lance*, 67–80.
5 Shriver, *Point of the Lance*, 68.
6 SSPI 1965.01.25 Poverty Southwest, 2.
7 SSPI 1965.01.25 Poverty Southwest, 2.
8 SSPI 1965.01.25 Poverty Southwest, 2.
9 Stossel, *Sarge*, 198–208.
10 Stossel, *Sarge*, 200.
11 Stossel, *Sarge*, 242–4.
12 Peace Corps, "Congress OK's $59 Million for Peace Corps," 5.
13 Stossel, *Sarge*, 203–5.
14 Stossel, *Sarge*, 209–17.
15 Stossel, *Sarge*, 246–51.
16 Stossel, *Sarge*, 204–6, 218–25, 233–35, 269–73, 450–1.
17 Stossel, *Sarge*, 218–25, 233–5.
18 Stossel, *Sarge*, 270.
19 Stossel, Sarge, 450.
20 Shriver, "Memorandum to President Johnson," October 12, 1965, cited in Stossel, *Sarge*, 451.
21 Stossel, *Sarge*, 251–8.
22 Stossel, *Sarge*, 247.
23 SSPI 1963.10.11 Commonwealth Club, 4.
24 SSPI 1986.09.20 Volunteers, 6.
25 SSPI 1986.09.20 Volunteers, 6–7.
26 SSPI 1965.12.07 International Living, 2–3. For other accounts of how Peace Corps works through transformative experiences, see SSPI 1963.05.30 Roosevelt, 3; SSPI 1963.11.19 YMCA, 2–3; and Shriver, *Point of the Lance*, 202–5.
27 SSPI 1963.06.09 Springfield, 4; see also SSPI 1961.07.24 Higher Education, 2–3; and Shriver, *Point of the Lance*, 79–80.
28 Shriver, *Point of the Lance*, 89–91.
29 Shriver, *Point of the Lance*, 80.
30 SSPI 1965.01.25 Poverty Southwest, 3–4.

31 For a brief account of these events, see Doran, "General Editors' Preface," vii.
32 Lonergan, *Insight*, 711.
33 For an application of these ideas to the field of conflict resolution, see Melchin and Picard, *Transforming Conflict through Insight.*
34 See Lonergan, *Insight*, 709–25.
35 Lonergan, *Method in Theology*, 105.
36 See Lonergan, *Insight*, 719–25.
37 Lonergan, *Method in Theology*, 108–9, 119.
38 Lonergan, *Method in Theology*, 360.
39 Lonergan, *Method in Theology*, 361.
40 Lonergan, *Method in Theology*, 361.
41 SSPI 1986.09.20 Volunteers, 6.
42 SSPI 1986.09.20 Volunteers, 7.
43 SSPI 1986.09.20 Volunteers, 6.
44 Shriver, "Memorandum to President Johnson," October 12, 1965, cited in Stossel, *Sarge*, 451.
45 SSPI 1986.09.20 Volunteers, 6.
46 SSPI 1986.09.20 Volunteers, 7.
47 Stossel, *Sarge*, 203–5, 209–17, 246–51.
48 Stossel, *Sarge*, 204–6, 218–25, 233–5, 269–73, 450–1.
49 SSPI 1963.10.11 Commonwealth Club, 4; see also SSPI 1965.01.25 Poverty Southwest, 3–4.
50 SSPI 1965.12.07 International Living, 2.
51 See, e.g., Stossel, *Sarge*, 93, 212–17, 238–9, 246–51, 288–96.
52 SSPI 1965.12.07 International Living, 3.
53 Lonergan's original analysis of charity was worked out in his study of Thomas Aquinas in *Grace and Freedom*, published initially as a set of articles in *Theological Studies* in 1941–1942. His transposition via interiority was developed further in his understanding of Aquinas in *Verbum*, again published initially as a set of articles in *Theological Studies* between 1946 and 1949. See "Editors' Preface," in *Verbum*, ix-xii.
54 SSPI 1963.06.09 Springfield, 4.
55 SSPI 1965.12.07 International Living, 3.
56 SSPI 1965.01.25 Poverty Southwest, 3–4.
57 The relevant references can be found in the notes to Chapter 4, note numbers 76 and 77.
58 Melchin and Picard, *Transforming Conflict through Insight*, 76–101.
59 SSPI 1965.01.25 Poverty Southwest, 3–4. For an analysis of some of these features of the Peace Corps, see Price and Bartoli, "Spiritual Values, Sustainable Security, and Conflict Resolution."
60 SSPI 1965.12.07 International Living, 3.

61 SSPI 1963.11.19 YMCA, 2.
62 SSPI 1963.11.19 YMCA, 2.
63 SSPI 1963.11.19 YMCA, 2.
64 SSPI 1963.11.19 YMCA, 2–3.

6. The Way Forward

1 Rawls, *Political Liberalism*, 3–4.
2 Our reasoning for proposing Lonergan over Rawls and Habermas is three-fold: (i) the solution for achieving universal accessibility must be workable; (ii) it must apply to both the procedures and the substance of discourse; and (iii) it must provide resources for objective ethical judgements. The critique of Rawls's solution, we suggest, is articulated by Habermas. The original position appears attractive, but cannot be implemented adequately under the veil of ignorance. This is because the movement towards over-lapping consensus cannot be achieved by limiting or constraining under-standing and judgement. Rather it requires expanding and heightening understanding and judgement. Rawls's image of justice being blind to self-interest is misleading. The fairness of justice is not achieved by blind-ness, it is achieved by a move towards expanding horizons. For Habermas, this expansion arises in a discourse process that follows the rules set out in a discourse ethic. We agree with the critics who challenge Habermas's solu-tion. A discourse ethic alone, as much as it adds to the analysis, still remains excessively procedural. It fails to provide a method that is as applicable to the substance of discourse as it is to the procedures of discourse. This, we argue, is related to the serious difficulties raised by conservatives who call for the recognition of objective moral values. The methods of Rawls and Habermas, we argue, purchase universality by sacrificing objectivity. Loner-gan's philosophical method aims explicitly to satisfy all three criteria.
3 Lonergan, *Method in Theology*, chap. 4.
4 A good example of the method at work is provided by Patrick Byrne in *The Ethics of Discernment*.
5 SSPI 1986.09.20 Volunteers, 6–7.
6 Shriver, "Memorandum to President Johnson," October 12, 1965, cited in STOSSEL, *Sarge*, 451.

Bibliography

(All online documents accessed March 2019)

Speeches by Sargent Shriver, Online,
Sargent Shriver Peace Institute (SSPI)

SSPI 1955.02.09 Kenwood
"Speech at Kenwood and Murray Schools PTA." Kenwood School, February 9, 1955. http://www.sargentshriver.org/speech-article/speech-at-kenwood-and-murray-schools-pta

SSPI 1956.01.16 Finance Committee
"Speech to Finance Committee, City Council of Chicago." Chicago, IL, January 16, 1956. http://www.sargentshriver.org/speech-article/speech-to-finance-committee-city-council-of-chicago

SSPI 1956.02.28 Junior Association
"Speech to the Junior Association of Commerce and Industry." Chicago, IL, February 28, 1956. http://www.sargentshriver.org/speech-article/speech-to-the-junior-association-of-commerce-and-industry

SSPI 1956.03.06 Women's Aid
"Speech to Chicago Women's Aid." Chicago, IL, March 6, 1956. http://www.sargentshriver.org/speech-article/speech-to-chicago-womens-aid

SSPI 1956.04.25 Racial Harmony
"Exploring Future of Racial Harmony - Cultural Level." DePaul University, April 25, 1956. http://www.sargentshriver.org/speech-article/exploring-future-of-racial-harmony-cultural-level

SSPI 1956.05.07 Youth Citizenship
"Speech to YMCA Youth Citizenship Luncheon." Red Lacquer Room, Palmer House, May 7, 1956. http://www.sargentshriver.org/speech-article/speech-to-ymca-youth-citizenship-luncheon

SSPI 1956.06.16 Veterans

"Address to Illinois Veterans of Foreign Wars." Chicago, IL, June 16, 1956. http://www.sargentshriver.org/speech-article/address-to-illinois-veterans-of -foreign-wars

SSPI 1956.10.26 Vocational Education

"Remarks at First Vocational Education Conference of Large City Superinten- dents of Schools." Chicago, IL, October 26, 1956. http://www.sargentshriver .org/speech-article/remarks-at-first-vocational-education-conference-of-large -city-superintendents-of-schools

SSPI 1956.11.12 Education Chicago

"Education in Chicago, Today and Tomorrow." The City Club, YMCA, Farwell Hall, November 12, 1956. http://www.sargentshriver.org/speech-article /education-in-chicago-today-and-tomorrow

SSPI 1956.11.19 School Boards

"Address to the Forty-Second Annual Conference of the Illinois Association of School Boards." Chicago, IL, November 19, 1956. http://www.sargent- shriver.org/speech-article/address-to-the-forty-second-annual-conference-of- the-illinois-association-of-school-boards

SSPI 1956.11.30 Mary McDowell

"Address to The Mary McDowell Settlement House." Chicago, IL, November 30, 1956. http://www.sargentshriver.org/speech-article/address-to-the-mary -mcdowell-settlement-house

SSPI 1957.03.04 Livingston

"Address before the Livingston County Institute." Pontiac, IL, March 4, 1957. http://www.sargentshriver.org/speech-article/address-before-the-livingston -county-institute

SSPI 1957.03.09 Public Relations

"Public Relations and Public Schools." Bloomington, IL, March 9, 1957. http:// www.sargentshriver.org/speech-article/public-relations-and-public-schools

SSPI 1957.03.14 Citizenship

"Citizenship." Grand Ballroom, Sheraton Hotel, Chicago, IL, March 14, 1957. http://www.sargentshriver.org/speech-article/citizenship

SSPI 1957.03.14 Dunbar

"Address to Dunbar Vocational School." Chicago, IL, March 14, 1957. http:// www.sargentshriver.org/speech-article/address-to-dunbar-vocational-school

SSPI 1957.03.21 Ancient Mystery

"The Ancient Mystery of Guiltless Suffering." Chicago, IL, March 21, 1957. http://www.sargentshriver.org/speech-article/the-ancient-mystery-of -guiltless-suffering

SSPI 1957.03.30 Career Conference

"Career Conference Speech." Illinois Institute of Technology, March 30, 1957. http://www.sargentshriver.org/speech-article/career-conference-speech

SSPI 1957.04.17 Leadership

"Leadership in Education." Chicago Historical Society, April 17, 1957.
http://www.sargentshriver.org/speech-article/leadership-in-education
SSPI 1957.06.09 Education America
"Article Concerning Education in America." Chicago Tribune Magazine,
June 9, 1957. http://www.sargentshriver.org/speech-article/article-concern
ing-education-in-america
SSPI 1957.07.09 Education Future
"Education for the Future - A Cooperative Approach." Northwestern Univer-
sity, July 9, 1957. http://www.sargentshriver.org/speech-article/education-
for-the-future-a-cooperative-approach
SSPI 1957.09.03 Champaign
"Address to Champaign Community Schools General Staff Meeting." Cham-
paign, IL, September 03, 1957. http://www.sargentshriver.org/speech
-article/speech-at-champaign-community-schools-general-staff-meeting
SSPI 1957.10.13 Rutledge
"Dedication of Rutledge Hall, Lincolnwood School." Lincolnwood, IL, Octo-
ber 13, 1957. http://www.sargentshriver.org/speech-article/dedication-of
-rutledge-hall-lincolnwood-school
SSPI 1957.10.28 Teachers Union
"Twentieth Anniversary Birthday Greetings to the Chicago Teachers Union."
Medinah Temple, October 28, 1957. http://www.sargentshriver.org/speech
-article/twentieth-anniversary-birthday-greetings-to-the-chicago-teachers-union
SSPI 1957.11.18 Saints Church
"Remarks About Race to Saints Faith, Hope and Charity Church." Winnetka,
IL, November 18, 1957. http://www.sargentshriver.org/speech-article
/address-to-saints-faith-hope-and-charity-church
SSPI 1958.01.21 Big Sisters
"Speech to Jewish Big Sisters." Standard Club, January 21, 1958.
http://www.sargentshriver.org/speech-article/speech-to-jewish-big-sisters
SSPI 1958.02.06 Problems
"The Problems of Education in Chicago." Standard Club | February 6, 1958.
http://www.sargentshriver.org/speech-article/the-problems-of-education-in
-chicago
SSPI 1958.02.07 Schoolmasters
"Address to the Illinois Schoolmasters Club Meeting." Illinois State Normal
University, February 7, 1958. http://www.sargentshriver.org/speech-article
/address-to-the-illinois-schoolmasters-club-meeting
SSPI 1958.02.11 Christians and Jews
"Address to the Annual High School National Conference of Christians and
Jews." Kankakee, IL, February 11, 1958. http://www.sargentshriver.org
/speech-article/address-to-the-annual-high-school-national-conference-of
-christians-and-jews

SSPI 1958.04.27 Men Money
"Men, Money and Missions in the Far East." Rockford, IL, April 27, 1958.
http://www.sargentshriver.org/speech-article/men-money-and-missions-in
-the-far-east
SSPI 1958.10.07 Everyone
"Everyone Wants to Get into the Act." University of Illinois, Urbana, October
7, 1958. http://www.sargentshriver.org/speech-article/everyone-wants-to-get
-into-the-act
SSPI 1958.10.26 Hoey Award
"Presentation of the James J. Hoey Award by New York Catholic Interracial
Council." New York University, October 26, 1958. http://www.sargentshriver
.org/speech-article/presentation-of-the-james-j-joey-award-by-new-york
-catholic-interracial-council
SSPI 1959.02.03 Your Brother
". . . And Your Brother shall Live With You." Delaware, February 3, 1959.
http://www.sargentshriver.org/speech-article/and-your-brother-shall-live
-with-you
SSPI 1959.06.04 Procopius
"St. Procopius College Commencement Speech." Lisle, IL, June 4, 1959.
http://www.sargentshriver.org/speech-article/st-procopius-college
-commencement-speech
SSPI 1961.03.24 Youth Forum
"Speech to the New York Herald Tribune Youth Forum." New York, March
24, 1961. http://www.sargentshriver.org/speech-article/speech-to-the-new-
york-herald-tribune-youth-forum
SSPI 1961.06.01 Interracial
"Address to the Catholic Interracial Council." Chicago, IL, June 1, 1961.
http://www.sargentshriver.org/speech-article/address-to-the-catholic
-interracial-council
SSPI 1961.06.04 Notre Dame
"University of Notre Dame Commencement Address." South Bend, IN, June
4, 1961. http://www.sargentshriver.org/speech-article/university-of-notre-
dame-commencement-address
SSPI 1961.06.07 DePaul
"DePaul University Commencement Address." Chicago, IL, June 7, 1961.
http://www.sargentshriver.org/speech-article/depaul-university
-commencent-address
SSPI 1961.06.29 Student Education
"Speech to the Student National Education Association." Atlantic City, NJ,
June 29, 1961. http://www.sargentshriver.org/speech-article/speech-to-the
-student-national-education-association
SSPI 1961.07.24 Higher Education

"Speech at the Institute of Higher Education, Board of Education, Methodist Church." Nashville, TN, July 24, 1961. http://www.sargentshriver.org /speech-article/speech-at-the-institute-of-higher-education-board-of -education-methodist-church
SSPI 1961.09.12 Agricultural
"Speech Before the National Association of County Agricultural Agents." New York City, September 12, 1961. http://www.sargentshriver.org/speech -article/speech-before-the-national-association-of-county-agricultural-agents
SSPI 1961.10.13 Corn Picking
"Speech at the National Corn Picking Contest." Worthington, MN, October 13, 1961. http://www.sargentshriver.org/speech-article/speech-at-the-national-corn-picking-contest
SSPI 1961.10.13 Wisconsin
"Wisconsin Speech (Draft)." Wisconsin, October 13, 1961. http://www .sargentshriver.org/speech-article/wisconsin-speech-draft
SSPI 1961.10.18 Women
"Women in the Corps." New York City, October 18, 1961. http://www .sargentshriver.org/speech-article/women-in-the-corps
SSPI 1962.02.09 Student Editors
"Statement to the Student Editors of the Conference on International Affairs." New York City, February 9, 1962. http://www.sargentshriver.org/speech-arti cle/statement-to-the-student-editors-of-the-conference-on-international-affairs
SSPI 1962.03.06 Higher Education
"Speech to the 17th National Conference on Higher Education." Chicago, IL, March 6, 1962. http://www.sargentshriver.org/speech-article/speech-to -the-17th-national-conference-on-higher-education
SSPI 1962.06.02 St. Louis
"St. Louis University Commencement Speech." Kiel Auditorium, June 2, 1962. http://www.sargentshriver.org/speech-article/st-louis-university -commencement-speech
SSPI 1962.06.03 Kansas State
"Kansas State University Commencement Address." Manhattan, KS, June 3, 1962. http://www.sargentshriver.org/speech-article/kansas-state-university -commencement-address
SSPI 1962.06.26 Women's Clubs
"Address to the 71st Annual Convention of Women's Clubs." Washington, DC, June 26, 1962. http://www.sargentshriver.org/speech-article/address-to -the-71st-annual-convention-of-womens-clubs
SSPI 1963.01.15 Religion and Race
"Speech to the National Conference on Religion and Race." Chicago, IL, January 15, 1963. http://www.sargentshriver.org/speech-article/speech-to-the-national-conference-on-religion-and-race

SSPI 1963.02.16 Georgetown
  "Speech at Georgetown University." Washington DC, February 16, 1963.
  http://www.sargentshriver.org/speech-article/speech-at-georgetown-university
SSPI 1963.02.24 Knights of Columbus
  "Knights of Columbus." Chicago IL, February 24, 1963. http://www.sargentshriver.
  org/speech-article/address-to-the-knights-of-columbus-in-1963
SSPI 1963.05.28 Salem
  "Address to Salem College." Salem WV, May 28, 1963. http://www.sargent
  shriver.org/speech-article/address-to-salem-college
SSPI 1963.05.30 Roosevelt
  "Speech at Eleanor Roosevelt Memorial Service." Hyde Park, NY, May 30, 1963.
  http://www.sargentshriver.org/speech-article/speech-at-eleanor-roosevelt
  -memorial-service
SSPI 1963.06.09 Springfield
  "Springfield College Commencement Address." Springfield MA, June 9,
  1963. http://www.sargentshriver.org/speech-article/springfield-college
  -commencement-address
SSPI 1963.06.12 Fordham
  "The Meeting of Church and State (Fordham Commencement Address)."
  New York City, June 12, 1963. http://www.sargentshriver.org/speech-article/
  the-meeting-of-church-and-state-fordham-commencement-address
SSPI 1963.08.27 Student Association
  "Address to the National Student Association." Bloomington, IN, August 27,
  1963. http://www.sargentshriver.org/speech-article/address-to-the-national
  -student-association
SSPI 1963.10.11 Commonwealth Club
  "Speech Before the Commonwealth Club of California." San Francisco, CA,
  October 11, 1963. http://www.sargentshriver.org/speech-article/speech
  -before-the-commonwealth-club-of-california
SSPI 1963.10.28 Hadassah
  "Address to the Hadassah Convention." Washington, DC, October 28, 1963.
  http://www.sargentshriver.org/speech-article/growth-of-an-international
  -movement
SSPI 1963.11.19 YMCA
  "Address at the Annual Dinner of the YMCA of Greater New York." New York
  City, November 19, 1963. http://www.sargentshriver.org/speech-article
  /address-at-the-annual-dinner-of-the-ymca-of-greater-new-york
SSPI 1963.12.11 Foreign Policy
  "Address to the Foreign Policy Association." New York City, December 11,
  1963. http://www.sargentshriver.org/speech-article/address-to-the-foreign
  -policy-association
SSPI 1964.01.28 Secret

"The Secret of Your Greatness." Bangkok, Thailand, January 28, 1964.
  http://www.sargentshriver.org/speech-article/the-secret-of-your-greatness
SSPI 1964.04.19 Dedication
  "Dedication of the Vatican Pavilion at the New York World's Fair." New York
  City, April 19, 1964. http://www.sargentshriver.org/speeches/address-by
  -sargent-shriver-opening-of-the-vatican-exhibit
SSPI 1964.11.15 Einstein
  "Address by Sargent Shriver at the Albert Einstein School of Medicine." New
  York City, November 15, 1964. http://www.sargentshriver.org/speech-article/
  address-by-sargent-shriver-at-the-albert-einstein-school-of-medicine
SSPI 1965.01.25 Poverty Southwest
  "Address to the National Conference on Poverty in the Southwest." Tucson,
  AZ, January 25, 1965. http://www.sargentshriver.org/speech-article/address
  -to-the-national-conference-on-poverty-in-the-southwest
SSPI 1965.12.07 International Living
  "Address to the Dinner of the Experiment in International Living." New York
  City, December 7, 1965. http://www.sargentshriver.org/speech-article
  /address-to-the-dinner-of-the-experiment-in-international-living
SSPI 1966.02.12 Xavier Alumni
  "Address at the Xavier Alumni Association Diamond Jubilee Banquet." New
  Orleans, LA, February 12, 1966. http://www.sargentshriver.org/speech-arti
  cle/address-at-the-xavier-alumni-association-diamond-jubilee-banquet
SSPI 1966.06.05 Illinois Wesleyan
  "Commencement Address at Illinois Wesleyan University." Bloomington, IL,
  June 5, 1966. http://www.sargentshriver.org/speech-article/commence
  ment-address-at-illinois-wesleyan-university
SSPI 1966.10.12 Catholic Charities
  "Address at the National Conference of Catholic Charities Annual Conven-
  tion." New Orleans, LA, October 12, 1966. http://www.sargentshriver.org/
  speech-article/address-at-the-national-conference-of-catholic-charities
  -annual-convention
SSPI 1967.04.17 Yale
  "Address before the 89th Annual Yale Daily News Banquet." New Haven, CT,
  April 17, 1967. http://www.sargentshriver.org/speech-article/address-before
  -the-89th-annual-yale-daily-news-banquet
SSPI 1967.10.04 University of California
  "Address at the University of California." Berkeley, CA, October 4, 1967.
  http://www.sargentshriver.org/speech-article/address-at-the-university
  -of-california
SSPI 1972.10.11 Brave Ones
  "Where Have All the Brave Ones Gone?" October 11, 1972. http://www
  .sargentshriver.org/speech-article/where-have-all-the-brave-ones-gone

SSPI 1981.09.22 Job Corps
"Address at the National Job Corps Competition Expo Lunch." Washington, DC, September 22, 1981. http://www.sargentshriver.org/speech-article/address-at-the-national-job-corps-competition-expo-lunch

SSPI 1982.07.01 Dedication
"Dedication for the Catholic Bishops' Pastoral Letter on War and Peace." Washington, DC, July 1, 1982. http://www.sargentshriver.org/speech-article/dedication-for-the-catholic-bishops-pastoral-letter-on-war-and-peace

SSPI 1982.11.14 Bishops Economy
"Address to the National Conference of Catholic Bishops Committee on Catholic Teaching and the American Economy." Washington, DC, November 14, 1982. http://www.sargentshriver.org/speech-article/address-to-the-national-conference-of-catholic-bishops-committee-on-catholic-teaching-and-the-american-economy

SSPI 1986.09.20 Volunteers
"Speech at the National Conference of Returned Peace Corps Volunteers and Staff." Washington, DC, September 20, 1986. http://www.sargentshriver.org/speech-article/speech-at-the-national-conference-of-returned-peace-corps-volunteers-and-staff

SSPI 2002.09.17 Washington and Lee
"Speech at Washington and Lee University." Lexington, VA, September 17, 2002. http://www.sargentshriver.org/speech-article/speech-at-washington-and-lee-university

SSPI 2002.11.16 Knights
"Address to the Knights of St. Gregory." Hartford, CT, November 16, 2002. http://www.sargentshriver.org/speech-article/address-to-the-knights-of-st-gregory

US Supreme Court Cases

Everson v. Board of Education of the Township of Ewing, 330 U.S. 1 (1947).
Cantwell v. Connecticut, 310 US 296 (1940).
Zorach v. Clauson, 343 U.S. 306, 318 (1952).
Engel v. Vitale, 370 U.S. 421 (1962).
School District of Abington Township, Pennsylvania v. Schempp, 374 U.S. 203 (1963).
Wallace v. Jaffree, 472 U.S. 38 (1985).
McCreary County, Kentucky v. American Civil Liberties Union of Kentucky, 545 U.S. 844 (2005).

Books, Articles, and Other Resources

Alfani, Roger, Andrea Bartoli, and Mauro Garofalo. "Seeking Peace through Insights: The Community of Sant'Egidio in the Central African Republic." *Theoforum* 50 (no. 2, 2020): 207–21.

Bartoli, Andrea. "The Insight Approach: Applications to Violence and Geno-
cide." In *Practicing Insight Mediation*, by Cheryl Picard, 159–63. Toronto:
University of Toronto Press, 2016.

Braman, Brian. *Meaning and Authenticity*. Toronto: University of Toronto Press, 2008.

Bredeck, Martin J. *Imperfect Apostles*. New York: Garland Publishing, 1988.

Byrne, Patrick. *The Ethics of Discernment: Lonergan's Foundations for Ethics*. Toronto:
University of Toronto Press, 2016.

Childress, James. "Conscientious Objection." In *The Westminster Dictionary of
Christian Ethics*, eds. James Childress and John Macquarrie, 118–20. Philadelphia: Westminster Press, 1986.

Childress, James, and John Macquarrie, eds. *The Westminster Dictionary of Christian Ethics*. Philadelphia: Westminster Press, 1986.

Collins, John. "The Biblical Vision of the Common Good." In *The Common Good
and US Capitalism*, eds. Oliver Williams and John Houck, 50–69. Lanham,
MD: University Press of America, 1987.

Commonweal. *Catholicism in America*. New York: Harcourt, Brace and Company,
1954.

Conn, Walter. *Conscience: Development, and Self-Transcendence*. Birmingham, AL:
Religious Education Press, 1981.

Cord, Robert. "The Nationalization of the Bill of Rights." In *The Supreme Court
and the Criminal Process*, eds. Peter Lewis and Kenneth Peoples, 58–63. Philadelphia: W.B. Saunders, 1978.

Cronin, John. *Social Principles and Economic Life*. Milwaukee: Bruce Publishing
Company, 1959.

Crysdale, Cynthia, ed. *Lonergan and Feminism*. Toronto: University of Toronto
Press, 1994.

Curran, Charles. *American Catholic Social Ethics*. Notre Dame: University of Notre
Dame Press, 1982.

–. *The Catholic Moral Tradition Today*. Washington: Georgetown University
Press, 1999.

–. *Catholic Social Teaching 1891-Present*. Washington, DC: Georgetown University
Press, 2002.

–. "The Common Good and Official Catholic Social Teaching." In *The Common
Good and U.S. Capitalism*, eds. Oliver Williams and John Houck, 111–29. Lanham, MD: University Press of America, 1987.

–. "Modern Roman Catholic Moral Theology." In *The Westminster Dictionary of
Christian Ethics*, eds. James Childress and John Macquarrie, 388–93. Philadelphia: Westminster Press, 1986.

–. "Natural Law." In *Themes in Fundamental Moral Theology*, 27–80. Notre Dame:
University of Notre Dame Press, 1977.

–. "Utilitarianism, Consequentialism, and Moral Theology." In *Themes in
Fundamental Moral Theology*, 121–44. Notre Dame: University of Notre Dame
Press, 1977.

Curran, Charles, Robert Hunt, and the "Subject Professors," with John Hunt and Terrence Connelly. *Dissent* In *and* For *the Church: Theologians and Humanae Vitae*. New York: Sheed & Ward, 1969.

Curran, Charles, and Richard McCormick, eds. *Readings in Moral Theology No. 2: The Distinctiveness of Christian Ethics*. New York: Paulist Press, 1980.

Doran, Robert. "General Editors' Preface." In Bernard Lonergan, *Early Works on Theological Method 3*, eds. Robert Doran and Daniel Monsour, trans. Michael Shields, vii-viii. Vol. 24 of Collected Works of Bernard Lonergan. Toronto: University of Toronto Press, 2013.

Douglass, R. Bruce, and David Hollenbach, eds. *Catholicism and Liberalism*. Cambridge, UK: Cambridge University Press, 1994.

Douthat, Ross. "Sargent Shriver's Christian Politics." *The New York Times* (Jan. 20, 2011). https://douthat.blogs.nytimes.com/2011/01/20/sargent-shrivers -christian-politics/

Dubois, E.T. *Portrait of Léon Bloy*. London: Sheed and Ward, 1950.

Finnis, John. *Fundamentals of Ethics*. Washington: Georgetown University Press, 1983.

Fischer, Fritz. *Making Them Like Us: Peace Corps Volunteers in the 1960s*. Washington, DC: Smithsonian Institution Press, 1998.

Fitzpatrick, Joseph. *Philosophical Encounters: Lonergan and the Analytic Tradition*. Toronto: University of Toronto Press, 2005.

Flanagan, Joseph. *Quest for Self-Knowledge*. Toronto: University of Toronto Press, 1997.

Fuchs, Lawrence H. *"Those Peculiar Americans": The Peace Corps and the American National Character*. New York: Meredith Press, 1967.

Gleason, Philip. "American Catholics and Liberalism, 1789–1960." In *Catholicism and Liberalism*, eds. R. Bruce Douglass and David Hollenbach, 45–75. Cambridge, UK: Cambridge University Press, 1994.

Gutiérrez, Gustavo. *We Drink from Our Own Wells*. Trans. Matthew O'Connell. Maryknoll, NY: Orbis Books, 1985.

Habermas, Jürgen. *Between Facts and Norms*. Trans. William Rehg. Cambridge, MA: M.I.T. Press, 1996 orig. 1992].

–. *Moral Consciousness and Communicative Action*. Trans. C. Lenhardt and S. Weber Nicholsen. Cambridge, MA: M.I.T. Press, 1990 [orig. 1983].

–. "Popular Sovereignty as Procedure." Trans. William Rehg. In *Deliberative Democracy*, eds. James Bohman and William Rehg, 35–65. Cambridge, MA.: The MIT Press, 1997.

–. "Three Normative Models of Democracy." In *Democracy and Difference*, ed. Seyla Benhabib, 21–30. Princeton: Princeton University Press, 1996.

Hair, Madalyn. *Freedom Under Siege*. Los Angeles: Tarcher, 1974.

Haughey, John. "Responsibility for Human Rights: Contributions from Bernard Lonergan." *Theological Studies* 63 (2002): 764–85.

Healey, Robert. "Thomas Jefferson's 'Wall': Absolute or Serpentine?" In *Equal Separation: Understanding the Religion Clauses of the First Amendment*, ed. Paul Weber, 123–48. New York: Greenwood Press, 1990.

Hefling, Charles. "Creation." In *The New Dictionary of Catholic Social Thought*, eds. Judith Dwyer and Elizabeth Montgomery, 249–54. Collegeville, MN: Liturgical Press, 1994.

Hitchcock, James. *The Supreme Court and Religion in American Life.* Princeton: Princeton University Press, 2004.

Hoffman, Elizabeth Cobbs. *All You Need is Love: The Peace Corps and the Spirit of the 1960s.* Cambridge, MA: Harvard University Press, 1998.

Hollenbach, David. *Claims in Conflict.* New York: Paulist Press, 1979.

–. *The Common Good and Christian Ethics.* Cambridge: Cambridge University Press, 2002.

–. "A Communitarian Reconstruction of Human Rights: Contributions from Catholic Tradition." In *Catholicism and Liberalism*, eds. R. Bruce Douglass and David Hollenbach, 127–50. Cambridge, UK: Cambridge University Press, 1994.

–. *Justice, Peace, and Human Rights.* New York: Crossroad, 1988.

–. *Nuclear Ethics.* New York: Paulist Press, 1983.

–. "Public Theology in America: Some Questions for Catholicism after John Courtney-Murray." *Theological Studies* 37 (1976): 290–303.

Hollenbach, David, Robin Lovin, John Coleman, and J. Bryan Hehir. "Theology and Philosophy in Public: A Symposium on John Courtney Murray's Unfinished Agenda." *Theological Studies* 40 (1979): 700–15.

Hughes, Glenn. *Transcendence and History.* Columbia, MO: University of Missouri Press, 2003.

Hughson, Thomas. *The Believer as Citizen.* New York: Paulist Press, 1993.

Johnson, Luke Timothy. "The Commonweal Catholic: It Started with Origen." *Commonweal* (Oct. 24, 2014): 16–19.

Jull, Marnie. "Aspiring to Change: Insight, Conflict and Change-Making." *Theoforum* 50 (no. 2, 2020): 223–40.

Keulman, Kenneth. *The Balance of Consciousness.* University Park, PA: Pennsylvania State University Press, 1990.

Kittler, Glenn. *The Peace Corps.* New York: Paperback Library, 1963.

Komonchak, Joseph. "Vatican II and the Encounter between Catholicism and Liberalism." In *Catholicism and Liberalism*, eds. R. Bruce Douglass and David Hollenbach, 76–99. Cambridge, UK: Cambridge University Press, 1994.

Lawrence, Frederick. "Finnis on Lonergan: A Reflection." *Villanova Law Review* 57 (2012): 849–72.

–. "'The Modern Philosophic Differentiation of Consciousness' or What is the Enlightenment?" In *Lonergan Workshop* 2, ed. Fred Lawrence, 231–79. Chico, CA: Scholars Press, 1981.

Lonergan, Bernard. "Cognitional Structure." In *Collection*, eds. Frederick Crowe
and Robert Doran, 205–21. Vol. 4 of Collected Works of Bernard Lonergan.
Toronto: University of Toronto Press, 1993 [orig. 1967].

–. *Collection.* Eds. Frederick Crowe and Robert Doran. Vol. 4 of Collected Works
of Bernard Lonergan. Toronto: University of Toronto Press, 1993 [orig.
1967].

–. "Doctrinal Pluralism." In *Philosophical and Theological Papers 1965–1980*, eds.
Robert Croken and Robert Doran, 70–104. Vol. 17 of Collected Works of
Bernard Lonergan. Toronto: University of Toronto Press, 2004.

–. *Grace and Freedom.* Eds. Frederick Crowe and Robert Doran. Vol. 1 of Collected Works of Bernard Lonergan. Toronto: University of Toronto Press,
2000 [orig. 1971].

–. *Insight: A Study of Human Understanding.* Eds. Frederick Crowe and Robert
Doran. Vol. 3 of Collected Works of Bernard Lonergan. Toronto: University
of Toronto Press, 1992 [orig. 1957].

–. "Merging Horizons: System, Common Sense, Scholarship." In *Philosophical
and Theological Papers 1965–1980*, eds. Robert Croken and Robert Doran,
49–69. Vol. 17 of Collected Works of Bernard Lonergan. Toronto: University
of Toronto Press, 2004.

–. *Method in Theology.* Toronto: University of Toronto Press, 1990 [orig. 1972].

–. *Phenomenology and Logic.* Ed. Philip McShane. Vol. 18 of Collected Works of
Bernard Lonergan. Toronto: University of Toronto Press, 2001.

–. *Philosophical and Theological Papers 1958–1964.* Eds. Robert Croken, Frederick
Crowe, and Robert Doran. Vol. 6 of Collected Works of Bernard Lonergan.
Toronto: University of Toronto Press, 1996.

–. *Philosophical and Theological Papers 1965–1980.* Eds. Robert Croken and
Robert Doran. Vol. 17 of Collected Works of Bernard Lonergan. Toronto:
University of Toronto Press, 2004.

–. *Philosophy of God, and Theology.* London: Darton, Longman & Todd, 1973.
Republished in *Philosophical and Theological Papers 1965–1980*, eds. Robert
Croken and Robert Doran, 159–218. Vol. 17 of Collected Works of Bernard
Lonergan. Toronto: University of Toronto Press, 2004.

–. "Revolution in Catholic Theology." In *A Second Collection*, eds. William Ryan
and Bernard Tyrrell, 231–8. Toronto: University of Toronto Press, 1996 [orig.
1974].

–. "Sacralization and Secularization." In *Philosophical and Theological Papers
1965–1980*, eds. Robert Croken and Robert Doran, 259–81. Vol. 17 of Collected Works of Bernard Lonergan. Toronto: University of Toronto Press,
2004 [orig. 1974].

–. *A Second Collection.* Eds. William Ryan and Bernard Tyrrell. Toronto: University of Toronto Press, 1996 [orig. 1974].

–. "Theology in its New Context." In *A Second Collection*, eds. William Ryan and Bernard Tyrrell, 55–67. Toronto: University of Toronto Press, 1996 [orig. 1974].

–. *Topics in Education*. Ed. Frederick Crowe. Vol. 10 of Collected Works of Bernard Lonergan. Toronto: University of Toronto Press, 1993.

–. "The Transition from a Classicist World-View to Historical-Mindedness." In *A Second Collection*, eds. William Ryan and Bernard Tyrrell, 1–10. Toronto: University of Toronto Press, 1996 [orig. 1974].

–. *Understanding and Being*. Eds. Frederick Crowe, Robert Doran, Thomas Daly, Elizabeth Morelli, and Mark Morelli. Vol. 5 of Collected Works of Bernard Lonergan. Toronto: University of Toronto Press, 1990 [orig. 1980].

–. *Verbum: Word and Idea in Aquinas*. Eds. Frederick Crowe and Robert Doran. Vol. 2 of Collected Works of Bernard Lonergan. Toronto: University of Toronto Press, 1997 [orig. 1967].

The Lonergan Review I (no. 1, 2009), II (no. 1, 2010), III (no. 1, 2011), VII (no. 1, 2016).

Mahoney, John. *The Making of Moral Theology*. Oxford: Clarendon Press, 1987.

Maritain, Jacques. *Christianity, Democracy, and the American Ideal: A Jacques Maritain Reader*. Ed. James Kelly. Manchester, NH: Sophia Institute Press, 2004.

–. *Man and the State*. Chicago: University of Chicago Press, 1951.

–. *The Person and the Common Good*. Trans. John Fitzgerald. Notre Dame: University of Notre Dame Press, 1985 [orig. 1946].

–. *The Range of Reason*. London: Geoffrey Bles, 1953.

–. *Ransoming the Time*. New York: Charles Scribner's Sons, 1941.

–. *The Social and Political Philosophy of Jacques Maritain*. Eds. Joseph Evans and Leo Ward. Notre Dame: University of Notre Dame Press, 1976.

Mathews, William. *Lonergan's Quest*. Toronto: University of Toronto Press, 2005.

McAuley, Thomas. "A Note on Popularized Mindfulness, Mindfulness in Thich Nhat Hahn, and Mindful Appropriation of the Cognitive-Existential Operations of Consciousness According to Bernard Lonergan." *Theoforum* 50 (no. 2, 2020): 323–36.

McCarthy, Colman. "Shriver: The Lightweight Label." *The Washington Monthly* 8 (June 1976): 4–10. http://www.unz.org/Pub/WashingtonMonthly-1976 jun-00004

McCarthy, Michael. *The Crisis of Philosophy*. Albany: State University of New York Press, 1989.

McInerny, Ralph. "Maritain, Jacques." In *The New Dictionary of Catholic Social Thought*, eds. Judith Dwyer and Elizabeth Montgomery, 563–5. Collegeville, MN: Liturgical Press, 1994.

–. "The Primacy of the Common Good." In *The Common Good and U.S. Capitalism*, eds. Oliver Williams and John Houck, 70–83. Lanham, MD: University Press of America, 1987.

Melchin, Derek. "Insight, Learning, and Dialogue in the Transformation of Religious Conflict: Applications from the Work of Bernard Lonergan." PhD diss., McGill University, 2008.

Melchin, Kenneth. "Charity and Justice in Economic Life." *Theoforum* 43 (2012): 135–52.

–. "Insight, Conflict, and Spirituality." In *Practicing Insight Mediation*, by Cheryl Picard, 155–9. Toronto: University of Toronto Press, 2016.

–. *Living with Other People.* Ottawa: Novalis; Collegeville, MN.: Liturgical Press, 1998.

–. "Reaching Toward Democracy: Theology and Theory When Talk Turns to War." *Catholic Theological Society of America, Proceedings* 58 (2003):41–59.

–. "Revisionists, Deontologists, and the Structure of Moral Understanding." *Theological Studies* 51 (1990): 389–416.

Melchin, Kenneth, and Cheryl Picard. *Transforming Conflict Through Insight.* Toronto: University of Toronto Press, 2008.

Melchin, Kenneth, and James Price. "Religion and Politics in the Early Public Life of Sargent Shriver." *Theoforum* 50 (no. 2, 2020): 337–66.

Metz, Johannes Baptist. *Faith in History and Society.* Trans. David Smith. New York: Seabury, 1980.

Meynell, Hugo. *Introduction to the Philosophy of Bernard Lonergan.* 2nd ed. Toronto: University of Toronto Press, 1991.

–. *Redirecting Philosophy: Reflections on the Nature of Knowledge from Plato to Lonergan.* Toronto: University of Toronto Press, 1998).

Morelli, Mark D. *Self-Possession: Being at Home in Conscious Performance.* Second edition. Los Angeles: Encanto Editions, 2019.

Murnion, William. "Aquinas and Maritain on the Act of Understanding." *The Lonergan Review* IV (2013): 54–82.

Murray, John Courtney. *We Hold These Truths.* Kansas City, MO: Sheed and Ward, 1988 [orig. 1960].

National Catholic Welfare Conference. "Racial Discrimination and the Christian Conscience." American Bishops Statement on Racism. Washington, DC, 1958. http://cuomeka.wrlc.org/exhibits/show/the-catholic-church –bishops–/documents/-racial-discrimination-and-the

Noonan, John. "Contraception." In *The Westminster Dictionary of Christian Ethics*, eds. James Childress and John Macquarrie, 124–6. Philadelphia: Westminster Press, 1986.

Peace Corps. "Congress OK's $59 Million for Peace Corps." *Peace Corps Volunteer* 1 (no. 1 November 1962): 5. http://peacecorpsonline.org/historyofthe peacecorps/primarysources/19621101%20Volunteer_Nov.pdf

Peddle, David. "Spirituality, Insight and the Sermon on the Mount: On the Saying 'Judgeth not lest ye be judged'." *Theoforum* 50 (no. 2, 2020): 281–321.

Picard, Cheryl. "Learning about Learning: The Value of 'Insight'." *Conflict Resolution Quarterly* 20 (2003): 477–84.

–. "Lonergan's Philosophy of Insight and its Significance for Conflict." *Theoforum* 50 (no. 2, 2020): 193–206.

–. *Practicing Insight Mediation.* Toronto: University of Toronto Press, 2016.

Picard, Cheryl, and Marnie Jull. "Learning Through Deepening Conversations: A Key Strategy of Insight Mediation." *Conflict Resolution Quarterly* 29 (2011): 151–76.

Picard, Cheryl, and Kenneth Melchin. "Insight Mediation: A Learning-Centered Mediation Model." *Negotiation Journal* 23 (2007): 35–53.

Pius XI, Pope. *Quadragesimo anno.* Encyclical of Pope Pius XI on Reconstruction of the Social Order. May 15, 1931. http://w2.vatican.va/content/pius-xi/en /encyclicals/documents/hf_p-xi_enc_19310515_quadragesimo-anno.html

Pius XII, Pope. *Summi pontificatus.* Encyclical of Pope Pius XII on the Unity of Human Society. October 20, 1939. http://w2.vatican.va/content/pius-xi i/en/encyclicals/documents/hf_p-xii_enc_20101939_summi-pontificatus.html

Porter, Jean. *The Recovery of Virtue.* Louisville, KY: Westminster/John Knox Press, 1990.

Price, Jamie. "Method in Analyzing Conflict Behavior: The Insight Approach." *Revista de Mediación* 11 (no. 1, 2018): 1–9.

–. "Method in Peacemaking." In *Peacemaking: From Practice to Theory,* vol. 2, eds. Susan Allen Nan, Zachariah Cherian Mampilly, and Andrea Bartoli, 610–21. Santa Barbara, CA: 2012.

–. "Explaining Human Conflict: Human Needs Theory and the Insight Approach." In *Conflict Resolution and Human Needs,* eds. Kevin Avruch and Christopher Mitchell, 108–23. London: Routledge, 2013.

–. "Practical Idealism: How Sargent Shriver Built the Peace Corps." *Commonweal* (Feb. 10, 2012): 18–21.

–. "Sargent Shriver, Insight Skills, and Retaliatory Violence." In *Practicing Insight Mediation,* by Cheryl Picard, 149–55. Toronto: University of Toronto Press, 2016.

Price, Jamie, and Andrea Bartoli. "Spiritual Values, Sustainable Security, and Conflict Resolution." In *The Routledge Handbook of Religion and Security,* eds. Chris Seiple, Dennis Hoover, and Pauletta Otis, 160–70. London: Routledge, 2013.

Price, Jamie, and Kenneth Melchin. "Recovering Sargent Shriver's Vision for Poverty Law: The Illinois Familycare Campaign and the Insight Approach to Conflict Resolution and Collaboration." *Clearinghouse Review* 43 (January–February 2010): 468–78.

Price, Jamie, and Megan Price. "Insight Policing and the Role of the Civilian in Police Accountability." *Clearinghouse Review* (August 2015): 1–8.

Price, Megan. "Intentional Peace: The Role of Human Consciousness in the Emergence of Peace and Conflict." In *Exploring Spirituality, Emergent Creativity, and Reconciliation*, ed. Gloria Neufeld Redekop, 267–82. Lanham, MD: Lexington Books, 2019.

–. "The Practical Value of Linking the Personal and the Social in Efforts to Change Complex Social Conflict." *Theoforum* 50 (no. 2, 2020): 241–58.

–. "The Process and Partnerships behind Insight Policing." *Criminal Justice Policy Review* 27 (no. 5, 2016): 553–67.

Price, Vieve Radha, and Chukwuma Obasi. "An Insight Approach to Theatre and Artistry: A Journey of Discovery." *Theoforum* 50 (no. 2, 2020): 259–79.

Rawls, John. *A Theory of Justice*. Cambridge, MA: Harvard University Press, 1971.

–. *Political Liberalism*. New York: Columbia University Press, 1996.

Redmon, Coates. *Come As You Are: The Peace Corps Story*. San Diego: Harcourt Brace Jovanovich, Publishers, 1986.

Reeves, Craig. "Natural Law." *Oxford Bibliographies*. http://www.oxfordbiblio graphies.com/view/document/obo-9780199796953/obo-9780199796953 -0024.xml

Reeves, T. Zane. *The Politics of the Peace Corps and VISTA*. Tuscaloosa: University of Alabama Press, 1988.

Rehg, William. *Insight and Solidarity*. Berkeley: University of California Press, 1997.

Rice, Gerard T. *The Bold Experiment: JFK's Peace Corps*. Notre Dame: University of Notre Dame Press, 1985.

Sargent Shriver Peace Institute. "Letters Page." http://www.sargentshriver.org /letters

Shriver, Sargent. *Point of the Lance*. New York: Harper & Row, 1964.

Smith, Janet. *Humane Vitae: A Generation Later*. Washington: The Catholic University of America Press, 1991.

Snell, R. J. "Performing Differently: Lonergan and the New Natural Law." In *Lonergan Workshop* 25, ed. Fred Lawrence, 365–87. Chestnut Hill, MA: Boston College, 2011.

Stossel, Scott. "The Good Works of Sargent Shriver." *The Atlantic* (Jan. 18, 2011). http://www.theatlantic.com/politics/archive/2011/01/the-good -works-of-sargent-shriver/69677

–. *Sarge: The Life and Times of Sargent Shriver*. Washington: Smithsonian Books, 2004.

Suitts, Steve. *Hugo Black of Alabama*. Montgomery, AL: New South Books, 2005.

Taylor, Charles. *The Ethics of Authenticity*. Cambridge, MA: Harvard University Press, 1992.

–. "The Politics of Recognition." In *Multiculturalism: Examining the Politics of Recognition*, ed. Amy Gutmann, 25–73. Princeton: Princeton University Press, 1994.

–. *A Secular Age.* Cambridge, MA: Harvard University Press, 2007.

–. *Sources of the Self.* Cambridge, MA: Harvard University Press, 1989.

Temple, William. *Christianity and Social Order.* London: Shepheard-Walwyn /SPCK, 1976 [orig. 1942].

Theoforum 43 (nos. 1–2, 2012), 45 (no. 1, 2014), 50 (no. 2, 2020).

Voegelin, Eric. *Anamnesis.* Trans. G. Niemeyer. Notre Dame: University of Notre Dame Press, 1978 [orig. 1966].

–. *The New Science of Politics.* Chicago: University of Chicago Press, 1974 [orig. 1952].

Wald, Kenneth. *Religion and Politics in the United States.* Lanham, MD: Rowman & Littlefield, 2007.

Walzer, Michael. *Spheres of Justice.* New York: Basic Books, 1983.

West, Charles. "The Common Good and the Participation of the Poor." In *The Common Good and U.S. Capitalism,* eds. Oliver Williams and John Houck, 20–49. Lanham, MD: University Press of America, 1987.

Williams, Oliver, and John Houck, eds. *The Common Good and U.S. Capitalism.* Lanham, MD: University Press of America, 1987.

Index

Abington v. Schempp (1963), 52–3;
  Clark's ruling in, 55–7
Americanism, 29
American patriotism, 63
American politics, 20; Catholics and,
  27–31
Aquinas, Thomas, 5, 26, 46, 78;
  charity, 81; Lonergan's study of,
  158n53; Shriver reading work of,
  152n26; theology of, 121
Aristotelian-Thomist architecture,
  truth, 6
Aristotle, philosophy of, 79
authenticity, 6, 92; language of, 102;
  pursuit of, 90

Baldwin, James, 61
Bartoli, Andrea, 96, 97, 98
being religious, definition of, 8–9
Bill of Rights (1791), 7, 32
Black, Hugo, 147n61; avoiding
  perception of influence, 33–4;
  Everson v Board of Education
  (1947), 32–3, 52, 53; neutrality
  and wall of separation, 34–5
Bloy, Léon, 152n25, 153n27
Boyle, Joseph, 85, 86

Canal Zone, 108, 109
capitalism, 78, 80
Catholic(s): American politics and,
  27–31; language of nature and grace,
  11–12; religion and politics and,
  76–82; theologians, 82–4, 86, 145n40;
  theology, 35, 62, 77–8, 86, 118

Catholic Church, 5, 40, 75
Catholic Interracial Council (CIC),
  40–1; John F. Kennedy Award, 42
Catholicism: classic, 5; conservative,
  5;conversion to, 25; liberal, 5–6;
  Shriver's, 82; tenets of, 42
Catholicism and Liberalism
  (Komonchak), 27
Catholic Worker program, Dorothy
  Day's, 81
Champaign Community Schools, 37
charity, 78; Catholic language of, 62,
  70, 85, 99, 117; Catholic tradition,
  78, 81–2; Lonergan's analysis of,
  123; religious virtue of, 12; Shriver's
  critique of, 123; spiritual logic of,
  122; theology of Thomas Aquinas, 81;
  transformative experience of, 117–18
Chicago Board of Education, 24, 26,
  37, 40
Chicago Knights of Columbus, 51, 65
Chicago Merchandise Mart, 16, 48
Chicago Religion and Race
  Conference, 66
Chicago School Board, 16
Chicago Teachers Historical
  Association, 44, 46
Christian faith, inclusive challenge, 85
Christian Family Movement, 25
Christian humanism, 29, 144n37,
  145n38
Chulalongkorn University, 68
Clark, Justice Tom, 53, 54–5; *Abington
  v. Schempp* (1963), 52–3, 55–7
classicism, 5, 13, 83

Cold War, 14, 24, 45, 107
Commonweal (magazine), 28, 29, 31,
    143n29, 144n30
Commonwealth Club of California,
    16, 69
communism, 29, 78, 80
compassion: habits of, 101; language
    of, 12, 99; love and, 11–13, 60–1;
    personal, 42; in politics, 105, 139;
    service and, 70–1, 73; spirituality
    and, 62–7, 72, 128; term, 119, 130;
    transformative experience of, 95
comprehensive doctrines, 20, 134,
    134–6
Conference on School Administration
    and Educational Leadership,
    Northwestern University, 35
Constitution (1789), 7, 32
contraception, natural law ethics, 82–3
Curran, Charles, 153nn26–7, 153n35;
    analysis of, 85; natural law, 83,
    153nn35–7

Day, Dorothy, 31, 144n29, 146n44;
    Catholic Worker program, 81
Democratic Party, 41
democratic pluralism, 30, 31, 135
DePaul University, 24, 49
diversity, 3; coming to terms with,
    82–9; consciousness of, 83;
    cultural, 36; discovery of, 13; of
    humanity, 36; inclusive challenge,
    85; interiority and, 90–5; religious,
    37, 46; Shriver's vision of religious
    resources guarding, 35–40
Douthat, Ross, 25

education, public, 35, 104
Establishment Clause, 54, 55, 57
Ethics of Authenticity, The (Taylor), 90
Everson v. Board of Education (1947),
    32–3, 52, 53
exemplary figures, going forward, 134,
    139–40
Experiment in International Living,
    37, 113–14, 121

Fifth Amendment, 32
Finnis, John, 85, 86, 89
First Amendment, 32; Black's
    interpretation of, 34–5; Free
    Exercise Clause of, 53; metaphor of
    wall of separation, 147n60; religious
    clauses of, 3, 7
Fordham University, 16, 21, 58, 59, 66
Foreign Affairs (magazine), 69
Fourteenth Amendment, due process
    clause of, 32
Fourth Degree Exemplification and
    Banquet, Knights of Columbus, 45
Frankfurter, Justice Felix, 58
Free Exercise Clause, First
    Amendment, 53

Gadamer, Hans Georg, 86, 89
Georgetown University, 115
Gibbons, Cardinal, 25
Gingrich, Newt, 55
God: Catholic, 35, 39, 73, 80;
    charity from, 81, 85; City of, 76;
    cooperation with, 51; Fatherhood
    of, 42, 49; gift of his love, 118;
    kicking, out of school, 55–7; name
    of, 76; persons created in image of,
    103; relationship with, 12; science
    revealing wonders of, 6; victory
    over evil, 79
Grace and Freedom (Lonergan), 158n53
Gregorian University, 115
Grisez, Germain, 85, 86

Habermas, Jürgen, 86, 87, 88, 89, 101,
    136, 159n2
Head Start, Shriver and, 23
hearts of citizens, 14, 24, 31, 45,
    146n47
Heschel, Abraham, 59
Hollenbach, David, 87, 88, 89
Holy Spirit, 6, 75, 81
Humanae vitae (Paul VI), 82, 85, 86
human experience, words denoting
    sphere of, 60
humanism, Christian, 29, 144n37

humanity, unity-in-diversity, 38–9
human nature, 39, 46, 81, 91, 116
Humphrey, Hubert, 67

Illinois Association of Secondary
  School Principals, 38, 43
Illinois State Normal University, 36, 37
Inclusive, word, 85
Insight (Lonergan), 46, 90, 93, 115,
  124, 155n68
insight approach: conflict as
  deformation, 124; de-linking of
  threats-to-cares, 125–6; interiority
  and conflict, 95–100; mediators, 125;
  Peace Corps and, 123–31; personal
  relations by volunteers, 130–1; threat-
  to-care and openness-to-care, 126–8,
  130; understanding peace, 126
interiority, 9–10; of citizens, 11;
  diversity and, 90–5; focus of, 10;
  focus on, 11; insight approach
  to conflict and, 95–100; method
  and, 13–15; method of, 101–2,
  104–5; problem of evil, 116–17;
  questioning of science, 93–5;
  spirituality and, 115–18; turn to, 14,
  44–7; values and, 92–3

James J. Hoey Award for Interracial
  Justice, 41
Jansenism, 84
Jefferson, Thomas; Hugo Black
  sharing focus of, 33; interiority and,
  9; religion and politics, 7–8, 101; on
  religious conviction, 32
Jewish Big Sisters Standard Club, 26
Job Corps, Shriver and, 23, 41
Johnson, Lyndon, 48, 111
John XXIII (Pope), 51, 58
Josephson, William, 110
Jull, Marnie, 96
justice and peace, 6; language of, 12;
  natural capacities for, 62; Peace
  Corps and, 50–1, 55, 62, 71; Shriver
  in pursuit of, 22–3, 55, 60–1, 64, 66,
  71; turning to interiority, 73

Kennedy, Bobby, 42
Kennedy, Eunice, 48
Kennedy, John F., 6; assassination of,
  48; Coretta King and, 42; debate with
  Nixon, 67; presidential campaign
  of, 27, 40, 41, 48; Shriver and Peace
  Corps, 6, 15, 67–8, 106–7; speech at
  Cow Palace, 67, 106
Kennedy, Joseph P., 110; Shriver and,
  15–16
King, Coretta Scott, 41–2
King, Martin Luther, Jr., 41–2, 59
Knights of Columbus, 45
knowledge, 24, 27, 38, 94; of dangers
  to avoid, 126; of dignity of man,
  49; gaining, 78, 91; guiding the
  living, 116; natural, of world, 84,
  91; Peace Corps volunteers sharing,
  64; pursuit of, 91; self-, 89, 112; of
  transformative experiences, 89;
  worldly, 101, 114, 122
Komonshak, Joseph, 27
Korean War, 65

Lawrence, Frederick, 89
learning, 65, 131, 137–8; construction
  of conflict, 19, 98–9; contributing
  and, 126; listening and, 110;
  mediation skills, 96; natural
  law and, 89; role in conflict, 97;
  transformative, 89, 111–12, 122;
  yesterday's, 116
Lee v. Weisman (1992), 56
Leo XIII (Pope), 78
liberalism: Catholic suspicion of, 27;
  core affirmation of, 5; philosophy
  of, 134; separation of church and
  state, 28
Livingston County Institute, 24
Lonergan, Bernard, 13, 20, 74;
  Insight, 46, 90, 93, 115; method
  of interiority, 91–2, 99, 101, 103;
  philosophical method of, 136;
  questioning of science, 93–5; on
  shift to interiority, 23; study of
  Aquinas, 91; turn to interiority, 89

Lonergan Review, The (journal), 96
Lonergan Workshop (journal), 96
Lord's Prayer, 52, 55

McCarthy, Colman, 144n37
McCarthyism, 29
MacIntyre, Alasdair, 86, 89
Mahoney, John, Catholic moral
   theology, 83–4
Maritain, Jacques, 12, 100; essays of,
   145n38; ideas of, 29–31; natural law,
   79, 80, 146n42; natural law approach,
   144n37; personalist ideas, 78
Mary McDowell Settlement House, 47
Mater et magistra, papal encyclical, 65
May, William, 85, 86
mediator strategies, lines of
   questioning, 98–9
Melchin, Derek, 96, 98, 124
Melchin, Kenneth, 96, 97, 98
Method: Journal of Lonergan Studies
   (journal), 96
Method in Theology (Lonergan), 115,
   136, 155n68
Moore, G. E., natural law, 85–6
Moyers, Bill, 58
Murray, John Courtney, 87, 146n47,
   152n24
Mystical Body of Christ, 65, 81

National Catholic Conference for
   Interracial Justice (NCCIJ), 41
National Conference on Religion and
   Race, 10, 21, 50
natural law: Catholic approaches, 86;
   Catholic framework of, 72; Catholic
   tradition, 78, 79–81, 82–4; diversity,
   87–9; ethics of contraception, 82–3;
   learning and, 89; moral "oughts,"
   85–6; requiring New Natural Law,
   86; Thomist framework, 29–30;
   traditional Catholic doctrine of, 39,
   44; transposition of, 91–2
natural-supernatural distinction, 84;
   Catholic tradition, 78–9
neutrality, Justices Clark and Black, 54

New York Herald Tribune Youth
   Forum, 48, 49, 62
New York World's Fair, 66
Nixon, Richard, 129–30; debate with
   Kennedy, 67
Northwestern University, 35, 37
Notre Dame University, 42, 49

Opus Dei, 25

Panama, Peace Corps and, 108–10, 131
Panama Canal, 108–9
Paul VI (Pope), 82
peace: pursuit of, 4, 75; pursuit of
   justice and, 14, 62, 79; question
   for peacemaking, 17–18; Shriver's
   commitment to, 6, 11, 73; as unity-
   in-diversity, 38; *see also* justice and
   peace
Peace Corps, 107–10; breaking
   down barriers, 71; core ideas, 21;
   development of, 6–7; formula
   for practical idealism, 16–17;
   formula guiding, 112–13; free
   discussion and debate in, 110–11;
   functioning of, 110–15; infusion of
   spiritual values into secular affairs,
   16; insight approach, 123–31;
   interiority and spirituality, 115–18;
   language of spirit and spiritual
   values, 64; launch of, 28; mission
   of, 107; mission of volunteers,
   68–9; organizational autonomy of,
   111; personal relations of, 120–1;
   planning and inception of, 110;
   policies and programs of, 70–1;
   resolving conflicts and building
   peace, 123–31; Shriver and, 6–7,
   12, 15–19, 21, 23, 99, 102, 105,
   106–7; Shriver's appointment to,
   48–9; Shriver's speeches at, 62–5;
   Shriver's vision of, 22; Shriver's
   vision of diversity, 35–6; Shriver's
   vocation and years with, 49–52;
   simple rules of, 112, 120; simple
   rules of volunteers, 17–19, 69, 112,

120; spiritual values and, 118–23; transformative experience of, 119–20; transformative experiences of volunteers, 121–3; transformative learning in, 111–12

personalist, 30, 78, 146n47

Peru, Peace Corps and, 126–8, 131

philosophical method, 134, 136–9

physicalism, 83

Picard, Cheryl, 96, 97, 98, 124

Pius XI (Pope), 78

Pius XII (Pope), 39, 83

political backlash, prayer in schools and, 55–7

Political Liberalism (Rawls), 134, 135, 136

politics: bringing religion into, 3; comprehensive doctrines, 134–6; exemplary figures, 134, 139–40; philosophical method, 134, 136–9; Shriver on relevance of religion for, 12–13; spiritualizing, 95–6; *see also* religion and politics

Poverty Law, Shriver and, 23

practical idealism, Shriver's formula for, 69

Practicing Insight Mediation (Picard), 96

prayer in schools, political backlash and, 55–7

Price, James, 96, 97

Price, Megan, 96

public education, 35, 104

Quadragesimo anno (Pius XI), 78, 152n26

questioning: mediator strategies, 98–9; of science, 93–5

race riots: America, 108, 109; Panama, 108, 109

racism, 103; campaign against, 40–4; poverty and, 110

Rahner, Karl, 84

Rawls, John, 86, 87, 88, 100, 134, 159n2

Regis College, 115

religion and politics: care and precision in navigating, 21; interiority and conflicts, 13–14;

navigating challenges of, 7–9; revisiting, 100–4; Shriver on, 75, 76–82; Shriver on wall of separation, 52–5; Shriver's language of, 71–4; Shriver's speeches, 14; wall of separation, 31–5, 47

religious laissez faire, 50, 60–1

religious leaders, social and ethical values of, 103–4

Republican Party, 41

Rerum novarum (Leo XIII), 78

Ricoeur, Paul, 86

Roosevelt, Theodore, 108

St. John's Catholic Parochial School, 26

St. Louis University, 66

St. Procopius College, 27

St. Thomas More Society, 26

Salem College, 63

science, questioning of, 93–5

Second Vatican Council, 5, 19, 28, 78

Secular Age, 9

shrinking planet, 36

Shriver, Hilda, 25, 28, 144n29

Shriver, Robert Sargent, 25, 28, 144n29

Shriver, Sargent, 4–7, 134; campaign against racism, 40–44; Catholicism of, 82–3; Catholic tradition of, 72–3, 75, 76–82, 99, 100–1, 107, 139; charity and justice in public life, 14; from charity to spirituality and compassion, 62–7; "Citizenship" topic, 24–5; commitment to natural law, 145n40; on "dark places of the human heart," 11; death of, 15; "Education for the Future," 37; as exemplary figure, 134, 139–40; formula for practical idealism, 69; human nature and, 81; importance of religious resources, 39–40; influence of Dorothy Day, 81; influence of faith on political program development, 23; interiority and conflict, 95–100; language of, 71–4; linking charity and compassion, 66–7; Peace Corps

Shriver, Sargent (*cont.*)
  and, 6–7, 21, 96, 99, 105, 106–7;
  Peace Corps years of, 49–52; as
  peacemaker, 15–19; public life in
  Chicago, 21; relevance of religion
  for politics, 12–13; on religion and
  politics, 76–82; religion-politics
  relations, 9, 47; religious resources
  for guarding diversity, 35–40;
  religious vocation to public life, 14,
  24–7, 44, 81; on separation of church
  and state, 10–11; simple rules for
  volunteers, 17–19; on spirituality and
  politics, 57–61; turn to interiority,
  45–6; understanding his calling,
  14–15; vision of religion and politics,
  22; on wall of separation, 52–5
Shriver's Socratic Seminar, 111, 120
simple rules, Peace Corps volunteers,
  17–19, 69, 112, 120
Sixteenth Annual Vocational
  Conference, "Citizenship" topic,
  24–5
Skinner, Richard Dana, 28
Smith, Janet, 86
Snell, R.J., 89
Special Olympics, Shriver and, 23
spirituality, 6; focus on charity, 26;
  from charity to, 62–7; interiority
  and, 31, 92, 95, 115–18; language
  of, 12, 72–3; Peace Corps and,
  118–23; of peacebuilding, 122;
  role of, 97, 105, 107, 123; Shriver
  on politics and, 23, 49, 57–61, 118,
  128, 131
Springfield College, 114
stewardship, Shriver on role of, 25
Stewart, Justice Potter, 53, 56
Stossel, Scott, Shriver's biographer,
  20, 25, 110, 152n26
sublation, 103
Summi pontificatus (Pius XII), 39
Supreme Court: *Abington v. Schempp*
  (1963), 55–7; challenges,
  21; decisions, 3, 20, 57; on
  Establishment Clause, 57; *Everson*

v. Board of Education (1947),
  32–3; jurisdiction of, 32; "wall of
  separation," 35, 52

Taylor, Charles, 9, 84, 86, 88, 89; *The
  Ethics of Authenticity*, 90
Ten Commandments, 56
Thailand (Bangkok), Peace Corps
  and, 68, 107, 131
Theoforum (journal), 96
Theory of Justice, A (Rawls), 134
Thomist natural law framework,
  29–30, 80
totalitarianism, 29, 80
Towering Task, The (Josephson and
  Wiggins), 110
Tracy, David, 87
Transforming Conflict through Insight
  (Melchin and Picard), 96, 97, 124
transposition, term, 67
"Treaty," 111, 120

Unitarians, 53
United Nations Universal Declaration
  of Human Rights, 12
unity-in-diversity: of humanity, 38–9;
  peace as, 38
unity of humankind, 36, 38
University of Illinois, 38, 43

Vatican II, 5
Vatican Pavilion, 66
Venezuela, Peace Corps and, 126,
  128–31
vicious cycle of alienation, 114, 121,
  126
VISTA, Shriver and, 23
vocation to public life, Shriver's
  religious, 14, 24–7, 44, 81
Voegelin, Eric, 9

Wallace v. Jafree (1985), 56
wall of separation, 47, 133; church
  and state, 3, 5; Justice Black on,
  52; Justice Clark on, 55; religion,
  schools and, 31–5; Shriver on, 52–5

Wall Street Journal (newspaper), 15, 68
War on Poverty, 41, 48, 108; Shriver and, 41
Watt, Donald, "Experiment in International Living," 37
Wiggins, Warren, 110

Wofford, Harris, 42
World War II, 26, 39, 40, 107

Yale Daily News (newspaper), 31
Yale Law School, 15
YMCA, 77, 128–9